Staff Ride Handbook for The Vicksburg Campaign, December 1862–July 1863

Dr. Christopher R. Gabel
and the Staff Ride Team,
Combat Studies Institute

Combat Studies Institute
U.S. Army Command and General Staff College
Fort Leavenworth, Kansas 66027-1352

Library of Congress Cataloging-in-Publication Data

Gabel, Christopher R. (Christopher Richard), 1954-
  Staff ride handbook for the Vicksburg Campaign, December 1862-July 1863/ Christopher R. Gabel and the Staff Ride Team, Combat Studies Institute.
    p. cm.
Includes bibliographical references.
1. Vicksburg (Miss.)–History–Seige, 1863.2. Vicksburg National Military Park
    (Miss.)–Guidebooks.3.Staff ride–Mississippi–Vicksburg. I. U.S. Army Command and General Staff College. Combat Studies Institute. Staff Ride Team. II. Title.

CONTENTS

Illustrations v
Tables... vii
Introduction... ix
    I. Civil War Armies...................................... 1
    II. Vicksburg Campaign Overview......................... 69
    III. Suggested Route and Vignettes 83
    IV. Support for a Staff Ride to Vicksburg 181
Appendixes
    A. Orders of Battle 185
    B. Biographical Sketches 203
    C. Medal of Honor Conferrals in the Vicksburg Campaign ... 213
Bibliography... 215

ILLUSTRATIONS

Figures

1. Regimental line of battle from march column 38

Maps

1. Vicksburg campaign key terrain features. 68
2. Vicksburg campaign overview 75
3. Snyder's (Haynes') Bluff, stand 1 82
4. Sketch of rebel fortifications at Haynes' Bluff. 85
5. Chickasaw Bayou battlefield, stands 2 and 3. 89
6. Grant's Canal, stand 4 96
7. Bayou expeditions. 97
8. *Cairo* and Fort Hill, stands 5 and 6 102
9. Grand Gulf, stands 7 and 8 109
10. Batteries at Grand Gulf captured by the United States Mississippi Squadron, 3 May 1863 113
11. Bruinsburg/Port Gibson, stands 9 and 10 117
12. Willows, stand 11 127
13. Raymond, stands 12 and 13 132
14. Champion Hill, stands 14-18 143
15. Big Black River, stand 19. 154
16. Vicksburg siege, stands 20-23 160

TABLES

1. Federal and Confederate organized forces.   6
2. Typical staffs.   8
3. Confederate and Federal effective strengths in the
   Vicksburg campaign, 30 April-4 July 1863 11
4. Mississippi River squadron: representative vessels. 20
5. Types of artillery available in the Vicksburg campaign. 30
6. Sample of Federal Logistical Data. 47

INTRODUCTION

Ad bellum Pace Parati: prepared in peace for war. This sentiment was much on the mind of Captain Arthur L. Wagner as he contemplated the quality of military education at the Infantry and Cavalry School at Fort Leavenworth, Kansas, during the 1890s. Wagner believed that the school's curricula during the long years of peace had become too far removed from the reality of war, and he cast about for ways to make the study of conflict more real to officers who had no experience in combat. Eventually, he arrived at a concept called the "Staff Ride," which consisted of detailed classroom study of an actual campaign followed by a visit to the sites associated with that campaign. Although Wagner never lived to see the Staff Ride added to the Leavenworth curricula, an associate of his, Major Eben Swift, implemented the Staff Ride at the General Service and Staff School in 1906. In July of that year, Swift led a contingent of twelve students to Chattanooga, Tennessee, to begin a two-week study of the Atlanta campaign of 1864.

The Staff Ride concept pioneered at Leavenworth in the early years of the twentieth century remains a vital part of officer professional development today. At the U.S. Army Command and General Staff College, the Army War College, ROTC detachments, and units throughout the world, U.S. Army officers are studying war vicariously in peacetime through the Staff Ride methodology. That methodology (in-depth preliminary study, rigorous field study, and integration of the two) need not be tied to a formal schoolhouse environment. Units stationed near historic battlefields can experience the intellectual and emotional stimulation provided by standing on the hallowed ground where soldiers once contended for their respective causes. Yet units may find themselves without many of the sources of information on a particular campaign that are readily available in an academic environment. For that reason, the Combat Studies Institute has begun a series of handbooks that will provide practical information on conducting Staff Rides to specific campaigns and battles. These handbooks are not intended to be used as a substitute for serious study by Staff Ride leaders or participants. Instead, they represent an effort to assist officers in locating sources, identifying teaching points, and designing meaningful field study phases. As such, they represent a starting point from which a more rigorous professional development experience may be crafted.

The Vicksburg campaign of 1862-63 is an effective vehicle for a Staff Ride. It raises a variety of teaching points, at both the operational and tactical levels, that are relevant to today's officers. Several different types of combat occurred in the course of the campaign. In addition, the campaign featured prominent participation by the Navy, thus raising a joint dimension. It also offers examples of combat support and combat service support activities, most notably military engineering and logistics.

The Staff Ride Handbook for the Vicksburg Campaign, December 1862-July 1863, provides a systematic approach to the analysis of this key Civil War campaign. Part I describes the organization of the Union and Confederate Armies, detailing their weapons, tactics, and logistical, engineer, communications, and medical support. It also includes a description of the U.S. Navy elements that featured so prominently in the campaign.

Part II consists of a campaign overview that establishes the context for the individual actions to be studied in the field.

Part III consists of a suggested itinerary of sites to visit in order to obtain a concrete view of the campaign in its several phases. For each site, or "stand," there is a set of travel directions, a discussion of the action that occurred there, and vignettes by participants in the campaign that further explain the action and which also allow the student to sense the human "face of battle."

Part IV provides practical information on conducting a Staff Ride in the Vicksburg area, including sources of assistance and logistical considerations. Appendix A outlines the order of battle for the significant actions in the campaign. Appendix B provides biographical sketches of key participants. Appendix C provides an overview of Medal of Honor conferral in the campaign. An annotated bibliography suggests sources for preliminary study.

I. CIVIL WAR ARMIES
Organization

The U.S. Army in 1861

The Regular Army of the United States on the eve of the Civil War was essentially a frontier constabulary whose 16,000 officers and men were organized into 198 companies scattered across the nation at seventy-nine different posts. At the start of the war, 183 of these companies were either on frontier duty or in transit, while the remaining 15, mostly coastal artillery batteries, guarded the Canadian border and Atlantic coast or one of the twenty-three arsenals. In 1861, this Army was under the command of Lieutenant General Winfield Scott, the seventy-five-year-old hero of the Mexican-American War. His position as general in chief was traditional, not statutory, because secretaries of war since 1821 had designated a general to be in charge of the field forces without formal Congressional approval. The field forces themselves were controlled through a series of geographic departments whose commanders reported directly to the general in chief. This department system, frequently modified, would be used by both sides throughout the Civil War for administering regions under army control.

Army administration was handled by a system of bureaus whose senior officers were, by 1860, in the twilight of long careers in their technical fields. Six of the ten bureau chiefs were over seventy years old. These bureaus, modeled after the British system, answered directly to the War Department and were not subject to the orders of the general in chief. Predecessors of many of today's combat support and combat service support branches, the following bureaus had been established by 1861:

Quartermaster	Medical
Ordnance	Adjutant General
Subsistance	Paymaster
Engineer	Inspector General
Topographic Engineer*	Judge Advocate General

*(Merged with the Engineer Bureau in 1863.)

During the war, Congress elevated the Office of the Provost Marshal and the Signal Corps to bureau status and created a Cavalry Bureau. Note that no operational planning or intelligence staff existed: American commanders before the Civil War had never required such a structure.

This system provided suitable civilian control and administrative support to the small field army prior to 1861. Ultimately, the bureau system would respond effectively, if not always efficiently, to the mass mobilization required over the next four years. Indeed, it would remain essentially intact until the early twentieth century. The Confederate government, forced to create an army and support organization from scratch, established a parallel structure to that of the U.S. Army. In fact, many important figures in Confederate bureaus had served in one of the prewar bureaus.

Raising the Armies

With the outbreak of war in April 1861, both sides faced the monumental task of organizing and equipping armies that far exceeded the prewar structure in size and complexity. The Federals maintained control of the Regular Army, and the Confederates initially created a regular force, mostly on paper. Almost immediately, the North lost many of its officers to the South, including some of exceptional quality. Of 1,108 Regular officers serving as of 1 January 1861, 270 ultimately resigned to join the South. Only a few hundred of the 15,135 enlisted men, however, left the ranks.

The Federal government had two basic options for the use of the Regular Army. It could be divided into training and leadership cadre for newly formed volunteer regiments or be retained in units to provide a reliable nucleus for the Federal Army in coming battles. At the start, Scott envisioned a relatively small force to defeat the rebellion and therefore insisted that the Regulars fight as units. Although some Regular units fought well, at the First Battle of Bull Run and in other battles, Scott's decision ultimately limited the impact of regular units upon the war. Battle losses and disease soon thinned the ranks of Regulars, and officials could never recruit sufficient replacements in the face of stiff competition from the states, which were forming volunteer regiments. By November 1864, many Regular units had been so depleted that they were withdrawn from front-line service. The war, therefore, was fought primarily with volunteer officers and men, the vast majority of whom had no previous military training or experience.

Neither side had difficulty in recruiting the numbers initially required to fill the expanding ranks. In April 1861, President Abraham Lincoln called for 75,000 men from the states' militias for a three-month period. This figure probably represented Lincoln's informed guess as to how many troops would be needed to quell the rebellion quickly. Almost 92,000 men responded, as the states recruited their "organized" but untrained militia companies. At the First Battle of Bull Run in July 1861, these ill-trained and poorly equipped soldiers generally fought much better than they were led. Later, as the war began to require more manpower, the Federal government set enlisted quotas through various "calls," which local districts struggled to fill. Similarly, the Confederate Congress, in March 1861, authorized the acceptance of 100,000 one-year volunteers. One-third of these men was under arms within a month. The Southern spirit of voluntarism was so strong that possibly twice that number could have been enlisted, but sufficient arms and equipment were not then available.

As the war continued and casualty lists grew, the glory of volunteering faded, and both sides ultimately resorted to conscription to help fill the ranks. The Confederates enacted the first conscription law in American history in April 1862, followed by the Federal government's own law in March 1863. Throughout these first experiments in American conscription, both sides administered the programs in less than a fair and efficient way. Conscription laws tended to exempt wealthier citizens, and initially, draftees could hire substitutes or pay commutation fees. As a result, the health, capability, and morale of the average conscript were poor. Many eligible men, particularly in the South, enlisted to avoid the onus of being considered a conscript. Still, conscription or the threat of conscription ultimately helped provide a sufficient quantity of soldiers for both sides.

Conscription was never a popular program, and the North, in particular, tried several approaches to limit conscription requirements. These efforts included offering lucrative bounties (fees) to induce volunteers to fill required quotas. In addition, the Federals offered a series of reenlistment bonuses, including money, thirty-day furloughs, and the opportunity for veteran regiments to maintain their colors and be designated as "veteran" volunteer infantry regiments. The Federals also created an Invalid Corps (later renamed the Veteran Reserve Corps) of men unfit for front-line service who performed essential rear-area duties. The Union also recruited almost 179,000 blacks, mostly in federally organized volunteer regiments. By February 1864, blacks were being conscripted in the North as well. In the South, the recruiting or conscripting of slaves was so politically sensitive that it was not attempted until March 1865, far too late to influence the war.

Whatever the faults of the manpower mobilization, it was an impressive achievement, particularly as a first effort on that scale. Various enlistment figures exist, but the best estimates are that approximately two million men enlisted in the Federal Army during 1861-65. Of that number, 1 million were under arms at the end of the war. Because Confederate records are incomplete or lost, estimates of their enlistments vary from 600,000 to over 1.5 million. Most likely, between 750,000 and 800,000 men served the Confederacy during the war, with a peak strength never exceeding 460,000. Perhaps the greatest legacy of the manpower mobilization efforts of both sides was the improved Selective Service system that created the armies of World Wars I and II.

The unit structure into which the expanding armies were organized was generally the same for Federals and Confederates, reflecting the common roots for both armies. The Federals began the war with a Regular Army organized into an essentially Napoleonic, musket-equipped structure. Each of the ten prewar infantry regiments consisted of ten 87-man companies with a maximum authorized strength of 878. At the beginning of the war, the Federals added nine Regular infantry regiments with a newer "French Model" organizational structure. The new regiments contained three battalions, with a maximum authorized strength of 2,452. The new Regular battalion, with eight 100-man companies, was, in effect, equivalent to the prewar regiment. Essentially an effort to reduce staff officer slots, the new structure was unfamiliar to most leaders, and both sides used a variant of the old structure for newly formed volunteer regiments. The Federal War Department established a volunteer infantry regimental organization with a strength that could range from 866 to 1,046 (varying in authorized strength by up to 180 infantry privates). The Confederate Congress fixed its ten-company infantry regiment at 1,045 men. Combat strength in battle, however, was always much lower because of casualties, sickness, leaves, details, desertions, and straggling.

The battery remained the basic artillery unit, although battalion and larger formal groupings of artillery emerged later in the war in the eastern theater. Four understrength Regular regiments existed in the

U.S. Army at the start of the war, and one Regular regiment was added in 1861, for a total of sixty batteries. Nevertheless, most batteries were volunteer organizations. A Federal battery usually consisted of six guns and had an authorized strength of 80 to 156 men. A battery of six twelve-pounder Napoleons could include 130 horses. If organized as "horse" or flying artillery, cannoneers were provided individual mounts, and more horses than men could be assigned to the battery. Their Confederate counterparts, plagued by limited ordnance and available manpower, usually operated with a four gun battery, often with guns of mixed types and calibers. Confederate batteries seldom reached their initially authorized manning level of 80 soldiers.

Prewar Federal mounted units were organized into five Regular regiments (two dragoon, two cavalry, and one mounted rifle), and one Regular cavalry regiment was added in May 1861. Originally, ten companies comprised a regiment, but congressional legislation in July 1862 officially reorganized the Regular mounted units into standard regiments of twelve "companies or troops" of 79 to 95 men each. Although the term "troop" was officially introduced, most cavalrymen continued to use the more familiar term "company" to describe their units throughout the war. The Federals grouped two companies or troops into squadrons, with four to six squadrons making a regiment. Confederate cavalry units, organized on the prewar model, authorized ten 76-man companies per regiment. Some volunteer cavalry units on both sides also formed into smaller cavalry battalions. Later in the war, both sides began to merge their cavalry regiments and brigades into division and corps organizations.

For both sides, unit structure above regimental level was similar to today's structure, with a brigade controlling three to five regiments and a division controlling two or more brigades. Federal brigades generally contained regiments from more than one state, while Confederate brigades often had several regiments from the same state. In the Confederate Army, a brigadier general usually commanded a brigade, and a major general commanded a division. The Federal Army, with no rank higher than major general until 1864, often had colonels commanding brigades and brigadier generals commanding divisions.

The large numbers of organizations formed, as shown in table 1, are a reflection of the politics of the time. The War Department in 1861 considered making recruiting a Federal responsibility, but this proposal seemed to be an unnecessary expense for the short war initially envisioned. Therefore, responsibility for recruiting remained with the states, and on both sides, state governors continually encouraged local constituents to form new volunteer regiments. This practice served to strengthen support for local, state, and national politicians and provide an opportunity for glory and high rank for ambitious men. Although such local recruiting created regiments with strong bonds among the men, it also hindered filling the ranks of existing regiments with new replacements. As the war progressed, the Confederates attempted to funnel replacements into units from their same state or region, but the Federals continued to create new regiments. Existing Federal regiments detailed men back home to recruit replacements, but these efforts could never successfully compete for men joining new local regiments. Thus, the newly formed regiments had no seasoned veterans to train the recruits, and the battle-tested regiments lost men faster than they could recruit replacements. Many regiments on both sides were reduced to combat ineffectiveness as the war progressed. Seasoned regiments were often disbanded or consolidated, usually against the wishes of the men assigned.

Table 1. Federal and Confederate Organized Forces

	Federal		*Confederate*	
Infantry	19	Regular Regiments	642	Regiments
	2,125	Volunteer Regiments	9	Legions*
	60	Volunteer Battalions	163	Separate Battalions
	351	Separate Companies	62	Separate Companies
Artillery	5	Regular Regiments	16	Regiments
	61	Volunteer Regiments	25	Battalions
	17	Volunteer Battalions	227	Batteries
	408	Separate Batteries		
Cavalry	6	Regular Regiments	137	Regiments
	266	Volunteer Regiments	1	Legion*
	45	Battalions	143	Separate Battalions
	78	Separate Companies	101	Separate Companies

*Legions were a form of combined arms team, with artillery, cavalry, and infantry. They were approximately the strength of a large regiment. Long before the end of the war, legions lost their combined arms organization.

The Leaders

Because the organization, equipment, tactics, and training of the Confederate and Federal Armies were similar, the performance of units in battle often depended on the quality and performance of their leaders. General officers were appointed by their respective central governments. At the start of the war, most, but certainly not all, of the more senior officers had West Point or other military school experience. In 1861, Lincoln appointed 126 general officers, of which 82 were, or had been, professional officers. Jefferson Davis appointed 89, of which 44 had received professional training. The remainder were political appointees, but of these only sixteen Federal and seven Confederate generals had no military experience.

Of the volunteer officers who composed the bulk of the leadership for both armies, colonels (regimental commanders) were normally appointed by state governors. Other field grade officers were appointed by their states, although many were initially elected within their units. Company grade officers were usually elected by their men. This long-established militia tradition, which seldom made military leadership and capability a primary consideration, was largely an extension of the states rights philosophy and sustained political patronage in both the Union and the Confederacy.

Much has been made of the West Point backgrounds of the men who ultimately dominated the senior leadership positions of both armies, but the graduates of military colleges were not prepared by such institutions to command divisions, corps, or armies. Moreover, though many leaders had some combat experience from the Mexican War era, few had experience above the company or battery level in the peacetime years prior to 1861. As a result, the war was not initially conducted at any level by "professional officers" in today's terminology. Leaders became more professional through experience and at the cost of thousands of lives. General William T. Sherman would later note that the war did not enter its "professional stage" until 1863.

Civil War Staffs

In the Civil War, as today, the success of large military organizations often depended on the effectiveness of the commanders' staffs. Modern staff procedures have evolved only gradually with the increasing complexity of military operations. This evolution was far from complete in 1861, and throughout the war, commanders personally handled many vital staff functions, most notably operations and intelligence. The nature of American warfare up to the mid-nineteenth century had not yet clearly overwhelmed the capabilities of single commanders.

Civil War staffs were divided into a "general staff" and a "staff corps." This terminology, defined by Winfield Scott in 1855, differs from modern definitions of the terms. Table 2 lists typical staff positions at army level, although key functions are represented down to regimental level. Except for the chief of staff and aides-de-camp, who were considered personal staff and would often depart when a commander was reassigned, staffs mainly contained representatives of the various bureaus, with logistical areas being best represented. Later in the war, some truly effective staffs began to emerge, but this was a result of the increased experience of the officers serving in those positions rather than a comprehensive development of standard staff procedures or guidelines.

Table 2. Typical Staffs

General Staff
    Chief of staff
    Aides
    Assistant adjutant general
    Assistant inspector general

Staff Corps
    Engineer
    Ordnance
    Quartermaster
    Subsistence
    Medical
    Pay
    Signal
    Provost marshal
    Chief of artillery

George B. McClellan, when he appointed his father-in-law as his chief of staff, was the first to use this title officially. Even though many senior commanders had a chief of staff, this position was not used in any uniform way, and seldom did the man in this role achieve the central, coordinating authority of the chief of staff in a modern headquarters. This position, along with most other staff positions, was used as an individual commander saw fit, making staff responsibilities somewhat different under each commander. This inadequate use of the chief of staff was among the most important shortcomings of staffs during the Civil War. An equally important weakness was the lack of any formal operations or intelligence staff. Liaison procedures were also ill-defined, and various staff officers or soldiers performed this function with little formal guidance. Miscommunication or lack of knowledge of friendly units proved disastrous time after time.

The Armies at Vicksburg

Major General Ulysses S. Grant's Army of the Tennessee was organized into four infantry corps. Major General Stephen A. Hurlbut's XVI Corps, however, remained headquartered in Memphis performing rear-area missions throughout the campaign, although nearly two divisions did join Grant during the siege. The remaining three corps, containing ten divisions with over 44,000 effectives, composed Grant's maneuver force during the campaign. Although some recently recruited "green" regiments participated, the bulk of Grant's army consisted of veteran units, many of which had fought with distinction at Forts Henry and Donelson, Shiloh, and Chickasaw Bayou. Of Grant's senior subordinates, the XV Corps commander, Major General William T. Sherman, was his most trusted. Ultimately to prove an exceptional operational commander, Sherman was an adequate tactician with considerable wartime command experience. He and Major General James B. McPherson, commander of XVII Corps, were West Pointers. McPherson was young and inexperienced, but both Grant and Sherman felt he held great promise. Grant's other corps commander, Major General John A. McClernand, was a prewar Democratic congressman who had raised much of his XIII Corps specifically so that he could command an independent Vicksburg expedition. A self-serving and politically ambitious man who neither enjoyed nor curried Grant's favor, he nonetheless was an able organizer and tactical commander who had served bravely at Shiloh. The division commanders were a mix of trained regular officers and volunteers who formed a better-than-average set of Civil War commanders.

Lieutenant General John C. Pemberton, a Pennsylvania-born West Pointer who had served with Jefferson Davis in the Mexican War, resigned his federal commission to join the South at the start of the war. Pemberton's army in the Vicksburg campaign consisted of five infantry divisions with no intermediate corps headquarters. Counting two brigades that briefly joined Pemberton's command during the maneuver campaign, he had over 43,000 effectives, many of whom had only limited battle experience. Of Pemberton's subordinates, Brigadier General John S. Bowen, a West Point classmate of McPherson's, was an exceptionally able tactical commander. Major General Carter L. Stevenson was also West Point trained, and the other division commander in the maneuver force, Major General William W. Loring, was a prewar Regular colonel who had worked his way up through the ranks. Significantly, none of these three men had any real respect for their commander and would prove to be less than supportive of him. Pemberton's other division commanders, Major Generals Martin L. Smith and John H. Forney, both West Pointers, would remain in or near the city, commanding Vicksburg's garrison troops throughout the campaign.

Although Pemberton's five divisions represented the main Confederate force in the Vicksburg campaign, his army came under the jurisdiction of a higher headquarters, General Joseph E. Johnston's Department of the West. Johnston, in 1861, had been the Quartermaster General of the Regular Army and one of only five serving general officers. He had commanded in the eastern theater early in the war until severely wounded. In November 1862 after several months of convalescence, he assumed departmental command in the west. Johnston assumed direct command in Mississippi on 13 May 1863 but was unable to establish effective control over Pemberton's forces. When Pemberton became besieged in Vicksburg, Johnston assembled an Army of Relief but never seriously threatened Grant.

Morale of the troops was a serious concern for both the Union and Confederate commanders. Grant's army suffered terribly from illness in the early months of the campaign, which it spent floundering in the Louisiana swamps. But the men recovered quickly once they gained the high ground across the river. Inured to hardship, these men were served by able commanders and hardworking staffs. Once movements started, morale remained high, despite shortfalls in logistical support.

Pemberton's men, although not always well served by their commanders, fought hard for their home region through the battle of Champion Hill. Although they briefly lost their resolve after that defeat, once behind the formidable works at Vicksburg, they regained a level of morale and effectiveness that only began to erode weeks later when they were faced with ever-increasing Federal strength and their own supply shortages.

Table 3. Confederate and Federal Effective Strengths in the Vicksburg Campaign, 30 April-4 July 1863

(Numbers Approximate)

Confederate

	Pemberton			*Johnston* (arrives 13 May)
1 May	43,600			
3 May	+3,200 Gregg's Brigade			
13 May	-3,200 Gregg to Johnston		+5,900	Gregg + Wilson Bdes
17 May	-5,800 Loring to Johnston		+5,800	Loring
1-22 May	-7,400 casualties			
21 May			+5,900	Walker (-)
26 May			+4,400	Jackson
1 June			+9,100	Breckinridge
21 June			+7,500	French
23 May-3 July	-900 KIA During Seige		-2,300	Misc. Losses/Detachments
4 July	29,500 Surrendered		36,300	

Federal
Grant's Strength in Mississippi

30 April	28,800	XIII Corps + 3/XVII
1 May	+5,100	7/XVII Corps
6-7 May	+11,100	XV Corps (-)
11 May	+5,900	2/XV
1-22 May	-8,800	Casualties
13-19 May	+4,200	6/XVII
4-30 June	+27,400	IX Corps, XVI Corps (-), Herron's Division
23 May-3 July	-500	Casualties during siege
30 June	73,095	"Present for duty" at or near Vicksburg on return of this date (93,565 "aggregate present")

Naval Power in the Vicksburg Campaign

Military Significance of the Rivers

Naval power was a decisive element in the western campaigns of the Civil War. Given the enormous size of the western theater of operations (680 miles in a straight line from Cairo, Illinois, to New Orleans) and the relative austerity of the road and rail nets, navigable waterways were the preferred method of movement for both commercial and military enterprises. In a situation analogous to twentieth-century "air superiority," control of the western rivers conferred significant military advantages, particularly with regards to mobility and firepower.

In an age when most military transportation moved by muscle power, the Mississippi River steamboat was a logistician's dream come true. Cargo capacity ranged from 250 tons for the smaller boats up to 1,700 for the largest. By contrast, a horse-drawn military wagon could move only about one ton, depending on the conditions of the roads. A Civil War-era freight train of ten cars might carry 100 tons of goods, but rail lines were few and difficult to maintain in the western theater. If camped on the banks of a navigable stream, a field army of 40,000 men and 18,000 horses could subsist handily on the daily deliveries of one large (500-ton) steamboat, which traveled on a river that was not vulnerable to sabotage and was rarely "out of order."

Moreover, riverboats could move the army itself. One riverboat could transport a regiment; ten could move an entire infantry division. Such troop movements might be operational in nature, such as the flow of reinforcements that came to Grant's army from other departments during the siege of Vicksburg; or tactical, as demonstrated during the Chickasaw Bayou battle when Sherman used riverboats to move troops from one part of the battlefield to another.

The rivers that moved supplies for the Army carried guns for the Navy—big guns, and lots of them. That portion of the Union's Mississippi squadron involved in the Vicksburg campaign possessed approximately 200 guns, which ranged from 24-pounder howitzers, to 11-inch smoothbores, and 100-pounder rifles. In comparison, Grant's army fielded 180 artillery pieces, mostly 12-pounders, when it first besieged Vicksburg. Pemberton's Confederates surrendered 172 pieces when the siege ended. Thus, the Mississippi River Squadron was by far the greatest source of artillery firepower in the theater.

It is important to understand that the Mississippi River was not a barrier to the Union ground forces involved in the Vicksburg campaign; rather, it was a superhighway. The free movement by river of both men and materiel was an essential precondition for Grant's campaign against Vicksburg. Conversely, when the Confederates lost the use of the rivers, their ability to wage war suffered. The U.S. Navy's presence along the Mississippi and its tributaries during the Vicksburg campaign seriously interfered with Confederate attempts to reinforce and resupply its ground elements opposing Grant. Unable to utilize water transport, the Confederates were forced to rely on the substandard roads and railroads. Moreover, the economic life of the Mississippi valley, and of the Confederacy as a whole, suffered significantly. Producers of commodities such as sugar and cotton were largely cut off from their markets in the east and overseas. By 1863, rather than producing cash crops that could not be transported, planters increasingly raised corn and hogs to feed themselves, commodities that they had imported by river before the war.

Confederate Naval Power

The U.S. Navy was able to exercise such pervasive control over the western rivers only because, by 1863, the Confederates lacked the means of challenging Union naval superiority. Such had not always been the case. In 1861, the Confederate War Department had established a "River Defense Fleet" in New Orleans, consisting of fourteen commercial riverboats converted into rams by strengthening their bows and stacking cotton bales on their decks as a form of armor (giving birth to the term "cottonclad"). Elsewhere on the Mississippi and its tributaries, about twenty-five other riverboats had artillery mounted on their decks making them into gunboats. Additionally, the Confederates laid keels for six new ironclad gunboats and began converting an existing boat into a seventh.

This imposing river force met with disaster in 1862. Two full-scale naval battles, one fought down river from New Orleans and the other upstream from Memphis, broke the back of Confederate naval power on the Mississippi. Every one of the fourteen rams of the River Defense Fleet was either destroyed in battle, captured, or burned to prevent capture. Only five of twenty-five gunboats survived into 1863, mostly by hiding upstream in such tributaries as the Red, Arkansas, White, and Yazoo Rivers. (Only one would remain by 1864.) The seven Confederate river ironclads fared little better. One was lost at the battle below New Orleans. Five were never commissioned, being captured or destroyed to prevent capture while still under construction. Just one, the *Arkansas,* saw action. Although its combat career lasted only three weeks, the *Arkansas* demonstrated that even one Confederate ironclad loose upon the Mississippi posed an intolerable threat to Union naval superiority. Measuring 165 feet in length, armed with a ram bow and eight guns, and protected by wood and iron armor measuring eighteen inches in thickness, her Achilles heel proved to be the power plant driving her twin screws. The *Arkansas'* own crew scuttled her on 5 August 1862 after her steam engines failed.

Thus, at the time of the Vicksburg campaign, there were no Confederate ironclads and only a handful of gunboats on the western rivers. In fact, the greatest threat to the U.S. Navy during this campaign was that of its own vessels falling into enemy hands. In February 1863, two Union boats—the ram *Queen of the West* and the ironclad *Indianola*—ran downstream past the Vicksburg batteries. Confederates captured *Queen of the West* when she ran aground and then used her to disable *Indianola,* which they attempted to refloat. *Queen of the West* was later destroyed in action on the Atchafalaya River. The Confederates scuttled *Indianola* on 26 February when a Union "monitor" ran the Vicksburg batteries, as if on its way to recapture *Indianola.* This "monitor" was in fact an unmanned, unpowered barge rigged out to resemble an ironclad.

Essentially, the Confederacy's only means of asserting control over the Mississippi River in 1863 resided in the fortified batteries at Vicksburg, Grand Gulf, and Port Hudson. The absence of a credible Confederate river fleet greatly magnified the operational and strategic significance of these points. They were, in effect, a substitute for naval power.

The Mississippi River Squadron

The Union naval force that played such a large role in the Vicksburg campaign began its existence as an Army organization known as the Western Flotilla. In 1861, the War Department began to procure combat vessels both by converting commercial boats and by contracting for new construction. The U.S. Navy, which at first wanted little to do with the river war, provided officers and some of the crews, but the Army owned the boats. The first three commanders of the Western Flotilla, though Navy officers, took orders from the Army department commander.

On 1 October 1862, the flotilla transferred from Army to Navy control. (The Army, however, retained possession of the unarmed riverboats that it used as transports.) The flotilla was redesignated the Mississippi River Squadron and received a new commander, David D. Porter, later that month. Porter held the rank of Flag Officer, which (at that time) was equivalent to a major general. Later, Porter was promoted to the rank of acting rear admiral, which theoretically made him the highest-ranking Union officer in the theater—Grant was still a two-star general.

Neither Porter's rank nor the separation of the squadron from Army control altered the fact that the war in the Mississippi Valley was primarily an Army war. In practice, the ground force commander initiated the majority of joint operations. However, it was a wise general who kept his naval counterpart intimately involved in the planning process. Since the squadron commander no longer took orders from the Army, he could effectively veto any plan that he considered unfeasible. Thus, it was best not to surprise him with a scheme that had not received Navy input. Under these circumstances, only the mutual trust and respect between Army and Navy commanders prevented disagreements from escalating into deadlock. By 1863, Grant understood what Porter could and could not be asked to do, and Porter understood the type of support that the Army needed. Both Grant and Porter knew that if they failed to cooperate effectively, their superiors in Washington would be sure to intervene. Neither man desired that.

At the time of the Vicksburg campaign, the Mississippi River Squadron numbered approximately sixty combat vessels. Of these, about twenty to twenty-five would be involved in the Vicksburg operation at any given time. The remainder could be found patrolling the Cumberland and Tennessee Rivers, interdicting Confederate trade along the Mississippi, and undergoing repairs. A grand total of approximately thirty-three Union combat vessels participated in the Vicksburg campaign at one time or another—thirteen ironclads, seven rams, eleven light draughts (commonly called "tinclads"), and two "timberclads." The variety of vessel types reflects the diversity of missions that the squadron executed.

For heavy combat, the squadron relied upon its ironclads. Their firepower and armor protection allowed them to trade blows with any enemy, ashore or afloat. Seven of the squadron's ironclads were built to a common design, created for the War Department in 1861 by a U.S.

Navy "constructor" named Samuel M. Pook. James B. Eads of St. Louis won the contract to build the seven "City Class" ironclads, so called because each was named after a midwestern river town. The seven were the *Cairo, Carondelet, Cincinnati, Louisville, Mound City, Pittsburg, and St. Louis* (later renamed the *Baron De Kalb*).

One of the City Class boats, the *Cairo* (pronounced *Kay-row*), is on display at the Vicksburg National Military Park. Visitors are often surprised by how large the *Cairo* is—175 feet long and 51 feet wide. She had a draft of only six feet (meaning that she could float in six feet of water). Two steam engines driving a center-mounted paddlewheel propelled the vessel to a top speed of approximately six knots. For armament, the *Cairo* mounted three 7-inch rifles, three 8-inch smoothbores, six 32-pounder smoothbores, and one 30-pounder Parrot rifle. The guns were located in a slope-sided casemate with three ports facing forward, four to each side, and two to the stern. (Thus, unlike seagoing vessels of the day, which could fire half their guns at one time with each broadside, the ironclad could train only roughly one-fourth of its armament on a given target.) The casemate was protected by 2½ of iron armor fixed over timbers two feet thick. Railroad rails provided additional protection on the rounded corners of the casemate. The octagonal pilothouse carried 1¼ inch of iron over timbers. Armor was thickest on the forward surfaces. The rear of the vessel was essentially unarmored as were the underwater surfaces. The *Cairo* sank in December 1862 after a "torpedo" (mine) blew a hole in her hull.

Three other ironclads, the *Tuscumbia, Chillicothe,* and *Indianola* were, like the Eads boats, specially designed and constructed to be ironclad gunboats. Their builder was Joseph Brown of Cincinnati. Unlike the Eads vessels, these were poorly constructed, lightly armed, and imperfectly armored. *Tuscumbia* was the worst of the lot—her hull had a twist to it, the deck sagged, and her already-inadequate armor plates tended to fall off when struck by artillery. The *Tuscumbia* carried only five guns, the *Chillicothe* two, and the *Indianola* four.

Another three ironclads, *Choctaw, Lafayette,* and *Benton,* were converted from commercial riverboats. They were stronger, safer, and more effective than Joseph Brown's vessels. Moreover, they were significantly larger than either the Eads or Brown ironclads. The *Choctaw* and *Lafayette* carried a layer of rubber, in addition to their iron armor, to help deflect projectiles (it did not work). The *Benton,* which sometimes served as Porter's flagship, was the Mississippi

River Squadron's most powerful vessel. She measured 202 feet long by 72 feet wide, and carried sixteen guns.

The ironclads' primary mission during the Vicksburg campaign was to silence Confederate fortified batteries ashore. At one time or another, Union ironclads pounded Haynes' Bluff, Vicksburg's river batteries, and Grand Gulf. The ironclads subdued none of these positions, but the fact that the Confederates deemed it necessary to build major fortifications to house these batteries is itself testimony to the power of ironclad gunfire.

The approved tactic for bombarding a fort was to fight it head-on from the downstream side of the fort—head-on to take advantage of the ironclad's heaviest armor (located on the forward surfaces), and from the downstream direction because the boats handled better with their bows facing the current. Moreover, by approaching the fort from downstream, any vessel disabled by enemy fire would drift to safety, away from the enemy guns. The range of engagement could be quite short—the ironclads might close to within 100 yards of the fortification, blasting with grape and exploding shell in an attempt to break down the earthen parapet (front wall) of the fort and disable its guns.

Ironclads were also highly effective in combat against other vessels on those increasingly rare occasions when Confederate boats challenged the Mississippi River Squadron. However, a different category of vessels existed strictly for combat against other boats. These were the rams. In 1862, a civil engineer named Charles Ellet, Jr., obtained a colonel's commission and authorization from the War Department to convert nine riverboats into rams. The necessary modifications involved reinforcing their hulls and filling their bows with timber so that they could survive deliberate collisions with enemy boats. The Ellet ram fleet had its day of glory on 6 June 1862 when it played a prominent part in the naval victory at Memphis. But since they carried little or no armament other than their rams, Ellet's vessels were of limited utility once the Confederate fleet had ceased to be an immediate threat. Even so, six Ellet rams were on hand for the Vicksburg campaign: the *Lancaster, Lioness, Monarch, Queen of the West, Switzerland,* and *Fulton*. The Ellet ram fleet, which remained an Army organization, was not technically a part of the Navy squadron, although it operated under Porter's orders.

Porter did possess one ram of his own: a Confederate vessel sunk at Memphis in 1862 but salvaged and returned to duty under the U.S. flag. This was the *General Price,* which differed from the Ellet rams in that it carried four heavy guns, making it more useful in joint operations than Ellet's boats.

The light draught vessels, or "tinclads," were, like the rams, modified riverboats, but by 1863, they were much more important to the day-to-day business of the squadron. Tinclads provided the naval presence that kept waterways under Union control, even when the riverbanks belonged to the Confederates. The tinclads got their name from the iron plating, ½-inch to ¾-inch thick, that protected the power plant and pilot house from small-arms fire. To drive off "bushwhackers," the typical tinclad mounted six 24-pounder howitzers facing to the sides, more than enough firepower to cope with most threats. Tinclads could even double as troop transports in joint operations, each one carrying up to 200 infantry. Their shallow draft enabled them to prowl waterways inaccessible to heavier war vessels. Some tinclads could float on as little as eighteen inches of water when lightly loaded.

The Mississippi River Squadron possessed thirty-four tinclads in June 1863, ten of which played roles in the Vicksburg campaign: the *Cricket, Forest Rose, Juliet, Linden, Glide, Marmora, Petrel, Rattler, Romeo,* and *Signal.* In addition, the "large tinclad" *Black Hawk,* which mounted thirteen guns, and two "timberclads," *Lexington* (eight guns) and *Tyler* (ten guns) were involved in operations around Vicksburg.

If the tinclads were the most versatile, certainly the most specialized instruments at Porter's disposal were the mortar boats. These were unpowered scows or rafts, each carrying one squat, kettle-shaped 13-inch siege mortar. The mortar itself weighed 17,120 pounds. With a full 20-pound charge, it could lob a 200-pound shell a distance of over two miles. During the siege of Vicksburg, thirteen mortar boats anchored on the western side of De Soto point, from where they maintained a steady barrage against the invested city

Naval Operations, 1863

By early 1863, Porter's Mississippi River Squadron controlled the Mississippi from St. Louis to Vicksburg. To the south, Rear Admiral David G. Farragut's Western Gulf Blockading Squadron dominated the river from its outlet to the Confederate fort at Port Hudson,

Louisiana. On 14 March 1863, Farragut succeeded in running upstream past Port Hudson in his flagship, the screw-sloop *Hartford*, in company with the small gunboat *Albatross*. The *Hartford* was powerful and fast, but being an ocean-going warship, she was ill-suited to conditions on the Mississippi. She measured 225 feet long by 44 feet wide and had a draft in excess of seventeen feet—far too deep for safe navigation on the western rivers. Her three masts looked absurd on the Mississippi, but her twenty-seven-gun armament commanded respect. Farragut's greatest contribution to the Vicksburg campaign was to blockade the mouth of the Red River until Porter's gunboats got below, thus severing a major military and commercial artery of the Confederacy.

On the night of 16-17 April 1863, Porter led a portion of the Mississippi River Squadron downstream past the batteries of Vicksburg in order to provide support and transportation for Grant's army, which was in the process of marching southward on the western side of the river. Seven ironclads ran the batteries—the *Carondelet, Pittsburg, Louisville, Mound City, Benton, Lafayette, and Tuscumbia*—along with one ram, the *General Price*, one tug, and three Army transports. Porter left behind the ironclad *De Kalb* and the tinclad fleet to keep the river safe upstream from Vicksburg. Two additional ironclads, the *Cincinnati* and *Choctaw*, arrived later from upriver to assist the *De Kalb*. The seven ironclads that ran the Vicksburg batteries tried, but failed, to silence the Confederate batteries at Grand Gulf on 29 April.

In May, when Grant's army crossed to the east bank of the Mississippi and marched inland, Porter subdivided the downstream portion of his force. The ironclads *Louisville, Tuscumbia, Mound City*, and *Carondelet* kept station at Grand Gulf, safeguarding Grant's line of communications. Porter himself led the ironclads *Benton, Lafayette*, and *Pittsburg*, plus the rams *General Price* and *Switzerland* (which had run the Vicksburg batteries in March), on operations up the Red River and its tributaries in conjunction with ground elements under Major General Nathaniel P. Banks. These joint operations on the Red River, plus the presence of ironclads at Grand Gulf, helped ensure that the Confederate defenders of Vicksburg received no reinforcements from west of the Mississippi during a critical period of the campaign.

In the last week of May, when Grant's army laid siege to Vicksburg by land, Porter's squadron besieged it by water. Not only did ironclads and mortarboats fire 11,500 projectiles in support of the siege, but also

Porter landed thirteen heavy cannon from his gunboats for the Army to use as siege artillery. These land batteries fired 4,500 rounds. And, of course, the squadron assured that supplies and reinforcements flowed to Grant's army without interference from the enemy.

The war on the western rivers did not end when Vicksburg fell to Grant on 4 July 1863. Union forces could occupy only key points along the Mississippi and other rivers. To the end of the war, "bushwhackers" and raiders continued to harass Union riverboat traffic, necessitating a continuous program of patrols and escorts by the tinclads and ironclads of the Mississippi River Squadron.

At war's end, however, the squadron vanished virtually without a trace. Whereas ocean-going vessels like the *Hartford* served on for years, even decades, the postwar Navy had no requirement whatsoever for a riverine force. Gunboats were converted (reconverted, in many cases) into commercial transports and steamed off into oblivion. Only the *Cairo,* encased in the protective muck of the Yazoo River for over a century, remains to illuminate a unique and fascinating chapter in American naval history.

Table 4. Mississippi River Squadron: Representative Vessels

Vessel Name	Type	Dimensions Length, Breadth, Draft	Armament	Armor (max)	Speed (knots)
Cairo	Ironclad (City Class)	175'/51'/6'	13 guns	2.5" Iron	6
Tuscumbia	Ironclad	178'/75'/7'	5 guns	6" Iron	8.6
Chillicothe	Ironclad	162'/50'/4'	2 guns	3" Iron	7
Indianola	Ironclad	175'/52'/5'	4 guns	3" Iron	6
Benton	Ironclad (conversion)	202'/72'/9'	16 guns	2.5" Iron	5.5
Choctaw	Ironclad (conversion)	260'/45'/8'	6 guns	1" Iron + 1" rubber	?
Layfayette	Ironclad (conversion)	280'/45'/8'	10 guns	2.5" Iron + 2" rubber	4
Queen of the West	Ellet Ram	181'/36'/6'	Ram 4 guns	None	?
General Price	Ram (captured)	182'/30'/13'	Ram 4 guns	None	10
Cricket	Tinclad	154'/28'/4'	6 guns	½" Iron	6
Black Hawk	Large Tinclad	260'/45'/6'	11 guns	½" Iron	?
Tyler	Timberclad	180'/45'/6'	10 guns	Wood planking	8

Weapons

Infantry

During the 1850s, in a technological revolution of major proportions, the rifle-musket began to replace the relatively inaccurate smoothbore musket in ever-increasing numbers, both in Europe and America. This process, accelerated by the Civil War, ensured that the rifled shoulder weapon would be the basic weapon used by infantrymen in both the Federal and Confederate armies.

The standard and most common shoulder weapon used in the American Civil War was the Springfield .58-caliber rifle-musket, models 1855, 1861, and 1863. In 1855, the U.S. Army adopted this weapon to replace the .69-caliber smoothbore musket and the .54-caliber rifle. In appearance, the rifle-musket was similar to the smoothbore musket. Both were single-shot muzzleloaders, but the rifled bore of the new weapon substantially increased its range and accuracy. The rifling system chosen by the United States was designed by Claude Minié, a French Army officer. Whereas earlier rifles fired a round, nonexpanding ball, the Minié system used a hollow-based cylindro-conoidal projectile, slightly smaller than the bore, which could be dropped easily into the barrel. When the powder charge was ignited by a fulminate of mercury percussion cap, the released propellant gases expanded the base of the bullet into the rifled grooves, giving the projectile a ballistic spin.

The Model 1855 Springfield rifle-musket was the first regulation arm to use the hollow-base .58-caliber Minié bullet. The slightly modified Model 1861 was the principal infantry weapon of the Civil War, although two subsequent models were produced in about equal quantities. The Model 1861 was fifty-six inches long, had a forty-inch barrel, and weighed 8.75 pounds. It could be fitted with a twenty-one inch socket bayonet (with an eighteen-inch blade, three inch socket) and a rear sight graduated to 500 yards. The maximum effective range of the Springfield rifle-musket was approximately 500 yards, although it had killing power at 1,000 yards. The round could penetrate 11 inches of white pine board at 200 yards and 3¾ inches at 1,000 yards, with a penetration of one inch being considered the equivalent of disabling a human being. Range and accuracy were increased by the use of the new weapon, but the soldiers' vision was still obscured by the dense clouds of smoke produced by its black powder propellant.

To load a muzzleloading rifle, the soldier took a paper cartridge in hand, tore the end of the paper with his teeth, poured the powder down the barrel, and placed a bullet in the muzzle. Then, using a metal ramrod, he pushed the bullet firmly down the barrel until seated. He then cocked the hammer and placed the percussion cap on the cone or nipple, which, when struck by the hammer, ignited the gunpowder. The average rate of fire was three rounds per minute. A well-trained soldier could possibly load and fire four times per minute, but in the confusion of battle, the rate of fire was probably slower, two to three rounds per minute.

In addition to the Springfields, over one hundred types of muskets, rifles, and rifled muskets—ranging up to .79-caliber—were used during the American Civil War. The numerous American-made weapons were supplemented early in the conflict by a wide variety of imported models. The best, most popular, and most numerous of the foreign weapons was the British .577-caliber Enfield rifle, Model 1853. Fifty-four inches long (with a 39-inch barrel), the rifle weighed 8.7 pounds (9.2 with the bayonet), could be fitted with a socket bayonet with an eighteen-inch blade, and had a rear sight graduated to a range of 800 yards. The Enfield design was produced in a variety of forms, both long and short barreled, by several British manufacturers and at least one American company. Of all the foreign designs, the Enfield most closely resembled the Springfield in characteristics and capabilities. The United States purchased over 436,000 Enfield-pattern weapons during the war. Statistics on Confederate purchases are more difficult to ascertain, but a report dated February 1863 indicates that 70,980 long Enfields and 9,715 short Enfields had been delivered by that time, with another 23,000 awaiting delivery.

While the quality of imported weapons varied, experts considered the Enfields and the Austrian Lorenz rifle-muskets very good. Some foreign governments and manufacturers took advantage of the huge initial demand for weapons by dumping their obsolete weapons on the American market. This practice was especially prevalent with some of the older smoothbore muskets and converted flintlocks. The greatest challenge, however, lay in maintaining these weapons and supplying ammunition and replacement parts for calibers ranging from .44 to .79. The quality of the imported weapons eventually improved as the procedures, standards, and astuteness of the purchasers improved. For the most part, the European suppliers provided needed weapons, and the newer foreign weapons were highly regarded.

All told, the United States purchased about 1,165,000 European rifles and muskets during the war, nearly all within the first two years. Of these, 110,853 were smoothbores. The remainder were primarily the French Minié rifles (44,250), Prussian rifles (59,918), and Austrian Model 1854s (266,294), Bokers (187,533), and Jagers (29,850). Estimates of total Confederate purchases range from 340,000 to 400,000. In addition to the Enfields delivered to the Confederacy (mentioned above), 27,000 Austrian rifles, 21,040 British muskets, and 2,020 Brunswick rifles were also purchased, with 30,000 Austrian rifles awaiting shipment.

Breechloaders and repeating rifles were available by 1861 and were initially purchased in limited quantities, often by individual soldiers. Generally, however, they were not issued to troops in large numbers because of technical problems (poor breech seals, faulty ammunition), fear by the Ordnance Department that the troops would waste ammunition, and the cost of rifle production. The most famous of the breechloaders was the single-shot Sharps, produced in both carbine and rifle models. The Model 1859 .52-caliber rifle was 47⅛ inches long, and weighed 8¾ pounds, while the carbine was .52 caliber and 39⅛ inches long and weighed 7¾ pounds. Both weapons used a linen cartridge and a pellet-primer-feed mechanism. Most Sharps carbines were issued to Federal cavalry units.

The best known of the repeaters was probably the seven-shot, .52-caliber Spencer, which also came in both rifle and carbine models. The rifle was 47 inches long and weighed 10 pounds, while the carbine was 39 inches long and weighed 8¼ pounds. The first mounted infantry unit to use Spencer repeating rifles in combat was Colonel John T. Wilder's "Lighting Brigade" on 24 June 1863 at Hoover's Gap, Tennessee. The Spencer was also the first weapon adopted by the U.S. Army that fired a metallic, rimfire, self-contained cartridge. Soldiers loaded rounds through an opening in the butt of the stock, which fed into the chamber through a tubular magazine by the action of the trigger guard. The hammer still had to be cocked manually before each shot.

Better than either the Sharps or the Spencer was the Henry rifle. Never adopted by the U.S. Army in large quantity, it was purchased privately by soldiers during the war. The Henry was a sixteen-shot, .44-caliber rimfire cartridge repeater. It was 43½ inches long and weighed 9¼ pounds. The tubular magazine located directly beneath the barrel had a fifteen-round capacity with an additional round in the chamber. Of the approximate 13,500 Henrys produced, probably 10,000 saw limited service. The government purchased only 1,731.

The Colt repeating rifle (or revolving carbine), Model 1855, also was available to Civil War soldiers in limited numbers. The weapon was produced in several lengths and calibers, the lengths varying from 32 to 42½ inches, while calibers were .36, .44, and .56. The .36 and .44 calibers were made to chamber six shots, while the .56 caliber had five chambers. The Colt Firearms Company was also the primary supplier of revolvers, the .44-caliber Army revolver and the .36-caliber Navy revolver being the most popular (over 146,000 purchased) because they were simple, sturdy, and reliable.

Cavalry

Initially armed with sabers and pistols (and, in one case, lances), Federal cavalry troopers quickly added the breechloading carbine to their inventory of weapons. However, one Federal regiment, the 6th Pennsylvania Cavalry, carried lances until 1863. Troopers preferred the easier-handling carbines to rifles and the breechloaders to awkward muzzleloaders. Of the single-shot breechloading carbines that saw extensive use during the Civil War, the Hall .52 caliber accounted for approximately 20,000 in 1861. The Hall was quickly replaced by a variety of carbines, including the Merrill .54 caliber (14,495), Maynard .52 caliber (20,002), Gallager .53 caliber (22,728), Smith .52 caliber (30,062), Burnside .56 caliber (55,567), and Sharps .54 caliber (80,512). The next step in the evolutionary process was the repeating carbine, the favorite by 1865 being the Spencer .52-caliber, seven-shot repeater (94,194). Because of the South's limited industrial capacity, Confederate cavalrymen had a more difficult time arming themselves. Nevertheless, they too embraced the firepower revolution, choosing shotguns and muzzleloading carbines as their primary weapons. In addition, Confederate cavalrymen made extensive use of battlefield salvage by recovering Federal weapons. However, the South's difficulties in producing the metallic-rimmed cartridges required by many of these recovered weapons limited their usefulness.

Artillery

Artillery in the Civil War era consisted of four general weapon types—guns, howitzers, mortars, and columbiads. Guns were long-barreled cannon that delivered high-velocity, flat-trajectory, long-range fire. Howitzers were lighter and shorter than guns, and used a smaller powder charge to fire explosive projectiles at shorter distances. Mortars, the shortest pieces, used a small powder charge to lob a large projectile at a very high angle. Columbiads combined characteristics of all three. They were generally of large caliber, possessed relatively long barrels, and used a large powder charge to fire a heavy projectile great distances.

Artillery was also categorized as to method of employment—field, siege (officially classified as "siege and garrison"), and seacoast. Field artillery, the lightest and most mobile, operated within tactical units as part of the standard combined arms team. Siege and seacoast artillery operated more or less independently of the other combat arms. Siege artillery units normally formed siege trains that were called to the front only under special circumstances. Seacoast artillery, the heaviest Civil War ordnance, was emplaced in fixed positions.

Field Artillery

In 1841, the U. S. Army selected bronze as the standard material for field pieces and at the same time adopted a new system of field artillery. The 1841 field artillery system consisted entirely of smoothbore muzzleloaders: 6- and 12-pounder guns; 12-, 24-, and 32-pounder howitzers; and 12-pounder mountain howitzers. A pre-Civil War battery usually consisted of six field pieces—four guns and two howitzers. A 6-pounder battery contained four 6-pounder guns and two 12-pounder howitzers, while a 12-pounder battery had four 12-pounder guns and two 24-pounder howitzers. The guns fired solid shot, shell, spherical case, grapeshot, and canister rounds, while howitzers fired shell, spherical case, grapeshot, and canister rounds.

The 6-pounder gun (effective range 1,523 yards) was the primary field piece used from the time of the Mexican War until the Civil War. By 1861, however, the 1841 system based upon the 6-pounder was obsolete. In 1857, a new and more versatile field piece, the 12-pounder gun-howitzer (Napoleon), Model 1857, appeared on the scene. Designed as a multipurpose piece to replace existing guns and howitzers, the Napoleon fired canister and shell like the 12-pounder howitzer and solid shot at ranges comparable to the 12-pounder gun. The Napoleon was a bronze, muzzleloading smoothbore with an effective range of 1,680 yards using solid shot (see table 5 for a comparison of artillery data). Served by a nine-man crew, the piece could fire at a sustained rate of two aimed shots per minute. With less than fifty Napoleons initially available in 1861, obsolete 6-pounders remained in the inventories of both armies for some time, especially in the western theater.

Another new development in field artillery was the introduction of rifling. Although rifled guns provided greater range and accuracy, they were somewhat less reliable and slower to load than smoothbores. (Rifled ammunition was semi-fixed, so the charge and the projectile had to be loaded separately.) Moreover, the canister load of the rifle did not perform as well as that of the smoothbore. Initially, some smoothbores were rifled on the James pattern, but they soon proved unsatisfactory because the bronze rifling eroded too quickly. Therefore, most rifled artillery was either wrought iron or cast iron with a wrought iron reinforcing band.

The most common rifled guns were the 10-pounder Parrott and the Rodman, or 3-inch, ordnance rifle. The Parrott rifle was a cast-iron piece, easily identified by the wrought-iron band reinforcing the breech. The 10-pounder Parrott was made in two models: the Model 1861 had a 2.9-inch rifled bore with three lands and grooves and a slight muzzle swell, while the Model 1863 had a 3-inch bore and no muzzle swell. The Rodman or Ordnance rifle was a long-tubed, wrought-iron piece that had a 3-inch bore with seven lands and grooves. Ordnance rifles were sturdier than the 10-pounder Parrott and displayed superior accuracy and reliability.

By 1860, the ammunition for field artillery consisted of four general types for both smoothbores and rifles: solid shot, shell, case, and canister. Solid shot for smoothbores was a round, cast-iron projectile; for rifled guns it took the form of an elongated projectile known as a bolt. Solid shot, with its smashing or battering effect, was used in a counterbattery role or against buildings and massed troop formations. The rifle's conical-shaped bolt lacked the effectiveness of the smoothbore's cannonball because it tended to bury itself upon impact instead of bounding along the ground like round shot.

Shell, also known as common or explosive shell, whether spherical or conical, was a hollow projectile filled with an explosive charge of black powder detonated by a fuse. Shell was designed to break into jagged pieces, producing an antipersonnel effect, but the low-order detonation seldom produced more than three to five fragments. In addition to its casualty producing effects, shell had a psychological impact when it exploded over the heads of troops. It was also used against field fortifications and in a counterbattery role. Case or case shot for both smoothbore and rifled guns was a hollow projectile with thinner walls than shell. The projectile was filled with round lead or iron balls set in a matrix of sulphur that surrounded a small bursting charge. Case was primarily used in an antipersonnel role. This type of round had been invented by Henry Shrapnel, a British artillery officer, hence the term "shrapnel."

Lastly, there was canister, probably the most effective round and the round of choice at close range (400 yards or less) against massed troops. Canister was essentially a tin can filled with iron balls packed in sawdust, with no internal bursting charge. When fired, the can disintegrated, and the balls followed their own paths to the target. The canister round for the 12-pounder Napoleon consisted of twenty-seven 1½ inch iron balls packed inside an elongated tin cylinder. At extremely close ranges, artillerymen often loaded double charges of canister.

Heavy Artillery—Siege and Seacoast

The 1841 artillery system listed eight types of siege artillery and another six types as seacoast artillery. The 1861 *Ordnance Manual* included eleven different kinds of siege ordnance. The principal siege weapons in 1861 were the 4.5-inch rifle; 18-, and 24-pounder guns; a 24-pounder howitzer and two types of 8-inch howitzers; and several types of 8- and 10-inch mortars. The normal rate of fire for siege guns and mortars was about twelve rounds per hour, but with a well-drilled crew, this could probably be increased to about twenty rounds per hour. The rate of fire for siege howitzers was somewhat lower, being about eight shots per hour.

The carriages for siege guns and howitzers were longer and heavier than field artillery carriages but were similar in construction. The 24-pounder model 1839 was the heaviest piece that could be moved over the roads of the day. Alternate means of transport, such as railroad or watercraft, were required to move larger pieces any great distance.

The rounds fired by siege artillery were generally the same as those fired by field artillery, except that siege artillery continued to use grapeshot after it was discontinued in the field artillery (1841). A "stand of grape" consisted of nine iron balls, ranging from two to about three and one-half inches in size depending on the gun caliber.

The largest and heaviest artillery pieces in the Civil War era belonged to the seacoast artillery. These large weapons were normally

A 13-inch mortar, now located on the grounds of the Grand Gulf Museum.

mounted in fixed positions. The 1861 system included five types of columbiads, ranging from 8- to 15-inch; 32- and 42-pounder guns; 8- and 10-inch howitzers; and mortars of 10- and 13-inches.

Wartime additions to the Federal seacoast artillery inventory included Parrott rifles, ranging from 6.4-inch to 10-inch (300-pounder). New columbiads, developed by Ordnance Lieutenant Thomas J. Rodman, included 8-inch, 10-inch, and 15-inch models. The Confederates produced some new seacoast artillery of their own- Brooke rifles in 6.4-inch and 7-inch versions. They also imported weapons from England, including 7- and 8-inch Armstrong rifles, 6.3-to12.5-inch Blakely rifles, and 5-inch Whitworth rifles.

Seacoast artillery fired the same projectiles as siege artillery but with one addition - hot shot. As its name implies, hot shot was solid shot heated in special ovens until red-hot, then *carefully* loaded and fired as an incendiary round.

Naval Ordnance

Like the Army, the U.S. Navy in the Civil War possessed an artillery establishment that spanned the spectrum from light to heavy. A series of light boat guns and howitzers corresponded to the Army's field artillery. Designed for service on small boats and launches, this class of weapon included 12- and 24-pounder pieces, both smoothbore and rifled. The most successful boat gun was a 12-pounder smoothbore howitzer (4.62-inch bore) designed by John A. Dahlgren, the Navy's premier ordnance expert and wartime chief of ordnance. Typically mounted in the bow of a small craft, the Dahlgren 12-pounder could be transferred, in a matter of minutes, to an iron field carriage for use on shore. This versatile little weapon fired shell and case rounds.

Naturally, most naval artillery was designed for ship killing. A variety of 32-pounder guns (6.4-inch bore) produced from the 1820s through the 1840s remained in service during the Civil War. These venerable smoothbores, direct descendants of the broadside guns used in the Napoleonic Wars, fired solid shot and were effective not only in ship-to-ship combat but also in the shore-bombardment role.

A more modern class of naval artillery weapons was known as "shellguns." These were large-caliber smoothbores designed to shoot massive exploding shells that were capable of dealing catastrophic damage to a wooden-hulled vessel. Shellguns could be found both in broadside batteries and in upper-deck pivot mounts, which allowed wide traverse. An early example of the shellgun, designed in 1845 but still in service during the Civil War, was an 8-inch model that fired a 51-pound shell.

John Dahlgren's design came to typify the shellgun class of weapons. All of his shellguns shared an unmistakable "beer-bottle" shape. The most successful Dahlgren shellguns were a 9-inch model (72.5-pound shell or 90-pound solid shot), an 11-inch (136-pound shell or 170-pound solid shot), and a 15-inch, which fired an awesome 330-pound shell or 440-pound solid shot. A pivot-mounted 11-inch shellgun proved to be the decisive weapon in the *U.S.S. Kearsarge's* 1864 victory over the *C.S.S. Alabama*. The famous U.S. Navy ironclad *Monitor* mounted two 11-inch Dahlgrens in its rotating turret. Later monitors carried 15-inch shellguns.

The U.S. Navy also made wide use of rifled artillery. These high-velocity weapons became increasingly important with the advent of ironclad warships. Some Navy rifles were essentially identical to Army models. For instance, the Navy procured Parrott rifles in 4.2-inch, 6.4-inch, 8-inch, and 10-inch versions, each of which had a counterpart in the Army as either siege or seacoast artillery. Other rifled weapons, conceived specifically for naval use, included two Dahlgren designs. The 50-pounder (with approximately 5-inch bore)

Table 5. Types of Artillery Available in the Vicksburg Campaign

FIELD ARTILLERY

Type	Model	Bore Dia. (in.)	Tube Length (in.)	Tube wt. (lbs.)	Carriage wt. (lbs.)	Range (yds) /deg. elev.
Smoothbores						
6-pounder	Gun	3.67	65.6	884	900	1,523/5°
12-pounder "Napoleon"	Gun-Howitzer	4.62	72.15	1,227	1,128	1,680/5°
12-pounder	Howitzer	4.62	58.6	788	900	1,072/5°
24-pounder	Howitzer	5.82	71.2	1,318	1,128	1,322/5°
Rifles						
10-pounder	Parrott	3.0	78	890	900	2,970/10°
3-inch	Ordnance	3.0	73.3	820	900	2,788/10°
20-pounder	Parrott	3.67	89.5	1,750		4,400/15°

SIEGE AND GARRISON

Type	Model	Bore Dia. (in)	Tube Length (in)	Tube wt. (lbs)	Projectile wt. (lbs)	Range (yds) /deg. elev.
Smoothbores						
8-inch	Howitzer	8.0	61.5	2,614	50.5 shell	2,280/12° 30'
10-inch	Mortar	10.0	28.0	1,852	87.5 shell	2,028/45°
12-pounder	Gun	4.62	116.0	3,590	12.3 shot	
24-pounder	Gun	5.82	124.0	5,790	24.4 shot	1,901/5°
Rifles						
18-pounder*	Gun (Rifled)	5.3	123.25			
30-pounder	Parrott	4.2	132.5	4,200	29.0 shell	6,700/25°

*The Confederate "Whistling Dick," an obsolete smoothbore siege gun, rifled and banded.

Table 5. Types of Artillery Available in the Vicksburg Campaign (Cont)

SEACOAST

Type	Model	Bore Dia. (in)	Tube Length (in)	Tube wt. (lbs)	Projectile wt. (lbs)	Range (yds) /deg. elev.
Smoothbores						
8- inch	Columbiad	8.0	124	9,240	65 shot	4,812/27° 30'
9- inch*	Dahlgren	9.0				
10- inch	Columbiad	10.0	126	15,400	128 shot	5,654/39° 15'
11- inch	Dahlgren	11.0	161	15,700		3,650/20°
32- pounder	Gun	6.4	125.7	7,200	32.6 shot	1,922/5°
42- pounder	Gun	7.0	129	8,465	42.7 shot	1,955/5°
Rifles						
6.4- inch	Brooke	6.4	144	9,120		
7- inch	Brooke	7.0	147.5	14,800		
7.5- inch**	Blakely	7.5	100			
100- pounder	Parrott	6.4	155	9,700	100 shot	2,247/5°

*A Confederate-produced copy of Dahlgren's basic design.

**The famous Confederate "Widow Blakely." Probably a British 42-pounder smoothbore shortened, banded, and rifled.

NAVAL*

Type	Model	Bore Dia. (in)	Tube Length (in)	Tube wt. (lbs)	Projectile wt. (lbs)	Range (yds) /deg. elev.
Smoothbores						
8- inch	Dahlgren	8	115.5	6,500	51 shell	1,657/5°
9- inch	Dahlgren	9	131.5	9,000	72.5 shell	1,710/5°
11- inch	Dahlgren	11	161	15,700	136 shell	1,712/5°
12- pounder	Howitzer	4.62	63.5	760	10 shell	1,085/5°
24- pounder	Howitzer	5.82	67	1,310	20 shell	1,270/5°
32-pounder	Gun	6.4	108	4,704	32 shot	1,756/5°
64- pounder	Gun	8	140.95	11,872		
Rifles						
30- pounder	Parrott	4.2	112	3,550	29 shell	2,200/5°
42-pounder**	Gun (rifled)	7	121	7,870	42 shot	
50- pounder	Dahlgren	5.1	107	6,000	50 shot	
100- pounder	Parrott	6.4	155	9,700	100 shot	2,200/5°
Mortar						
13- inch	Mortar	13	54.5	17,120	200 shell	4,200/45°

*Some naval guns served ashore as siege artillery. Moreover, many guns mounted on the boats of the Mississippi River Squadron were in fact Army field artillery and siege guns.

**Converted smoothbore.

was the better of the two Dahlgren rifles. An 80-pounder model (6-inch bore) was less popular, due to its tendency to burst.

The Confederacy relied heavily on British imports for its naval armament. Naval variants of Armstrong, Whitworth, and Blakely weapons all saw service. In addition, the Confederate Navy used Brooke rifles manufactured in the South. The Confederacy also produced a 9-inch version of the Dahlgren shellgun that apparently found use both afloat and ashore.

Weapons at Vicksburg

The wide variety of infantry weapons available to Civil War armies is clearly evident at Vicksburg. A review of the *Quarterly Returns of Ordnance* for April-June 1863 reveals that approximately three-quarters of Grant's Army of the Tennessee carried "first class" shoulder weapons, the most numerous of which were British 1853 Enfield rifle-muskets (.577 caliber). Other "first class" weapons used in the Vicksburg campaign included American-made Springfield rifle-muskets (.58 caliber), French rifle-muskets (.58 caliber), French "light" or "Liege" rifles (.577 caliber), U.S. Model 1840/45 rifles (.58 caliber), Dresden and Suhl rifle-muskets (.58 caliber), and Sharps breechloading carbines (.52 caliber). Approximately thirty-five Federal regiments (roughly one-quarter of the total) were armed primarily with "second class" weapons, such as Austrian rifle-muskets in .54, .577, and .58 calibers; U.S. Model 1841 rifled muskets (.69 caliber); U.S. Model 1816 rifled muskets altered to percussion (.69 caliber); Belgian and French rifled muskets (.69 and .71 calibers); Belgian or Vincennes rifles (.70 and .71 calibers); and both Austrian and Prussian rifled muskets in .69 and .70 calibers. Only one Federal regiment, the 101st Illinois Infantry, was armed with "third class" weapons, such as the U.S. Model 1842 smoothbore musket (.69 caliber), Austrian, Prussian, and French smoothbore muskets (.69 caliber), and Austrian and Prussian smoothbore muskets of .72 caliber. After the surrender of Vicksburg, the 101st Illinois, along with about twenty regiments armed with "second class" arms, exchanged its obsolete weapons for captured Confederate rifle-muskets.

Although the Confederate records are incomplete, it seems that some 50,000 shoulder weapons were surrendered at Vicksburg, mostly British-made Enfields. Other weapons included a mix of various .58-caliber "minié" rifles (Springfield, Richmond, Mississippi and Fayetteville models), Austrian and French rifle-muskets in .577 and

.58 calibers, Mississippi rifles, Austrian rifle-muskets (.54 caliber), various .69-caliber rifled muskets altered to percussion, Belgian .70-caliber rifles, and British smoothbore muskets in .75 caliber.

The diversity of weapons (and calibers of ammunition) obviously created serious sustainment problems for both sides. Amazingly, there is little evidence that ammunition shortages had much influence on operations (the Vicksburg defenders surrendered 600,000 rounds and 350,000 percussion caps), even though the lack of weapons standardization extended down to regimental levels.

Whereas there was little to differentiate Union from Confederate effectiveness so far as small arms were concerned, the Union forces at Vicksburg enjoyed a clear superiority in terms of artillery. When Grant's army closed on Vicksburg to begin siege operations, it held about 180 cannon. At the height of its strength during the siege, the Union force included some forty-seven batteries of artillery for a total of 247 guns—13 "heavy" guns and 234 "field" pieces. Twenty-nine of the Federal batteries contained six guns each; the remaining eighteen were considered four-gun batteries. Smoothbores outnumbered rifles by a ratio of roughly two to one.

No account of Union artillery at Vicksburg would be complete without an acknowledgment of the U.S. Navy's contributions. Porter's vessels carried guns ranging in size from 12-pounder howitzers to 11-inch Dahlgren shellguns. The *Cairo*, which is on display today at Vicksburg, suggests both the variety and the power of naval artillery in this campaign. When she sank in December 1862, the *Cairo* went down with three 42-pounder (7-inch bore) Army rifles, three 64-pounder (8-inch bore) Navy smoothbores, six 32-pounder (6.4-inch bore) Navy smoothbores, and one 4.2-inch 30-pounder Parrott rifle. Porter's firepower was not restricted to the water. During the siege, naval guns served ashore as siege artillery.

The Confederates possessed a sizeable artillery capability but could not match Federal firepower. Taken together, the Confederate forces under Pemberton and Johnston possessed a total of about 62 batteries of artillery with some 221 tubes. Pemberton's force besieged in Vicksburg included 172 cannon—approximately 103 fieldpieces, and 69 siege weapons. Thirty-seven of the siege guns, plus thirteen fieldpieces, occupied positions overlooking the Mississippi. (The number of big guns along the river dropped to thirty-one by the end of the siege—apparently some weapons were shifted elsewhere.) The thirteen field pieces were distributed along the river to counter amphibious assault. The heavy ordnance was grouped into thirteen distinct river-front batteries. These large river-defense weapons included twenty smoothbores, ranging in size from 32-pounder siege guns to 10-inch Columbiads, and seventeen rifled pieces, ranging from a 2.75-inch Whitworth to a 7.44-inch Blakely.

In most of the engagements during the Vicksburg campaign, the Union artillery demonstrated its superiority to that of the Confederates. During the siege, that superiority grew into dominance. The Confederates scattered their artillery in one- or two-gun battery positions sited to repel Union assaults. By declining to mass their guns, the Confederates could do little to interfere with Union siege operations. By contrast, Union gunners created massed batteries at critical points along the line. These were able both to support siege operations with concentrated fires and keep the Confederate guns silent by smothering the embrasures of the small Confederate battery positions. As the siege progressed, Confederate artillery fire dwindled to ineffective levels, whereas the Union artillery blasted away at will. As much as any other factor, Union fire superiority sealed the fate of the Confederate army besieged in Vicksburg.

Tactics

Tactical Doctrine in 1861

The Napoleonic Wars and the Mexican War were the major influences on American thinking at the beginning of the Civil War. The campaigns of Napoleon and Wellington provided ample lessons in battle strategy, weapons employment, and logistics, while American tactical doctrine reflected the lessons learned in Mexico (1846-48). However, these tactical lessons were misleading because in Mexico relatively small armies fought only seven pitched battles. Because these battles were so small, almost all the tactical lessons learned during the war focused at the regimental, battery, and squadron levels. Future Civil War leaders had learned little about brigade, division, and corps maneuver in Mexico, yet these units were the basic fighting elements of both armies in 1861-65.

The U.S. Army's experience in Mexico validated Napoleonic principles—particularly that of the offensive. In Mexico, tactics did not differ greatly from those of the early nineteenth century. Infantry marched in column and deployed into line to fight. Once deployed, an infantry regiment might send one or two companies forward as skirmishers, as security against surprise, or to soften the enemy's line. After identifying the enemy's position, a regiment advanced in closely ordered lines to within one hundred yards. There, it delivered a devastating volley, followed by a charge with bayonets. Both sides used this basic tactic in the first battles of the Civil War.

In Mexico, American armies employed artillery and cavalry in both offensive and defensive battle situations. In the offense, artillery moved as near to the enemy lines as possible—normally just outside musket range—in order to blow gaps in the enemy's line that the infantry might exploit with a determined charge. In the defense, artillery blasted advancing enemy lines with canister and withdrew if the enemy attack got within musket range. Cavalry guarded the army's flanks and rear but held itself ready to charge if enemy infantry became disorganized or began to withdraw.

These tactics worked perfectly well with the weapons technology of the Napoleonic and Mexican wars. The infantry musket was accurate up to 100 yards but ineffective against even massed targets beyond that range. Rifles were specialized weapons with excellent accuracy and range but slow to load and therefore not usually issued to line troops. Smoothbore cannon had a range of up to one mile with solid shot but were most effective against infantry when firing canister at ranges under 400 yards. Artillerists worked their guns without much fear of infantry muskets, which had a limited range. Cavalry continued to use sabers and lances as shock weapons.

American troops took the tactical offensive in most Mexican War battles with great success, and they suffered fairly light losses. Unfortunately, similar tactics proved to be obsolete in the Civil War because of a major technological innovation fielded in the 1850s—the rifle-musket. This new weapon greatly increased the infantry's range and accuracy and loaded as fast as a musket. The U.S. Army adopted a version of the rifle-musket in 1855, and by the beginning of the Civil War, rifle-muskets were available in moderate numbers. It was the weapon of choice in both the Union and Confederate Armies during the war, and by 1862, large numbers of troops on both sides had rifle-muskets of good quality.

Official tactical doctrine prior to the beginning of the Civil War did not clearly recognize the potential of the new rifle-musket. Prior to 1855, the most influential tactical guide was General Winfield Scott's three-volume work, Infantry Tactics (1835), based on French tactical models of the Napoleonic Wars. It stressed close-order, linear formations in two or three ranks advancing at "quick time" of 110 steps (eighty-six yards) per minute. In 1855, to accompany the introduction of the new rifle-musket, Major William J. Hardee published a two-volume tactical manual, *Rifle and Light Infantry Tactics.* Hardee's work contained few significant revisions of Scott's manual. His major innovation was to increase the speed of the advance to a "double-quick time" of 165 steps (151 yards) per minute. If, as suggested, Hardee introduced his manual as a response to the rifle-musket, then he failed to appreciate the weapon's impact on combined arms tactics and the essential shift the rifle-musket made in favor of the defense. Hardee's *Tactics* was the standard infantry manual used by both sides at the outbreak of war in 1861.

If Scott's and Hardee's works lagged behind technological innovations, at least the infantry had manuals to establish a doctrinal basis for training. Cavalry and artillery fell even further behind in recognizing the potential tactical shift in favor of rifle-armed infantry. The cavalry's manual, published in 1841, was based on French sources that focused on close-order offensive tactics. It favored the traditional cavalry attack in two ranks of horsemen armed with sabers or lances. The manual took no notice of the rifle-musket's potential, nor did it give much attention to dismounted operations. Similarly, the artillery had a basic drill book delineating individual crew actions, but it had no tactical manual. Like cavalrymen, artillerymen showed no concern for the potential tactical changes that the rifle-musket implied.

Regular Army infantry, cavalry, and artillery practiced and became proficient in the tactics that brought success in Mexico. As the first volunteers drilled and readied themselves for the battles of 1861, officers and noncommissioned officers taught the lessons learned from the Napoleonic Wars and validated in Mexico. Thus, the two armies entered the Civil War with a good understanding of the tactics that had worked in the Mexican War but with little understanding of how the rifle-musket might upset their carefully practiced lessons.

Early War Tactics

In the battles of 1861 and 1862, both sides employed the tactics proven in Mexico and found that the tactical offensive could still be successful—but only at a great cost in casualties. Men wielding rifled weapons in the defense generally ripped frontal assaults to shreds, and if the attackers paused to exchange fire, the slaughter was even greater. Rifles also increased the relative numbers of defenders, since flanking units now engaged assaulting troops with a murderous enfilading fire. Defenders usually crippled the first assault line before a second line of attackers could come forward in support. This caused successive attacking lines to intermingle with survivors to their front, thereby destroying formations, command, and control. Although both sides favored the bayonet throughout the war, they quickly discovered that rifle-musket fire made successful bayonet attacks almost impossible.

As the infantry found the bayonet charge to be of little value against rifle-muskets, cavalry and artillery made troubling discoveries of their own. Cavalry soon learned that the old-style saber charge did not work against infantry armed with rifle-muskets. Cavalry, however, retained its traditional intelligence-gathering and screening roles whenever commanders chose to make the horsemen the "eyes and ears" of the army. Artillery, on its part, found that it could not maneuver freely to canister range as it had in Mexico because the rifle-musket was accurate beyond that distance. Worse yet, at ranges where gunners were safe from rifle fire, artillery shot, shell, and case were far less effective than close-range canister. Ironically, rifled cannon did not give the equivalent boost to artillery effectiveness that the rifle-musket gave to the infantry. Moreover, the increased range of cannons proved no real advantage in the broken and wooded terrain over which so many Civil War battles were fought.

There are several possible reasons why Civil War commanders continued to employ the tactical offensive long after it was clear that the defensive was superior. Most commanders believed the offensive was the decisive form of battle. This lesson came straight from the Napoleonic Wars and the Mexican-American War. Commanders who chose the tactical offensive usually retained the initiative over defenders. Similarly, the tactical defensive depended heavily on the enemy choosing to attack at a point convenient to the defender and continuing to attack until badly defeated. Although this situation occurred often in the Civil War, a prudent commander could hardly count on it for victory. Consequently, few commanders chose to exploit the defensive form of battle if they had the option to attack.

The offensive may have been the decisive form of battle, but it was very hard to coordinate and even harder to control. The better generals often tried to attack the enemy's flanks and rear but seldom achieved success because of the difficulty involved. Not only did the

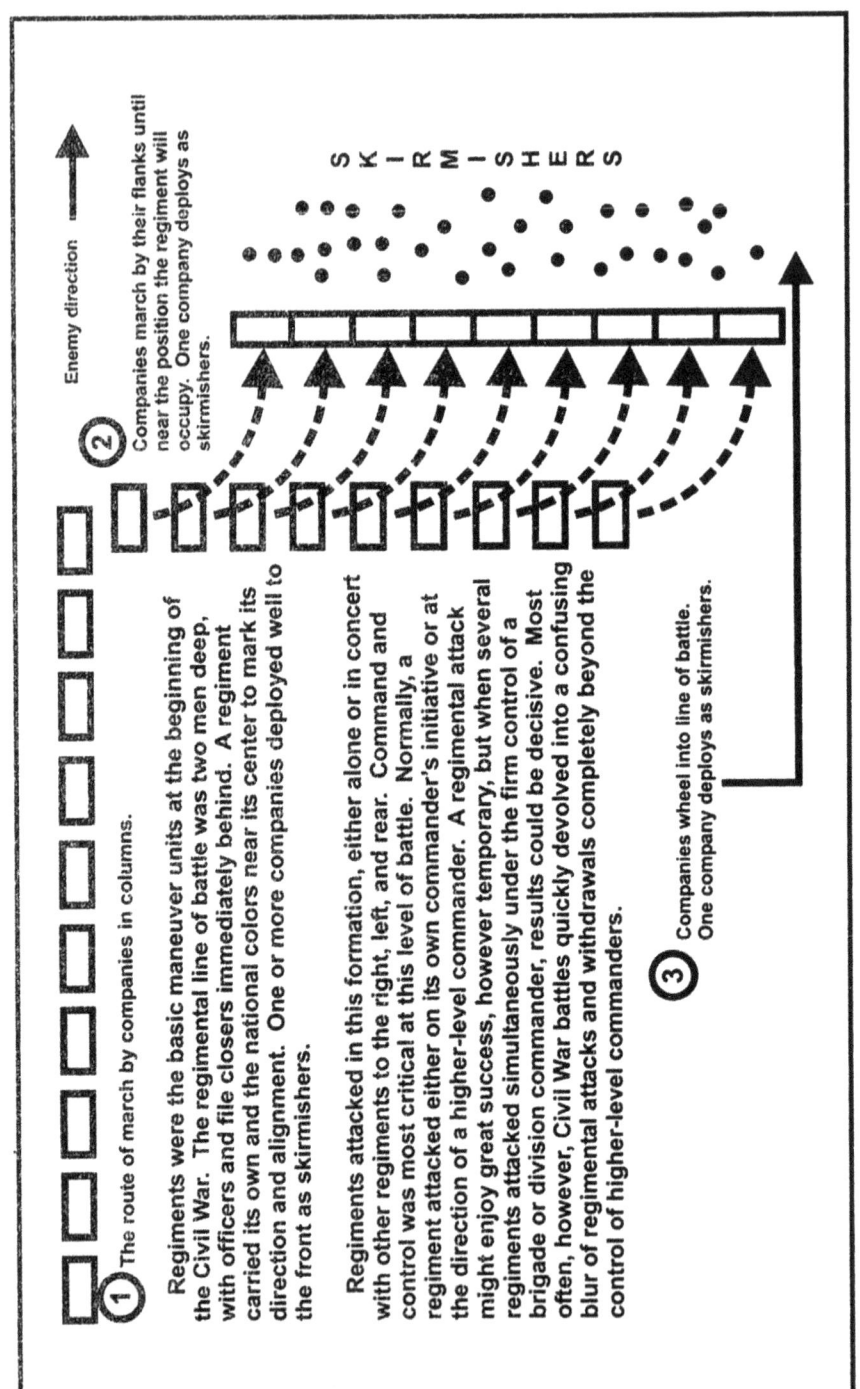

Figure 1. Regimental line of battle from the march column.

commander have to identify the enemy's flank or rear correctly, but also he had to move his force into position to attack and then do so in conjunction with attacks made by other friendly units. (For the procedure involved in moving a regiment into line of battle from march column, see figure 1.) Command and control of the type required to conduct these attacks was quite beyond the ability of most Civil War commanders. Therefore, Civil War armies repeatedly attacked each other frontally, with resulting high casualties because that was the easiest way to conduct offensive operations. When attacking frontally, a commander had to choose between attacking on a broad front or a narrow front. Attacking on a broad front rarely succeeded except against weak and scattered defenders. Attacking on a narrow front promised greater success but required immediate reinforcement and continued attack to achieve decisive results. As the war dragged on, attacking on narrow fronts against specific objectives became a standard tactic and fed the ever-growing casualty lists.

Later War Tactics

Poor training may have contributed to high casualty rates early in the war, but casualties remained high and even increased long after the armies became experienced. Continued high casualty rates resulted because tactical developments failed to adapt to the new weapons technology. Few commanders understood how the rifle-musket strengthened the tactical defensive. However, some commanders made offensive innovations that met with varying success. When an increase in the speed of the advance did not overcome defending firepower (as Hardee suggested it would), some units tried advancing in more open order. But this sort of formation lacked the appropriate mass to assault and carry prepared positions and created command and control problems beyond the ability of Civil War leaders to resolve. Late in the war, when the difficulty of attacking field fortifications under heavy fire became apparent, other tactical expedients were employed. Attacking solidly entrenched defenders often required whole brigades and divisions moving in dense masses to rapidly cover intervening ground, seize the objective, and prepare for the inevitable counterattack. Seldom successful against alert and prepared defenses, these attacks were generally accompanied by tremendous casualties and foreshadowed the massed infantry assaults of World War I. Sometimes, large formations attempted mass charges over short distances without halting to fire. This tactic enjoyed limited success at Spotsylvania Court House in May 1864. At Spotsylvania, a Union division attacked and captured an exposed portion of the Confederate line. The attack succeeded because the Union troops crossed the intervening ground quickly without artillery preparation and without stopping to fire their rifles. Once inside the Confederate defenses, the Union troops attempted to exploit their success by continuing their advance, but loss of command and control made them little better than a mob. Counterattacking Confederate units, in conventional formations, eventually forced the Federals to relinquish much of the ground gained.

As the war dragged on, tactical maneuver focused more on larger formations—brigade, division, and corps. In most of the major battles fought after 1861, brigades were employed as the primary maneuver formations. But brigade maneuver was at the upper limit of command and control for most Civil War commanders. Brigades might be able to retain coherent formations if the terrain were suitably open, but most often, brigade attacks degenerated into a series of poorly coordinated regimental lunges through broken and wooded terrain. Thus, brigade commanders were often on the main battle line trying to influence regimental fights. Typically, defending brigades stood in line of battle and blazed away at attackers as rapidly as possible. Volley fire usually did not continue beyond the first round. Most of the time, soldiers fired as soon as they were ready, and it was common for two soldiers to work together, one loading while the other fired. Brigades were generally invulnerable to attacks on their front and flanks if units to the left and right held their ground or if reinforcements came up to defeat the threat.

Two or more brigades constituted a division. When a division attacked, its brigades often advanced in sequence, from left to right or vice versa—depending on the terrain, suspected enemy location, and number of brigades available to attack. At times, divisions attacked with two or more brigades leading, followed by one or more brigades ready to reinforce the lead brigades or maneuver to the flanks. Two or more divisions constituted a corps that might conduct an attack as part of a larger plan controlled by the army commander. More often, groups of divisions attacked under the control of a corps-level commander. Division and corps commanders generally took a position to the rear of the main line in order to control the flow of reinforcements into the battle, but they often rode forward into the battle lines to influence the action personally.

Of the three basic branches, cavalry made the greatest adaptation during the war. It learned to use its horses for mobility, then dismount and fight on foot like infantry. Cavalry regained a useful battlefield role by employing this tactic, especially after repeating and breechloading rifles gave it the firepower to contend with enemy infantry. Cavalry also found a role off the battlefield, in long-range raids that interdicted enemy supply lines and diverted enemy troops, in a manner that foreshadowed air interdiction in the twentieth century. The campaign for Vicksburg included two excellent examples of this function. The first of these was a Confederate raid on the Union supply depot at Holly Springs, led by Major General Earl Van Dorn in December 1862, that effectively thwarted Grant's first offensive into Mississippi. The second was a Union raid from Tennessee to Baton Rouge, Louisiana, led by Colonel Benjamin H. Grierson, which diverted Confederate attention away from Grant's main effort in April 1863.

In contrast to the cavalry, which reasserted itself as an offensive arm, artillery found that it could best add its firepower to the rifle-musket and tip the balance even more in favor of the tactical defensive, but artillery never regained the importance to offensive maneuver that it held in Mexico. If artillery had developed an indirect firing system, as it did prior to World War I, it might have been able to contribute more to offensive tactics. Still, both sides employed artillery decisively in defensive situations throughout the war.

The most significant tactical innovation in the Civil War was the widespread use of field fortifications after armies realized the tactical offensive's heavy cost. It did not take long for the deadly firepower of the rifle-musket to convince soldiers to entrench every time they halted. Eventually, armies dug complete trenches within an hour of halting in a position. Within twenty-four hours, armies could create defensive works that were nearly impregnable to frontal assaults. In this respect, this development during the American Civil War was a clear forerunner of the kind of warfare that came to dominate World War I.

Summary

In the Civil War, the tactical defense dominated the tactical offense because assault formations proved inferior to the defender's firepower. The rifle-musket, in its many forms, provided this firepower and caused the following specific alterations in tactics during the war:

- It required the attacker, in his initial dispositions, to deploy farther away from the defender, thereby increasing the distance over which the attacker had to pass.

- It increased the number of defenders who could engage attackers (with the addition of effective enfilading fire.)

- It reduced the density of both attacking and defending formations.

- It created a shift of emphasis in infantry battles toward firefights rather than shock attacks.

- It caused battles to last longer because units could not close with each other for decisive shock action.

- It encouraged the widespread use of field fortifications. The habitual use of field fortifications by armies was a major American innovation in nineteenth-century warfare.

- It forced cavalry to the battlefield's fringes until cavalrymen acquired equivalent weapons and tactics.

- It forced artillery to abandon its basic offensive maneuver: that of moving forward to within canister range of defending infantry.

Tactics in the Vicksburg Campaign

The basic unit of operational maneuver for Union forces in the Vicksburg campaign was the corps. For the Confederates, it was the division (there being no corps echelon in Pemberton's order of battle). On the battlefield, the brigade was the basic tactical unit for both sides. (One obvious exception to this rule was the battle of Raymond, where the Confederate force was a single brigade, and the brigade commander deployed and maneuvered regiments.)

Union forces held the initiative at the operational level throughout the campaign. Not surprisingly, in most tactical encounters, Union forces were on the offensive. Union commanders relied heavily on frontal attacks—neither Grant nor his subordinates were noted for their tactical finesse. Frontal assaults in the Civil War were generally costly, but they sometimes worked, as the Vicksburg campaign demonstrates. At the battle of Port Gibson, the Union corps commander who ran the battle, Major General John A. McClernand, enjoyed a heavy numerical advantage over the Confederates, but rugged terrain and jungle-like vegetation greatly facilitated the defense. McClernand responded by packing his forces two, three, and four regiments deep, on whatever open ground was available—crowding out his artillery in the process.

Whether this was a conscious adaptation to circumstances or a blind urge on McClernand's part to gather more and more force is a matter of speculation. Although McClernand's men eventually drove the Confederates from the field in a series of frontal attacks, Port Gibson does not stand out as an example of effective offensive tactics.

Undoubtedly, the most successful frontal attack of the campaign occurred during the battle of the Big Black River on 17 May. Brigadier General Michael K. Lawler, a Union brigade commander, perceived a weak spot in the Confederate fieldworks opposing him. He formed his brigade into a formation reminiscent of the assault columns used by Napoleon: two regiments leading, with a third following closely in support, a fourth in reserve, and two regiments on loan from another brigade to pin the enemy with fire and serve as an exploitation force. Lawler utilized natural cover to bring his brigade close to the enemy, and when the attack came, it was vigorous and impetuous. The unsteady Confederate regiment facing Lawler broke and ran when this assault force reached its breastworks.

The Napoleonic influence can be seen on a larger scale as well. During the Union march from Port Gibson to Jackson, and then to Champion Hill, Grant deployed his corps on separate routes to facilitate movement, but close enough to support each other should Confederates be encountered in force. Napoleon referred to this practice as the bataillon carrée, which can best be summarized by the adage, "march dispersed, fight massed." As he closed on the Confederates at Champion Hill on 16 May, Grant contrived to bring three converging corps-size columns to bear upon the enemy in a classic "concentric attack." The outnumbered Confederates could have been attacked from three directions and possibly destroyed, but Union command, control, and communications were inadequate to the task of coordinating the action. Only one of the three Union columns ever became fully engaged.

But if Union tactical art was mediocre on average, Confederate skill was generally lower still. The Confederate forces defending Mississippi constituted a "department" and never were formally designated as an "army." Prior to the campaign, units were dispersed, having spent the winter in garrison and in fortified positions. Regiments had little recent experience operating together as brigades and divisions. Not until Grant crossed the Mississippi and moved into the interior did a major portion of the department assemble as a field army. Not surprisingly, the assembled forces had difficulty even forming up and marching as a unit, let alone fighting. At the battle of Champion Hill, the Confederate army was unresponsive and uncoordinated. Individual brigades and regiments fought hard and well, but higher-level command and control was lacking.

But at the lower echelons, some of the more imaginative and daring tactics of the Vicksburg campaign were executed, or at least attempted, by Confederates. Whereas Grant's forces relied almost exclusively on the frontal attack, on two occasions during the maneuver phase of the campaign, Confederate commanders attempted to attack their enemy in flank. During the battle of Port Gibson, Brigadier General John S. Bowen tried to thwart McClernand's steamroller tactics by leading a portion of Colonel Francis M. Cockrell's brigade in an attack against the Union right flank. But as was so often the case in the Civil War, by the time Cockrell's men reached their jump-off point, the enemy had begun to respond. After initial progress, Cockrell's men were stopped by Union reserves drawn up to oppose them. Later in the campaign, at the battle of Raymond, Confederate Brigadier General John Gregg attempted another flank attack. Unaware that his brigade confronted a Union corps, Gregg detached three of his five regiments and sent them off to attack the Union right. But when the flanking forces reached their jump-off position and realized the numerical odds against them, they opted not to attack.

When the campaign of maneuver ended and the siege of Vicksburg began, an entirely new set of tactics came into play. Whereas there was little formal doctrine for battlefield tactics in the Civil War (and none at all for operational maneuver), the sciences of fortification and siegecraft were well-established and understood by any military engineer trained at West Point. In keeping with the principles of fortification, the Confederates had erected strong earthwork fortifications that afforded interlocking fields of fire and commanded the approaches into Vicksburg. Trenches or "rifle pits" connected the major fortifications. After two failed assaults (by far the bloodiest frontal attacks of the campaign), the Union forces responded with a siege that was also the product of conventional doctrine. Grant established two separate forces, one to face outward and block any Confederate interference from outside, and the other to enclose Vicksburg and "reduce" its fortifications. Union troops crept up to the Confederate positions through zigzag trenches called "saps" or "approaches" and dug mines under some of the major fortifications.

But the siege ended before the last act of the doctrinal script was played out—there was no final assault.

Logistical Support

Victory on Civil War battlefields seldom hinged on the quality or quantity of tactical logistics. On the operational and strategic level, however, logistical capabilities and concerns always shaped the plans and sometimes the outcomes of campaigns. And as the war lengthened, the logistical advantage shifted inexorably to the North. The Federals controlled the majority of financial and industrial resources of the nation, and with their ability to import any needed materials, the Federals ultimately created the best-supplied army the world had yet seen. Despite suffering from shortages of raw materials, the Confederates, on their part, generated adequate ordnance, but they faltered gradually in their ability to acquire other war matériel. The food supply for Southern armies, moreover, was often on the verge of collapse, largely because limitations of the transportation network were compounded by political-military mismanagement. Still, the state of supply within field armies on both sides depended more on the caliber of the people managing resources than on the constraints of available matériel.

One of the most pressing needs at the start of the war was for sufficient infantry and artillery weapons. Large quantities of outmoded muskets were on hand for both sides, either in arsenals or private hands, but the Federals initially had only 35,000 modern rifle-muskets, while the Confederates had seized about 10,000. Purchasing agents rushed to Europe to buy existing stocks or contract for future production. This led to an influx of outmoded weapons, which resulted in many soldiers going into battle with Mexican War-era smoothbore muskets. As late as the fall of 1863, soldiers on both sides in the western theater were armed with muskets; several of Grant's regiments in the Vicksburg campaign noted exchanging their muskets for captured Confederate Enfields. Modern artillery pieces were generally available in adequate quantities, though the Confederates usually were outgunned. Although breechloading technology was available and the Confederates had imported some Whitworths from England, muzzleloading smoothbore or rifled cannon were the standard pieces used by both armies.

With most of the government arsenals and private manufacturing capability located in the North, the Federals ultimately produced sufficient modern firearms for their armies, but the Confederates also accumulated adequate quantities—either from battlefield captures or through the blockade. In addition, exceptional management within the Confederate Ordnance Bureau led to the creation of a series of arsenals throughout the South that produced large quantities of munitions and weapons.

The Northern manufacturing capability permitted the Federals eventually to produce and outfit their forces with repeating arms, the best of which had been patented before 1861. Initially, however, the North's conservative Ordnance Bureau would not risk switching to a new, unproved standard weapon that could lead to soldiers wasting huge quantities of ammunition in the midst of an expanding war. By 1864, after the retirement of Chief of Ordnance James Ripley and with President Lincoln's urging, Federal cavalry received seven-shot Spencer repeating carbines, which greatly increased its battle capabilities.

Both sides initially relied on the states and local districts to provide some equipment, supplies, animals, and foodstuffs. As the war progressed, more centralized control over production and purchasing emerged under both governments. Still, embezzlement and fraud were common problems for both sides throughout the war. The North, with its preponderance of railroads and developed waterways, had ample supply and adequate distribution systems. The South's major supply problem was subsistence. Arguably, the south produced enough food during the war to provide for both military and civilian needs, but mismanagement, parochial local interests, and the relatively underdeveloped transportation network often created havoc with distribution.

In both armies, the Quartermaster, Ordnance, Subsistence, and Medical Bureaus procured and distributed equipment, food, and supplies. The items for which these bureaus were responsible are not dissimilar to the classes of supply used today. Some needs overlapped, such as the Quartermaster Bureau's procurement of wagons for medical ambulances, but conflicts of interest usually were manageable. Department and army commanders requested needed resources directly from the bureaus, and bureau chiefs wielded considerable power as they parceled out occasionally limited resources.

When essential equipment and supplies could not be obtained through normal channels, some commanders used their own resources to procure them. One example of this practice was Colonel John T. Wilder, who personally contracted for Spencer rifles for his mounted brigade in the Army of the Cumberland. Wilder obtained an unsecured personal loan to purchase the weapons, and his men reimbursed him from their pay. The Federal government picked up the cost after the rifles' worth was demonstrated in the Tullahoma and Chickamauga campaigns.

Typically, matériel flowed from the factory to base depots as directed by the responsible bureaus. Supplies were then shipped to advanced depots, generally a city on a major transportation artery safely within the rear area of a department. During campaigns, the armies established temporary advance depots served by rail or river transportation. From these points, wagons carried the supplies forward to the field units. This principle is somewhat similar to the modern theater sustainment organization.

The management of this logistical system was complex and crucial. A corps wagon train, if drawn by standard six-mule teams, would be spread out from five to eight miles, based on the difficulty of terrain, weather, and road conditions. The wagons, which were capable of hauling 4,000 pounds in optimal conditions, could carry only half that load in difficult terrain. Sustenance for the animals was a major

Table 6. Sample of Federal Logistical Data

Item	Packing	Weight (lbs.)
Bulk ammunition:		
.58 caliber, expanding ball (500-grain bullet)	1,000 rounds per case	98
12-pounder Napoleon canister (14.8 lbs. per round)	8 rounds per box	161
"Marching" ration (per man per day):		
1 lb. hard bread (hardtack)		2
¾ lb. salt pork or ¼ lb. fresh meat		
1 oz. coffee		
3 oz. sugar and salt		
Forage (per horse per day):		
14 lbs. hay and 12 lbs. grain		26
Personal equipment:		
Includes rifle, bayonet, 60 rounds of ammunition, haversack, 3 days' rations, blanket, shelter half, canteen, personal items		50—60

restriction, because each animal required up to twenty-six pounds of hay and grain a day to stay healthy and productive. Bulky and hard to handle, this forage was a major consideration in campaign planning. Wagons delivering supplies more than one day's distance from the depot could be forced to carry excessive amounts of animal forage. If full animal forage was to be carried, the required numbers of wagons to support a corps increased dramatically with each subsequent day's distance from the forward depot. Another problem was created by herds of beef that often accompanied the trains or were appropriated en route. This provided fresh (though tough) meat for the troops but slowed and complicated movement.

The bulk-supply problems were alleviated somewhat by the practice of foraging, which, in the proper season, supplied much of the food for animals and men of both sides. Foraging was practiced with and without command sanction wherever an army went, and it became command policy during Grant's Vicksburg campaign.

Logistics in the Vicksburg Campaign

When Major General Earl Van Dorn's cavalry destroyed Grant's advance depot at Holly Springs in December 1862, it wrecked Grant's plan for an overland, railroad-centered attack to support Sherman's Chickasaw Bayou expedition. Although the outcome of that expedition would probably not have been altered, this episode illustrates how closely operational planning relied on a fixed logistical base for overland operations. Grant, in his memoirs, however, credits the Holly Springs raid with providing him the key to a less-conventional strategy. Forced to rely upon foraging and requisition in the surrounding countryside to feed his army in the weeks following Van Dorn's raid, Grant came to realize that the Mississippi valley, though relatively underpopulated, was indeed a rich agricultural area, abounding in beef, hogs, and grain. Thus, Grant credited Van Dorn with showing him the solution to his supply dilemma should he choose to operate far from any secure logistical pipeline. War matériel (weapons, ammunition, medical supplies, etc.) would still have to be hauled by wagons, along with some limited food items such as coffee and bread. The countryside, however, could sustain his army with bulky animal forage, meat, and other provisions.

In January 1863, Grant established an impressive logistics system running from his depots at Cairo, Illinois, and Memphis to advance bases established along the levees at Lake Providence, Milliken's

Bend, and Young's Point—the latter being just ten river miles from Vicksburg. Supplies as well as troops moved down river on a sizeable fleet of army-contracted riverboats. These transports varied considerably in size, but many were capable of carrying 300,000 pounds of supplies—the equivalent of 150 wagonloads. At the end of March, when Grant decided to move his army south of Vicksburg on the Louisiana side of the river, he hoped to have water transport most or all of the way. Union engineers, augmented by details from McClernand's and Sherman's corps, dug a canal at Duckport linking the Mississippi to the network of bayous paralleling the army's route of march. The canal was completed successfully, but falling water levels made it useless before it could do any good. As a last resort, Union logisticians pushed wagon trains along the sixty-three-mile route that McClernand's and McPherson's corps traveled, from Milliken's Bend to Bruinsburg. Some supplies were hauled by wagon from Milliken's Bend to Perkins' Plantation, just below New Carthage. There, they were loaded on riverboats that had run by the Vicksburg batteries, for delivery to the army downstream. About 11 May, over a week after the bulk of the army had crossed to the east bank, Sherman's men completed a new road from Young's Point to Bowers' Landing, across the base of De Soto point. This road shortened the wagon haul to twelve miles—still a two-day haul over the rough roads. From Bower's Landing, steamers carried supplies down the river to the newly won logistical base at Grand Gulf.

The net effect of these efforts was to give Grant two sets of well-stocked advance depots, one below Vicksburg and several just above the city. After Grant moved away from his new base at Grand Gulf, his army had only to reestablish links with the river and its supply problems would essentially disappear. The Confederates knew this, and expected Grant to stay close to the river during his advance toward Vicksburg. Thus, his movement inland came as a surprise.

In his postwar memoirs, Grant stated that he "cut loose" from his supply lines when he pushed inland from Grand Gulf. Many historians have taken those words at face value, asserting that Grant's men relied entirely upon food and forage gathered from the countryside. Grant, however, never cut completely loose from his supply lines, nor did he intend his words to convey that. As his army maneuvered east of the river, a steady stream of wagons carried supplies from Young's Point to Bower's Landing, where the supplies were loaded on steamboats and carried to Grand Gulf. From Grand Gulf, huge wagon trains, escorted by brigades hurrying forward to join the main force, carried supplies to the army. No "line of supply" existed only in the sense that Union troops did not occupy and garrison the supply route. An aggressive Confederate thrust into the area between Grand Gulf and Grant's army might have thwarted the Union campaign—Grant's men could forage for food, but only so long as they moved forward. Moreover, the barns and fields of Mississippi did not provide any ammunition to the foragers. One of the ironies of the campaign is that Pemberton's single offensive action, the attempt to strike south from Edwards toward Dillon's Plantation on 15 May, would probably have led him to Grant's ammunition train. However, heavy rains, confusion, and indecision led instead to the battle at Champion Hill.

During the campaign of maneuver, Grant was well served by his logistical staff in the rear and by the aggressive support of Rear Admiral David Porter. As Grant's army neared Vicksburg, Porter sensed the opportunity to establish a logistic base just north of Vicksburg on the Yazoo River at Johnson's Plantation (the site of Sherman's landing in the abortive Chickasaw Bayou expedition). The Navy's initiative led to supplies being on the ground by 18 May when Grant's army reached the outer works around the city. That, and efficient construction of roads from the plantation by Federal engineers, enabled Grant to fulfill a promise to provide hardtack for his troops by 21 May. At the same time, Porter's gunboats reduced the Warrenton batteries just a few miles below the city and enabled Grant's logisticians to move the lower supply base from Grand Gulf to Warrenton. These two bases cut the overland wagon haul to a maximum of six miles for units manning the siege lines. Thus, as Grant closed on Vicksburg, his supply situation changed dramatically, almost overnight, whereas the Confederates then had to rely almost completely on whatever stores had been placed in the city in advance.

Curiously, the Confederate logistical situation in the Vicksburg campaign was almost uniformly worse than that of the Union forces. The fact that the Confederates were conducting defensive operations within their own territory resulted in as many logistical problems as advantages. The bountiful forage discovered by Grant's troops was generally not available to the Confederate army, due in large part to the farmers' reluctance to part with their produce. In March, Pemberton complained of a shortage of beef, yet one of his staff officers noted an abundance of cattle in the region between Vicksburg and Jackson. Federal surgeons found apothecary shelves in Jackson well stocked with drugs, yet Confederate surgeons were critically short of medical supplies. The explanation, however, is simple: the invading Federals could take what they needed, whereas the defending Confederates could not so easily requisition from their own people.

Thus, the Confederates had to rely upon their established logistical systems and procedures. Confederate logistical doctrine in the Civil War called for armies to supply themselves, as far as possible, from the resources of the area in which they were stationed. There was no shortage of basic supplies in the Vicksburg region. The Mississippi Delta (the area between the Mississippi and Yazoo Rivers) and farmlands to the east produced large quantities of food for man and beast. The transportation net, with the main rail line running from Vicksburg to the major rail nexus at Jackson, and the numerous navigable waterways, offered the Confederates the ability to stockpile or shift supplies quickly. The telegraph network provided communications that could support the management of logistical resources. Depots and manufacturing centers in Jackson, Enterprise, and Columbus, Mississippi, helped support a variety of Confederate needs.

Three major factors, however, limited Pemberton's ability to optimize his logistical support. The first problem was the inefficiency of, and competing priorities between, the Confederate quartermaster and commissary departments. Many of the supplies from Pemberton's area were needed to support other military departments. Even so, the management of these resources was inefficient, and not enough funds were available for local purchase of food. Pemberton also had concerns about his own staff—officials in Richmond had received civilian complaints about Pemberton's Quartermaster. This problem, however vexing, did not prove insurmountable.

The second problem was largely beyond Pemberton's control—Union naval superiority. Prior to the war, most bulk commodities were moved by water. But in the course of the Vicksburg campaign, Porter's gunboats denied the Confederates the use of the Mississippi and its tributaries, thus throwing heavier demands on the overtaxed road and rail transport systems. Even before Grant's army crossed to the east bank of the Mississippi, Pemberton found it difficult to gather and distribute supplies.

The third and greatest problem hampering Confederate logistical efforts was Pemberton's lack of overall vision for the campaign. In the absence of a campaign plan, the Confederate logisticians, like Pemberton himself, could only react to Union initiatives. Supplies could not be positioned to support any particular scheme of maneuver.

After Grant seized and destroyed Jackson, all supplies became critical for Pemberton. With Porter on the Mississippi and with the eastward rail lines interdicted, Pemberton was effectively cut off from any resources beyond the immediate vicinity of his army. Fortunately, his largest supply depots were in Vicksburg, a fact that helps explain Pemberton's reluctance to risk the loss of the city. Rations that could be stretched out for perhaps two full months were stockpiled inside Vicksburg before 18 May. Ordnance officers had managed to gather significant quantities of small arms and ammunition as well. The main shortages in the city after the siege began were artillery, medical supplies, engineer tools, and percussion caps for rifle-muskets. The latter shortage was eased when couriers penetrated the Union siege lines with several hundred thousand caps.

As the siege progressed, the contrast between Union and Confederate logistics became increasingly pronounced. Confederate stockpiles dwindled, rations were cut, and ammunition expenditure curtailed. But the Union forces, situated as they were on North America's greatest transportation artery, received reinforcements and supplies in seemingly limitless quantities. Predictably, Confederate morale deteriorated until Pemberton felt that his troops had lost the ability and will to fight. Finally, logistics played a role in determining the final surrender terms. An important factor influencing Grant's decision to parole the entire Vicksburg garrison of over 29,000 men was the simple fact that the Confederate government, not the Federal army, would then have to deal with transporting and feeding those troops.

Engineer Support

Engineers on both sides performed many tasks essential to every campaign. Engineers trained at West Point were at a premium; thus, many civil engineers, commissioned as volunteers, supplemented the work being done by engineer officers. The Confederates, in particular, relied on civilian expertise because many of their trained engineer officers sought line duties. State or even local civil engineers planned and supervised much of the work done on local fortifications.

In the prewar U.S. Army, the Corps of Engineers contained a handful of staff officers and one company of trained engineer troops. This cadre expanded to a four-company Regular engineer battalion. Congress also created a single company of topographic engineers, which joined the Regular battalion when the engineer bureaus merged in 1863. In addition, several volunteer pioneer regiments, some containing up to 2,000 men, supported the various field armies. The Corps of Engineers also initially controlled the fledgling Balloon Corps, which provided aerial reconnaissance. The Confederate Corps of Engineers, formed as a small staff and one company of sappers, miners, and pontoniers in 1861, grew more slowly and generally relied on details and contract labor rather than established units with trained engineers and craftsmen.

Engineer missions for both sides included construction of fortifications; repair and construction of roads, bridges, and, in some cases, railroads; demolition; limited construction of obstacles; and construction or reduction-of-siege works. The Federal Topographic Engineers, a separate prewar bureau, performed reconnaissance and produced maps. The Confederates, however, never separated these functions in creating their Corps of Engineers. Experience during the first year of the war convinced the Federals that all engineer functions should be merged under a single corps because qualified engineer officers tended to perform all related functions. As a result, the Federals also merged the Topographic Engineers into their Corps of Engineers in March 1863.

Bridging assets included wagon-mounted pontoon trains that carried either wooden, canvas-covered, or inflatable rubber pontoon boats. Using this equipment, trained engineer troops could bridge even large rivers in a matter of hours. The most remarkable pontoon bridge of the war was the 2,200-foot bridge built by Army of the Potomac engineers in 1864 over the James River—one of over three dozen pontoon bridges built in support of campaigns in the east that year. In 1862, the Confederates began developing pontoon trains after they had observed their effectiveness. In fact, during the Atlanta campaign of 1864, General Joseph Johnston had four pontoon trains available to support his army.

Both armies in every campaign of the war traveled over roads and bridges built or repaired by their engineers. Federal engineers also helped clear waterways by dredging, removing trees, or digging canals. Fixed fortifications laid out under engineer supervision played critical roles in the Vicksburg campaign and in actions around Richmond and Petersburg. Engineers also supervised the siege works to reduce those fortifications.

While the Federal engineer effort expanded in both men and materiel as the war progressed, the Confederate efforts continued to be hampered by major problems. The relatively small number of organized engineer units available forced Confederate engineers to rely heavily on details or contract labor. Finding adequate manpower, however, was often difficult because of competing demands for it. Local slave owners were reluctant to provide labor details when labor was crucial to their economic survival. Despite congressional authorization to conscript 20,000 slaves as a labor force, state and local opposition continually hindered efforts to draft slave labor. Another related problem concerned the value of Confederate currency. Engineer efforts required huge sums for men and materiel, yet initial authorizations were small, and although congressional appropriations grew later in the war, inflation greatly reduced effective purchasing power. A final problem was the simple shortage of iron resources, which severely limited the Confederates' ability to increase railroad mileage or even produce iron tools.

In 1861, maps for both sides were also in short supply; for many areas in the interior, they were nonexistent. As the war progressed, the Federals developed a highly sophisticated mapping capability. Federal topographic engineers performed personal reconnaissance to develop base maps, reproduced them by several processes, and distributed them to field commanders. Photography, lithographic presses, and eventually photochemical processes gave the Federals the ability to reproduce maps quickly. Western armies, which usually operated far from base cities, carried equipment to reproduce maps on campaigns with their army headquarters. By 1864, annual map production exceeded 21,000 copies. Confederate topographic work never approached the Federal effort in quantity or quality. Confederate topographers initially used tracing paper to reproduce maps. Not until 1864 did the use of photographic methods become widespread in the South.

Engineers in the Vicksburg Campaign

The engineering operations conducted in support of the Vicksburg campaign were perhaps the most diverse and complex of the war. For much of the campaign, Federal engineers focused on mobility operations, while Confederate engineers emphasized countermobility, particularly in denying the Federals the use of streams and bayous in the swamps north of the city. Confederate engineers also supervised the construction and repair of the fortifications around the city. During the siege phase of the campaign, Grant's engineers focused on the reduction of those works, utilizing procedures such as sapping, mining, and other related tasks, as well as the improvement of roads and landings to enhance logistical support. This wide range of activities, which required engineers on both sides to construct roads, emplace or construct bridges, clear or obstruct waterways, construct field works, emplace batteries, divert the flow of rivers, and numerous other tasks, is made even more remarkable by the limited numbers of trained engineers available to accomplish them.

Grant's Army of the Tennessee contained three formally organized engineer units. The largest was the Missouri Engineer Regiment of the West. Organized initially in July 1861, its ranks held skilled railroad men, engineers, and ironworkers recruited from St. Louis and surrounding areas. By the time of the Vicksburg campaign, it had extensive experience in a variety of construction operations and had been involved in some minor skirmishing. The regiment, with a strength of roughly 900 men, constructed roads around Young's Point in February 1863 and in March cut levees on the west side of the river and constructed casemated battery positions opposite Vicksburg. In April, six companies of the regiment returned to Memphis to begin the repair of the Memphis and Charleston Railroad. Companies A, D, F, and I, which were designated the 2d Battalion, remained with Grant's main force during the decisive phases of the campaign. The other two formally organized engineer units were the Kentucky Company of Engineers and Mechanics and Company I of the 35th Missouri, which was designated as the army's pontoon company. Since Grant then had barely 500 "trained" engineers at his disposal for his operations below Vicksburg, most of his divisions detailed men for engineer tasks or designated one of their infantry companies as engineer troops. Known as "pioneer" companies and detachments, or as the "pioneer corps" of their parent divisions, these ad hoc units generally undertook missions requiring higher degrees of skill than those assigned to normal labor details.

The most strenuous engineer labors of the campaign took place between January and April 1863, as Grant sought ways to bypass the strong Confederate position at Vicksburg by creating flanking routes though the bayou country. Several of these efforts involved alternate water routes around the city. One scheme involved digging a canal that would divert the Mississippi through the peninsula directly opposite Vicksburg, a project initiated during Farragut's expedition in June 1862. Beginning in January 1863, details of infantry under engineer supervision labored the better part of two months before the rising river flooded them out. A month later, labor details working under engineer supervision cut the levee at Yazoo Pass to divert Mississippi River water into the Delta region in hopes that gunboats and transports could find a way to Vicksburg from the north. In March, the 1st Missouri Engineers used black powder to blow a gap in the western levee along the Mississippi River at Lake Providence. The plan was to flood enough of the countryside to link the bayous and rivers west of the Mississippi and thus provide an alternate route for steamboats all the way to the Red River. Once the levees were broken, the engineers used man-powered underwater saws, which swung pendulum-like from barge-mounted trestles, to cut off trees and stumps and allow passage of vessels. This backbreaking work required the men to spend much of their time in the water untangling the saws. It took the Missouri Engineers eight days to clear a two-mile stretch of bayou. Unfortunately, falling water levels led to the abandonment of the project.

Grant's subsequent march from Milliken's Bend to Hard Times, a distance of sixty-three miles through the swampy floodplain, entailed a vast amount of engineering work. Much of the roadbed had to be corduroyed (paved with logs laid side-by-side); stretches of quicksand required layers of planking to create sufficient buoyancy for wagons; and numerous water courses had to be bridged using materials found on site. Engineers and infantry details constructed eight major bridges, totaling more than 1,700 feet, along the road to Hard Times. Again, the shortage of qualified engineer troops meant that most of the actual labor involved details of infantry, under the supervision of engineer-trained officers. This road-building effort continued on the west bank even after Grant crossed the river at Bruinsburg and pushed inland.

During the campaign of maneuver on the east side of the river, Union bridge builders demonstrated their ingenuity to the fullest. Twenty-two trestle, suspension, pontoon, and raft bridges were employed in the campaign. Engineers used all available materials in their bridges, including boards pulled from buildings, cotton bales, telegraph wire, vines, cane, and flatboats, in addition to the supplies forwarded from engineer depots upriver. The pontoon company of Sherman's corps ultimately brought along its inflatable rubber pontoons, which were employed in the crossing of the Big Black River.

Once Grant decided to initiate a formal siege to reduce Vicksburg, he was faced with a critical shortage of trained engineer officers. Grant ordered all officers with West Point training or civil engineer experience to assist chief engineer Captain Frederick E. Prime and the other three engineer officers on Grant's staff. These men supervised infantry details at the different approaches, while the trained engineer units worked in the saps and trenches. Captain Andrew Hickenlooper, Major General John A. Logan's chief engineer, was able to procure experienced coal miners, drawn from the ranks, to construct the mine undertaken by Logan's division.

On the Confederate side, the engineering effort in this campaign came under the general authority of chief engineer Major Samuel H. Lockett, who arrived at Vicksburg in June 1862. At that time, Vicksburg's only fortifications consisted of a few batteries along the river. Union naval bombardments on 27-28 July 1862 persuaded the Confederate command to fortify the city on both the landward and river fronts. Lockett spent the month of August surveying the rough terrain and planning on how best to utilize it for defensive purposes. On 1 September 1862, the actual construction began, using hired or impressed slave labor. Lockett's fortified line extended nine miles, from the river above Vicksburg to the river below. Thirteen river batteries studded the bluffs overlooking the Mississippi. Snyder's (Haynes') Bluff to the north and Warrenton to the south were also fortified. In addition, the Confederates also constructed a set of floating barriers called "rafts" across the Yazoo River to block incursions by Union gunboats.

When Pemberton assumed command of the department on 1 November 1862, Lockett's responsibilities increased. He exercised authority over the entire area from Holly Springs to Port Hudson and from Vicksburg to Jackson. As part of his duties, Lockett surveyed defensive positions around Jackson and Edwards Station. In May 1863, after Grant had crossed the river, Lockett laid out defensive bridgeheads at several crossing sites along the Big Black River.

One other Confederate engineering effort is worthy of note. Brigadier General John S. Bowen, given command of Grand Gulf in

March 1863, used slave labor to shave the cliffs overlooking the mouth of the Big Black River and built a series of batteries and rifle pits that would withstand over one hundred tons of ordnance fired by Porter's gunboats during their unsuccessful bombardment of the position on 29 April.

As the campaign unfolded, Lockett continued to support the Confederate army, often on his own initiative. It was Lockett who found and repaired the washed-out bridge over Baker's Creek that gave Pemberton a withdrawal route after the battle of Champion Hill on 16 May. Lockett later prepared the railroad bridge over the Big Black for demolition and fired it on 17 May just before the Federals reached it after their destruction of the Confederate bridgehead. Following that disastrous engagement, Lockett rushed back to Vicksburg to supervise the repair of fortifications damaged by the winter rains. Once the siege began, Lockett was busy supervising the repair of fortifications damaged by Union artillery. When the Federals began mining efforts, Lockett responded with at least fifteen countermines, three of which he exploded.

Lockett operated with even fewer engineer assets than the meager number available to Grant. Although Lockett and his three-man staff equaled the number of engineers assigned to Grant's staff, and although he did have four other trained engineers as assistants, his troop assets included only one company of sappers and miners that numbered less than three dozen men. Most of the entrenching work had been done by a relatively small number of hired or impressed slave laborers. Apparently, Confederate infantrymen were less willing than their Union counterparts to dig and maintain earthworks. When Lockett reached Vicksburg on 18 May, he had only twenty-six sappers and miners, eight detailed mechanics, four overseers, and seventy-two slaves (twenty of whom were sick) to quickly repair nine miles of fortified lines. Lockett noted having only 500 shovels available.

Although the Confederate army at Vicksburg was obviously blessed with an engineer staff officer of talent and initiative, not all of Lockett's countrymen appreciated his efforts. General Joseph E. Johnston, when he toured the works around Vicksburg in December 1862, felt that "[t]he usual error of Confederate engineering had been committed there. An immense, entrenched camp, requiring an army to hold it, had been made instead of a fort requiring only a small garrison." This defect, however, was not Lockett's fault. He received little command guidance; therefore, he planned his defenses to suit the best engineering aspects of the terrain.

Topographical engineering played little role in this campaign for either side. Grant's topographic engineers became fully involved in the more crucial field engineering missions, and the speed of movements in May precluded useful mapping work. The Confederates, as was typical in most of the western theater, paid almost no attention to mapping or even detailed reconnaissance of their area of operations. As a result, Pemberton did not know the topography of his own department any better than Grant did during the campaign of maneuver.

Communications Support

Communications systems used during the Civil War consisted of line-of-sight signaling, telegraphic systems, and various forms of the time-honored courier methods. The telegraph mainly offered viable strategic and operational communications, line-of-sight signaling provided operational and limited tactical possibilities, and couriers were most heavily used for tactical communications.

The Federal Signal Corps was in its infancy during the Civil War, Major Albert C. Myer having been appointed the first signal chief in 1860. His organization grew slowly and became officially recognized as the Signal Corps in March 1863. It achieved bureau status by November of that year. Throughout the war, the Federal Signal Corps remained small, its maximum strength reaching just 1,500 officers and men, most of whom were on detached service with the corps. Myer also indirectly influenced the formation of the Confederate Signal Service. Among the men who assisted Myer in prewar testing of his wigwag signaling system was Lieutenant E. P. Alexander. (Myer's wigwag system, patented in 1858, used five separate, numbered movements of a single flag. Four-number groups represented letters of the alphabet and a few simple words and phrases. The system could also be employed at night by using kerosene torches.) Alexander used wigwag signals to the Confederates' advantage during the First Battle of Bull Run and later organized the Confederate Signal Corps. Officially established in April 1862, the Confederate Signal Corps was attached to the Adjutant and Inspector General Department. It attained the same size as its Federal counterpart, with nearly 1,500 men ultimately being detailed for service.

Myer also fought hard to develop a Federal field telegraph service. This field service utilized the Beardslee device, a magneto-powered machine operated by turning a wheel to a specific point. This sent an electrical impulse that keyed the machine at the other end to the same letter. Although less reliable than the standard Morse code telegraph key, the Beardslee could be used by an operator with only several hours' training and did not require bulky batteries for a power source. Myer's field telegraph units carried equipment on wagons that enabled its operators to establish lines between field headquarters. The insulated wire used could also be hooked into existing trunk lines, thus offering the potential to extend the reach of the civilian telegraph network. Control over the existing fixed telegraph system, however, remained with the U.S. Military Telegraph Service. Myer lost his struggle to keep the field telegraph service under the Signal Corps when Secretary of War Edwin M. Stanton relieved Myer as the signal chief in November 1863 and placed all telegraph activity under the Military Telegraph Service.

Although the Confederate Signal Corps' visual communications capabilities were roughly equal to those of the Federals, Confederate field telegraph operations remained too limited to be of operational significance. The Confederates' existing telegraph lines provided strategic communications capabilities similar to those of the Federals, but lack of resources and factories in the South for producing wire precluded their extending the prewar telegraph networks.

The courier system, using mounted staff officers or detailed soldiers to deliver orders and messages, remained the most viable tactical communications option, short of commanders meeting face to face. Although often effective, this system was fraught with difficulties, as couriers often were captured, killed, or delayed in route. Commanders sometimes misinterpreted or ignored messages, and situations often changed by the time messages were delivered. The weaknesses of the courier system, though not always critical in themselves, tended to compound commanders' errors or misjudgments during campaigns and battles.

Communications in the Vicksburg Campaign

Operating along river lines of communication meant that Grant's army often would leave behind its excellent strategic telegraph network. Memphis, two days by steamboat from Vicksburg, was the nearest telegraph station upriver, and the telegraph lines running north from Memphis often were cut by guerrillas. For much of the campaign, Cairo, Illinois, was the closest point that had reliable telegraph links with the East. Once Grant began operations south of Vicksburg, he essentially broke off his communications with Washington. President Lincoln, on 22 May 1863 (the day Grant launched his deliberate assault against Vicksburg), telegraphed Major General Stephen Hurlbutt at Memphis with a situation update based upon information gleaned from Confederate newspapers smuggled out of Richmond. The next day, Lincoln, who had not yet heard from Grant about his landing at Bruinsburg, finally received a telegraphic report. Grant's message, describing his operations since 30 April, had been sent upriver by courier on a steamer only after the Federal army had closed on the city on 18 May.

As for Federal tactical communications, Grant's signal corps detachment struggled to fill its ranks with detailed officers and men, but the full complement of forty-five officers was not assigned until late in the campaign. Signal officers operating with the field army probably provided their best service as scouts, since they usually advanced ahead of the main force, reconnoitering potential signal sites. The nature of the terrain generally precluded communications by flag, but stations set up along the riverbanks and at key areas along the line of march offered some limited local communications. Interestingly, Admiral Porter early saw the value of the army signal system. He detailed seven Navy officers to work with the signal corps. Thus Porter, on the river, could maintain a link with the army as long as the gunboats operated within visual range of army signal stations on shore.

Telegraph played no tactical role in the Vicksburg campaign. Although six field telegraph units were assigned to Grant's army, they did not arrive in Memphis until late June and did not reach Vicksburg until after the surrender. During the campaign of maneuver, Grant's most reliable means of tactical communication was the courier, and this method was fraught with problems. On 16 May, as the Federal army advanced on multiple routes toward Champion Hill, the courier system failed badly. When the northernmost of the three Union columns became fully engaged with the enemy, Grant, accompanying that column, sent a message to McClernand, three miles away, to bring the other two columns into action. But the courier carrying the message chose to take a twelve-mile route by road rather than riding three miles across country. As a result, four hours elapsed before McClernand's divisions pushed the enemy, and part of his force never attacked at all.

Another problem arose during the deliberate assault of the Vicksburg works on 22 May, when Grant's inability to communicate directly with McClernand led to confusion about the need to support a supposed success in McClernand's sector.

The Confederates, on the other hand, operated with an excellent network of fixed telegraphic communications until Grant cut the lines into Vicksburg as he advanced from the south and east. The existence of a civilian telegraph net allowed Pemberton to get by with a signal corps detachment of only three officers. Virtually every significant town was linked by telegraph line; thus, Pemberton initially had excellent operational as well as strategic communications. In December 1862, Confederate telegraphers, using a line running along the west bank of the Mississippi, alerted Pemberton to the approach of Sherman's Chickasaw Bayou expedition, enabling the Confederates to bring in reinforcements from other parts of the department.

Ironically, the effectiveness of his telegraph communications may have worked to Pemberton's disadvantage as the campaign progressed because the telegraph system also allowed him to receive contradictory advice from two key subordinates, Bowen and Stevenson. Bowen argued that the main Federal effort was coming from below Vicksburg, while Stevenson argued that it was coming above Vicksburg. The telegraph also provided Pemberton with conflicting instructions from Joseph Johnston and Jefferson Davis about whether he should defend or evacuate Vicksburg as Grant advanced on the city. Most important, the allure of the telegraph may well have been a factor in keeping Pemberton tied to his headquarters long after he should have taken the field in person.

After 4 May, when advancing Federals began to cut telegraph wires, the Confederates relied increasingly on couriers. This system also had its problems. One of the three couriers Johnston sent out on 13 May with an order directing Pemberton to join him at Clinton was actually a Federal spy, who instead delivered the message to the Federals. Thus Grant learned of the order before the other two couriers reached Pemberton!

Once Pemberton withdrew behind the works at Vicksburg, couriers became his only means of communication with the outside world. Although a few men were able to slip through Federal lines early in the siege, couriers ultimately were forced to use the river, clinging to floating logs or pieces of debris in order to enter and leave the city.

Messages conveyed by this dangerous route took from five to ten days to pass between Johnston and Pemberton, and often couriers destroyed their messages if capture seemed imminent. The last message Pemberton received from outside the city came in by courier on 23 June.

Medical Support

Federal and Confederate medical systems followed a similar pattern. Surgeons general and medical directors for both sides had served many years in the prewar Medical Department but were hindered by an initial lack of administrative experience in handling large numbers of casualties, as well as by the state of medical science in the midnineteenth century. Administrative procedures improved with experience, but throughout the war, the simple lack of knowledge about the true causes of disease and infection led to many more deaths than direct battlefield action.

After the disaster at the Battle of First Bull Run, the Federal Medical Department established an evacuation and treatment system developed by Surgeon Jonathan Letterman. At the heart of the system were three precepts: consolidation of field hospitals at division level, decentralization of medical supplies down to regimental level, and centralization of medical control of ambulances at all levels. A battle casualty evacuated from the front line normally received treatment at a regimental holding area immediately to the rear. From this point, wagons or ambulances carried wounded men to a division field hospital, normally within a mile of the battle lines. Seriously wounded men could then be further evacuated by wagon, rail, or watercraft to general hospitals, located usually in towns along the lines of communication in the armies' rear areas.

Although the Confederate system followed the same general principles, Confederate field hospitals were often consolidated at brigade rather than division level. A second difference lay in the established span of control of medical activities. Unlike their Federal counterparts, who had control over all medical activities within an army area, a Confederate army medical director had no control of activities beyond his own brigade or division field hospitals. A separate medical director for large hospitals was responsible for evacuation and control. In practice, both sets of medical directors resolved potential problems through close cooperation. By 1863, the

Confederacy had also introduced rear area "wayside hospitals," which were intended to handle convalescents en route home on furloughs.

Procedures, medical techniques, and medical problems for both sides were virtually identical. Commanders discouraged soldiers from leaving the battle lines to escort wounded back to the rear, but such practice was common, especially in less-disciplined units. The established technique for casualty evacuation was to detail men for litter and ambulance duty. Both armies used bandsmen, among others, for this task. Casualties would move or be assisted back from the battle line, where litter bearers evacuated them to field hospitals using ambulances or supply wagons. Ambulances were specially designed, two- or four-wheel carts with springs to limit jolts, but rough roads made even short trips agonizing for wounded men. Brigade and division surgeons staffed consolidated field hospitals. Hospital site considerations were the availability of water, potential buildings to supplement the hospital tents, and security from enemy cannon and rifle fire. The majority of operations performed at field hospitals in the aftermath of battle were amputations. Approximately 70 per cent of Civil War wounds occurred in the extremities, and the soft Minié ball shattered any bones that it hit. Amputation was the best technique then available to limit the chance of serious infection. The Federals were generally well supplied with chloroform, morphine, and other drugs, though shortages did occur on the battlefield. Confederate surgeons often lacked critical drugs and medical supplies.

Medical Support in the Vicksburg Campaign

Grant's Army of the Tennessee had adopted most of the Letterman system by March 1863. Thus, field hospitals were consolidated at the division echelon, and medical supplies were distributed down to regimental level. Ambulances were under positive medical control, with commissioned or noncommissioned officers in charge at division and brigade and ambulance drivers and assistants assigned to each regiment. When Regular army surgeon Madison Mills became Grant's medical director in March 1863, he inherited a growing field hospital established at Milliken's Bend. Mills established convalescent camps and opened more field hospitals there to support Grant's guidance that ill troops be kept with the command insofar as possible to enable them to rejoin their units upon recovery.

Federal surgeons were able to stockpile a significant amount of medical supplies in the depot established at Young's Point. Most were kept on the steamer *Des Arc,* which could move supplies to any secure drop-off point along the river. By May, Mills estimated that six months of medical supplies had been stockpiled. He was assisted in this by Grant's standing order that any steamer with space that moved down river from Memphis was to bring additional medical supplies. The medical department also received invaluable assistance from the U.S. Sanitary Commission in the form of supplies and evacuation of sick and wounded.

The river constituted an excellent evacuation as well as supply route. In addition to the 1,000-bed general hospital and convalescent camps established just north of Vicksburg, thousands of beds were available in general hospitals up river. Memphis alone had 5,000 available beds, with many more available in general hospitals in Cairo, Mound City, Paducah, Evansville, and St. Louis. Three steamers, *R. C. Wood, D. A. January,* and *City of Memphis,* served as hospital ships for evacuation to these upriver hospitals. A round trip to Memphis took four to five days.

The most severe medical problem facing Grant's army between January and July 1863 was disease, a problem severely exacerbated early in the campaign when the army occupied swampy encampments along the river. From January to March, high water forced the troops to crowd together on the tops of the levees. Unfortunately, the levees also served as roads, latrines, and graves. Thus, Grant's army experienced over 170,000 cases of serious illness during this encampment. One should be skeptical of historians' assertions that work on projects such as the canal helped put Grant's men in excellent shape for the campaigning to come. Reports from regiments engaged in these projects routinely list more men on the sick lists than were present for duty. Once Grant began to maneuver, however, the combination of continual movement and healthier terrain led to dramatic decreases in serious disease.

During the campaign of maneuver, surgeons were forced by the nature of operations to carry sick and wounded soldiers along with the marching columns or leave them behind to be captured. By the time Grant began the siege of Vicksburg, over 2,000 Federal wounded from the battles of Raymond, Jackson, and Champion Hill had been left under Confederate control. Nineteen Federal surgeons stayed behind to attend these men. Four additional Federal surgeons stayed to help attend the Confederate wounded from those battles, which indicates the critical shortage of doctors serving Pemberton's army. On 20 May, five wagons displaying a flag of truce and loaded with medical supplies rolled east from the Federal siege lines into Confederate territory to support the wounded from those earlier battles. After the surrender of Vicksburg on 4 July, fifty ambulances moved to Raymond under a flag of truce to recover many of these wounded.

Although the Federal corps commanders' emphasis on medical support varied, medical officers had adequate supplies throughout the campaign. Sherman's corps allocated enough wagons for medical needs. McClernand, on the other hand, accorded low priority to medical requirements, thus Surgeon Mills had to scramble to support his XIII Corps surgeons. Shortages of medical supplies were partly made up in Jackson and other towns as surgeons raided the stocks of local drug stores. There also seemed to be no shortage of food for the wounded. Surgeons reported an abundance of beef for making soup and an adequate supply of hard bread and vegetables. After the supply line to the river was fully reestablished on 21 May, even ice became available.

After Grant initiated the siege of Vicksburg, division hospitals were established a mile behind the lines, using combinations of buildings and tents. Water often came from cisterns because of a shortage of wells and springs. The policy of keeping wounded and sick soldiers close to their commands, whenever practicable, was maintained. A consolidated evacuation hospital near Johnson's plantation on the Yazoo River housed the seriously ill and wounded until medical steamers could move them up the Mississippi to general hospitals.

Except for the assaults of 19 and 22 May, when more than 3,000 Union soldiers were wounded, battle casualties averaged close to a hundred per week, numbers that the medical staffs could manage effectively. Upon the Confederate surrender on 4 July, however, the Federal surgeons were confronted with over 6,000 Confederate sick and wounded from the city. The well-established Federal hospital, supply, and evacuation network proved adequate to meet this new demand.

Relatively little specific information is available concerning Confederate medical efforts during the campaign. However, it is safe to assume that problems with sickness and disease, particularly for those units posted in the Delta, were of similar magnitude to those encountered by Union troops when they, too, camped on the floodplain. It is clear that the Confederate army suffered from supply shortages and from an inadequate number of trained surgeons. Since Federal surgeons reported finding large stocks of medical supplies in Jackson, it would seem that some of Pemberton's logistical problems hindered his medical staff as well. Reports on the medical condition of the army at the time of the surrender reveal that, within the city, the Confederates were "almost destitute" of medical supplies.

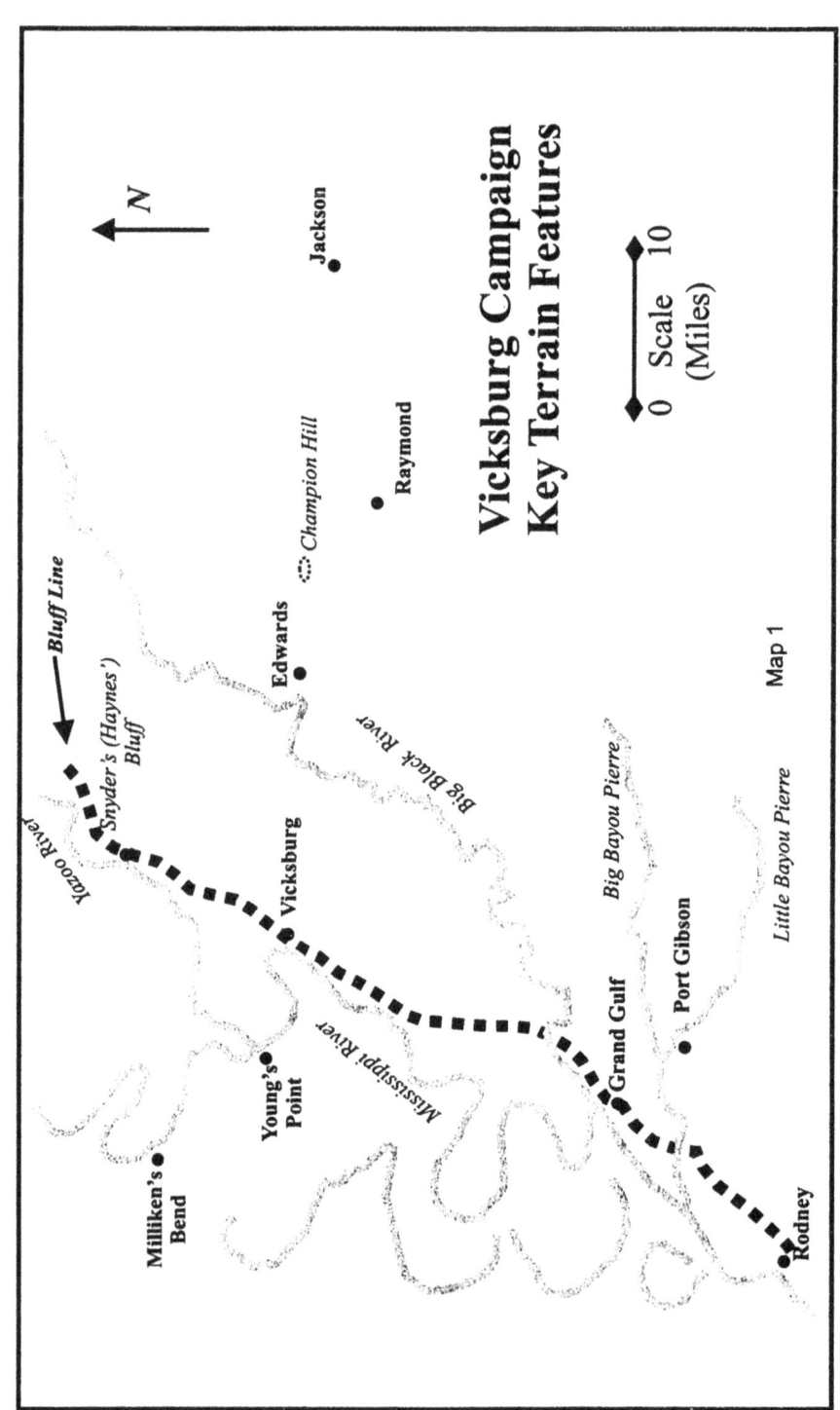

Map 1

II. VICKSBURG CAMPAIGN OVERVIEW

The central and dominating feature of the Vicksburg campaign is the mighty Mississippi River. This great waterway, which drains more than 1,234,000 square miles of the North American continent, shaped and constrained the Civil War in the West at every level—strategic, operational, and tactical. Strategically, opening the Mississippi River system to Union commerce was a key objective for the Lincoln administration and a potential death knell to Confederate aspirations of nationhood. Operationally, the river was the axis of advance and main line of communications for Union forces penetrating the Confederate heartland from north and south. By November 1862, the Confederates retained control over only the stretch of river between Vicksburg, Mississippi, and Port Hudson, Louisiana.

The Mississippi River created the terrain over which much of the Vicksburg campaign would be fought and thus influenced the tactical level of operations. The Mississippi is an "aggrading" stream, meaning that it is depositing sediments in its bed rather than eroding them away. In other words, it is building up the land, raising its own bed in the process, instead of cutting a channel down into the land. The process of sediment deposition occurs fastest at the banks where the river's waters run slowest, leading to the creation of natural levees flanking the channel. When the river rounds a bend, it tends to scour away at the outside of the bend and deposits sediment at the inside, thus moving itself laterally across the landscape. Periodically, the river breaks through its banks, seeking a shorter and lower course, where it begins again the process of building up its bed with sediments. Since the last Ice Age, when the Mississippi assumed its present configuration, the great river has wriggled back and forth across its vast floodplain, just as a rivulet of rainwater writhes upon a windowpane. It has deposited millions of tons of sediment and left a patchwork of waterways and abandoned natural levees to mark each change of its channel. Lake Providence, the Yazoo River, and the countless waterways of the "Delta" are all relics of Mississippi River channels in bygone ages (see map 1).

Periodically, the Mississippi floods, more or less inundating the entire floodplain, leaving only the tops of the levees above water and rendering temporarily navigable many of the tributaries and abandoned channels that abound in the river's proximity. Such was the case in the first quarter of 1863. Unusually heavy rains filled the floodplain with water and kept the river well above flood stage from mid-January until early April.

In the twentieth century, the U.S. Army Corps of Engineers has sought to contain the Mississippi within a set of fixed banks. Before that time, however, major changes of course were a frequent occurrence. Thus it is that much of the Mississippi's 1863 riverbed is today either slack water or dry land. The river settlements of Vicksburg, Grand Gulf, and Bruinsburg have all been deserted by the channel. Owing to the intervention of man, the floodplain, as a whole, is a much drier place today than it was in 1863.

The river channel is an imposing terrain feature. Averaging in 1863 about one-half mile in width, at the hairpin turns adjacent to Vicksburg and Grand Gulf, it narrowed to one-quarter mile and ran one hundred feet deep. Water velocity at these constricted points was about six knots, making for treacherous navigation.

Although the Mississippi represented one of the great transportation arteries on the continent, access to the river from the shore and vice versa was not easy. It is true that riverboats could tie up at any of the numerous plantation landings dotting the riverbanks. However, since these habitations relied on the river for access to the outside world, roads running inland from them were few and unreliable. When the bottomlands filled with water, road travel was all but impossible on the Mississippi floodplain.

The best interfaces between roads and the river occurred wherever the river touched the eastern edge of the floodplain. Here, there stood a line of bluffs running from Kentucky to Louisiana. In 1863, the river met this bluff line at Columbus, Kentucky; Memphis, Tennessee; Vicksburg, Grand Gulf, Rodney, and Natchez in Mississippi; and Port Hudson and Baton Rouge in Louisiana. Just north of Vicksburg, the Yazoo River, a navigable tributary of the Mississippi, touches this bluff line at a place called Haynes' Bluff. Not surprisingly, each of these places figured prominently in the Mississippi River campaigns. For the Confederates, such locations were the best spots for siting artillery to command the channel, thus closing the river to Union navigation. From the Union perspective, at these sites where river met bluff, armies could offload from riverboats directly onto high, dry ground, avoiding the watery maze of the floodplain. These rare interfaces between river and bluff constituted decisive terrain in 1863.

One other important characteristic of the terrain in the Vicksburg campaign is directly attributable to the Mississippi River. At the end of the last Ice Age, when the river flowed with 10 to 100 times its present volume, it assumed the form of a "braided stream," meaning that it followed multiple channels that threaded among a vast array of islets and sandbars. Westerly winds blowing across these alluvial features raised clouds of dust out of the floodplain and deposited the sediment in a belt reaching five to fifteen miles inland from the bluff line. These yellowish-brown deposits, two hundred feet thick at Vicksburg, are known as "loess" (pronounced "luss") soil. Loess has some remarkable properties. Relatively impermeable to water, it erodes easily but is capable of holding a vertical slope. Thus, the terrain of the loess region (including Vicksburg) has been carved by erosion into a fantastic array of razorback ridges and precipitous ravines. Furthermore, being easy to dig and requiring little bracing, the loess soil of Vicksburg facilitated tunneling and fortification construction during the war.

Just as the Mississippi River formed the land it occupies, so it shaped the campaigns waged for its control during the Civil War. The struggle for the western waters began in February 1862 when Union forces captured Forts Henry and Donelson on the Tennessee and Cumberland Rivers, respectively. These positions outflanked Columbus, Kentucky, the Confederacy's northernmost outpost on the

Loess soil in a Vicksburg road cut, showing its ability to hold a vertical slope.

Mississippi, which was promptly evacuated. The next Confederate strongpoints downstream, New Madrid and Island Number 10, fell in April 1862 to Union Army and Navy forces under Brigadier General John Pope and Flag Officer Andrew H. Foote. Pope, together with Foote's successor, Flag Officer Charles H. Davis, secured Forts Pillow and Randolph in June. Union forces occupied Memphis shortly thereafter. The next defensible terrain downstream from Memphis was at Vicksburg.

After Memphis, the Union flotilla under Davis proceeded to reconnoiter the river to Vicksburg, where on 30 June it met Flag Officer David G. Farragut's Western Gulf Blockading Squadron. Farragut had worked upstream with his ocean-going warships following the 1 May capture of New Orleans. Thus, the U.S. Navy controlled the entire Mississippi River in the early summer of 1862—except for a short stretch of water commanded by five batteries of Confederate guns at Vicksburg.

Farragut could not stay at Vicksburg. His expedition included only 3,200 Army troops, under Brigadier General Thomas Williams—too few to assault the bluffs and silence the guns. Williams' men tried but failed to cut a canal across the peninsula opposite Vicksburg that would have bypassed the city and its guns. Falling water levels—Farragut's blue-water sloops drew up to seventeen feet—and the appearance of a Confederate ironclad, the *Arkansas*, persuaded Farragut to return to New Orleans before his little fleet became stranded.

The U.S. Navy's appearance at Vicksburg alarmed the Confederate high command. Farragut's departure gave the Confederates an opportunity that they exploited fully. Under Captain Samuel Lockett, work began on improving the fortifications of Vicksburg, making it the "Gibraltar of the West," with works facing both landward and toward the river. The Confederates also erected a similar but smaller fortress some 250 miles downriver at Port Hudson, Louisiana, thus securing to the Confederacy the river between these two points.

In October 1862, Confederate Lieutenant General John C. Pemberton assumed command of the Department of Mississippi and East Louisiana. Pemberton's responsibilities included not only the river bastions at Vicksburg and Port Hudson but also the field forces confronting the Union Army of the Tennessee under Major General Ulysses S. Grant, which menaced northern Mississippi. Two flaws in the Confederate command structure would complicate Pemberton's life. First, the western boundary of his department rested upon the largest high-speed avenue of approach in North America—the Mississippi River. He had no authority over forces on the far shore. Second, Pemberton was authorized to report directly to Richmond, bypassing General Joseph E. Johnston, overall commander between the Appalachian Mountains and the Mississippi. When catastrophe loomed in 1863, the easily offended Johnston attempted to deny responsibility for Pemberton's situation.

Command arrangements on the Union side of the upcoming campaign appeared to be just as disordered. In mid-1862, command authority over Army contingents in the Mississippi Valley was divided between the Department of the Mississippi in the north and the Department of the Gulf in the south. In July, Major General Henry W. Halleck, commanding the Department of the Mississippi, was promoted to the position of general in chief and departed for Washington, without designating a successor. Instead, the huge department fragmented into four smaller departments, the smallest of which was Grant's Department of the Tennessee. Halleck intended to coordinate the Army commands west of the Appalachians from Washington. President Lincoln made things worse when he authorized Major General John McClernand, a prominent political general, to raise yet another force, with which McClernand promised to open the Mississippi. McClernand proceeded to assemble his "private" army at Memphis, within Grant's department.

Similarly, the two Navy components on the Mississippi operated independently of each other. Farragut and Flag Officer David D. Porter, commander of the newly designated Mississippi Squadron, both reported to the Navy Department in Washington. Needless to say, there was no joint commander on the Mississippi with the authority to direct the combined efforts of Army and Navy.

In practice, the Union command arrangement worked better than one might have expected. Porter and Grant proved to be congenial spirits who achieved through cooperation what could not be done by command. Moreover, in the course of the campaign, Halleck effectively enlarged the boundaries of Grant's small department to give him control over both banks of the Mississippi. He also directed neighboring departments to provide Grant with substantial reinforcements. Making a virtue of necessity, Grant exercised considerable latitude in his interpretation of instructions from

Washington. This was due in large part to his distance from the seat of power. On the Confederate side, Pemberton received plenty of advice from his superiors, but less in the way of tangible assistance.

In November 1862, Grant opened his first campaign against Mississippi. His plan involved advances on two axes, which were to converge in the Vicksburg-Jackson region. Grant led 45,000 troops southward from western Tennessee. His subordinate, Major General William T. Sherman, on his part, conducted a river-borne expedition from Memphis to the Yazoo River just above Vicksburg. Departing from the vicinity of La Grange, Tennessee, Grant's column methodically forced the Yalobusha and Tallahatchie River lines, rebuilding the Mississippi Central Railroad as it advanced. Pemberton, commanding 30,000 troops in Grant's path, seemed reluctant to give battle. On 20 December, Pemberton gained a reprieve when Confederate cavalry under Brigadier General Nathan B. Forrest and Major General Earl Van Dorn raided Grant's extended line of communications in several places. Van Dorn's destruction of the major Union advanced depot at Holly Springs, Mississippi, forced Grant to call off the overland campaign.

Sherman's river-borne expedition fared even worse. Much of his army consisted of raw recruits that he had "borrowed" from McClernand's independent command—without McClernand's knowledge. The expedition suffered a bloody repulse on 29 December at Chickasaw Bayou (see map 2).

Three days later, Sherman gave up the expedition, reembarked his troops, and returned to the Mississippi, where an irate John McClernand reclaimed his "borrowed" army. McClernand proceeded to lead an expedition up the Arkansas River that culminated in the capture of a Confederate fort at Arkansas Post on 10 January.

While contemplating further operations in the interior of Arkansas, McClernand received orders from Grant to return with his force to the Vicksburg area. McClernand disputed Grant's authority over him, but Grant had the backing of Halleck, so McClernand complied. Grant received further instructions from Halleck to combine his and McClernand's forces into one army of three corps, the corps commanders being McClernand, Sherman, and Major General James B. McPherson. (Major General Stephen A. Hurlbut commanded a fourth corps, the headquarters of which remained in Tennessee during the Vicksburg campaign.) Grant further decided that this united force

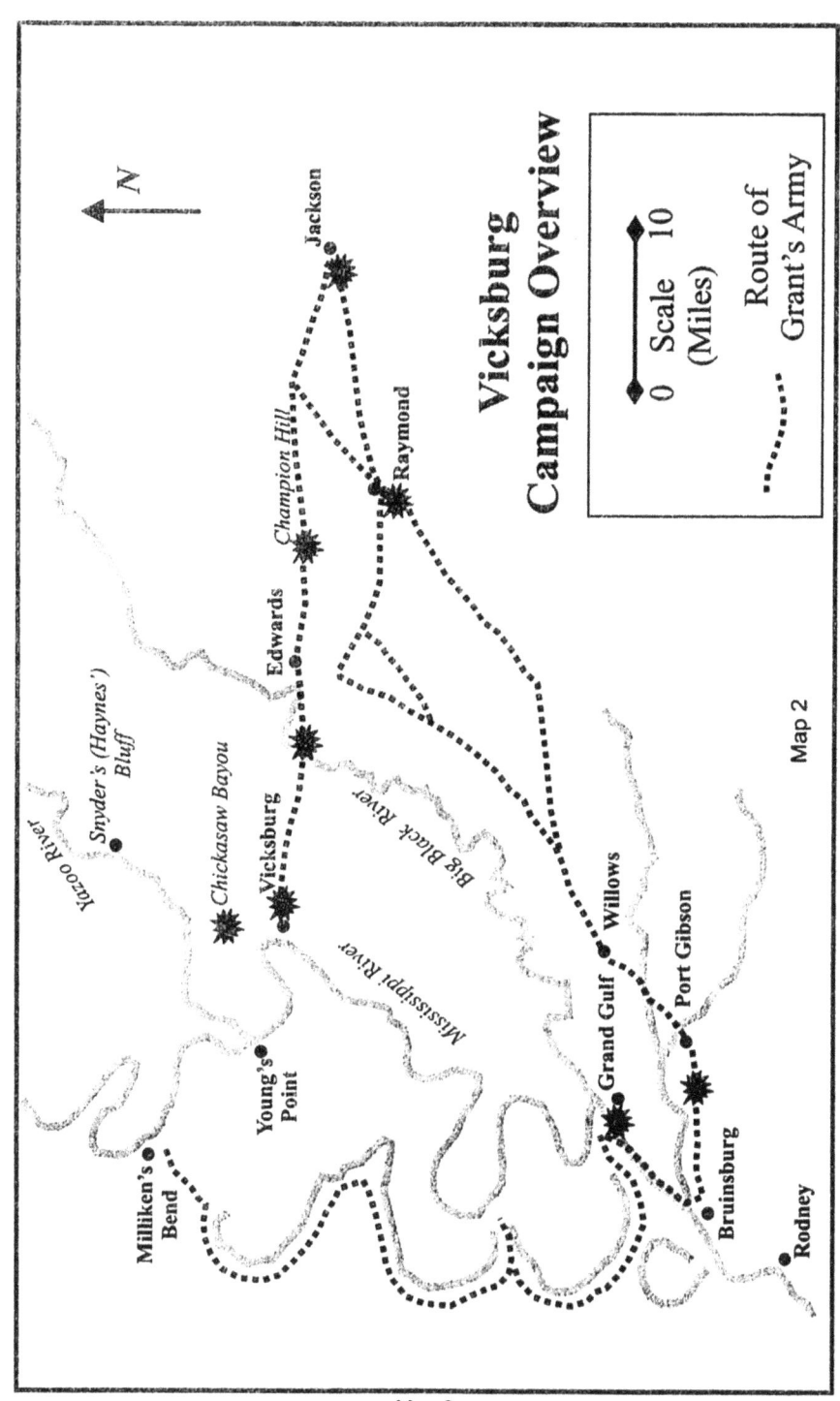

would operate against Vicksburg by way of the river, not overland. On 30 January, Grant opened headquarters at Young's Point, Louisiana, on the west bank of the Mississippi River, just ten miles above Vicksburg.

Grant's immediate problem was to get his army out of the floodplain and on to high ground on the Vicksburg side of the river. Heavy rains and unusually high river levels kept the floodplain more or less under water from January to April, effectively precluding any sort of direct approach across the lowlands. Instead, Grant explored ways to bypass the Vicksburg fortifications by water, so as to approach the city from the land side (see map 7 in stand 4 on page 97).

The first such project was an ill-fated attempt to complete the canal, begun in 1862 and intended to cut the peninsula opposite Vicksburg. Other projects involved opening navigable routes through the web of waterways on the Mississippi floodplain. The Lake Providence expedition was an attempt to bypass Vicksburg by way of an interconnected series of lakes, bayous, and rivers west of the Mississippi. Two other expeditions, Yazoo Pass and Steele's Bayou, probed the "Delta," a swampy, low-lying region lying between the Mississippi and the Yazoo. None of these experiments succeeded. By late March, when water levels began to drop, Grant gave up on the "bayou expeditions" and decided to outflank Vicksburg on foot.

On the Confederate side, confidence rose with every Union setback. By early April, the Confederates saw indications that Grant had given up the campaign and was returning his army to Memphis. But on 9 April, Pemberton learned that strong Union forces were marching southward from the Union camps on the west bank of the Mississippi. The purpose and extent of this movement was not clear to Pemberton, but it would prove to be more than just another bayou expedition. Grant was in fact bypassing Vicksburg with his main force. McClernand's corps led the way, stepping off on 31 March, with McPherson's following, while Sherman's corps protected the base of operations above Vicksburg. The route of march followed the natural levees lining the bayous, which were once part of the Mississippi but were now well west of the river.

On the night of 16-17 April, Porter ran the batteries at Vicksburg with eight of his gunboats and three transports, furnishing Grant with the means to cross to the east bank of the Mississippi below Vicksburg. Pemberton, lulled by the slow pace of events in the preceding three months and distracted by Union diversions elsewhere in his large department, failed to recognize the magnitude of this threat.

Pemberton's awakening came suddenly on 29 April when Porter's gunboats opened a devastating bombardment on the Confederate fortifications at Grand Gulf, the first point south of Vicksburg where the Mississippi touched the line of bluffs. McClernand's troops stood by on transports ready to land as soon as the Confederate guns fell silent. When, after five hours, the shore batteries were still firing, Grant called off the operation. The next morning, 30 April, Union troops landed unopposed twelve miles downstream from Grand Gulf at a plantation landing called Bruinsburg. By day's end, McClernand's corps had reached the top of the bluffs, placing Grant on high, dry ground on the Vicksburg side of the river with 22,000 men.

Although there were over 60,000 Confederate troops in the Department of Mississippi and East Louisiana, Pemberton could assemble only 8,000 troops in the Grand Gulf area to challenge the Union incursion. Brigadier General John S. Bowen, the commander at Grand Gulf, was at the head of his own two brigades, plus two more hurried forward from Vicksburg when he encountered McClernand's corps near Port Gibson on 1 May. For most of the day, Bowen's troops, outnumbered three to one, fought tenaciously among the razor-backed ridges and vine-choked ravines typical of the "loess hills" region. When McClernand, reinforced by elements of McPherson's corps, finally bulldozed Bowen from the battlefield, the Confederates were able to withdraw in relatively good order.

Union troops, McPherson's corps leading, occupied Port Gibson and crossed Little Bayou Pierre on 2 May, capturing a bridge over Big Bayou Pierre on 3 May. McPherson's advance outflanked the Confederate position at Grand Gulf, forcing Bowen to evacuate it. Porter's sailors promptly occupied Grand Gulf, which would serve as Grant's logistics base for the next two weeks.

His bridgehead east of the Mississippi secure, Grant paused from 3 to 9 May in the area between the Big Bayou Pierre and the Big Black River. In this interval, he evaluated his options for subsequent operations and allowed his supply train to catch up with the army. During this period, Sherman's corps joined with the main body. Sherman's arrival with two divisions gave Grant 42,000 men, with more reinforcements arriving regularly.

When Grant ordered the resumption of offensive operations, the Union axis of advance did not carry northward toward Vicksburg but rather northeastward, up the watershed between the Big Black and Bayou Pierre. Grant's objective was the railroad linking Vicksburg with Jackson (and the rest of the Confederacy). The Union force advanced on a wide front, foraging as it advanced: McClernand's corps on the left with its flank on the Big Black, Sherman's coming up in the center, and McPherson's on the right.

The Union advance met with little opposition, for Pemberton had chosen to interpret his instructions to defend Vicksburg literally. He kept two of his five divisions near the Vicksburg fortifications and put the other three to work fortifying and guarding the Big Black River near Edwards. Meanwhile, Confederate authorities began to order up reinforcements and directed General Joseph E. Johnston to take command personally in Mississippi. Johnston and the reinforcements were converging on Jackson, Mississippi, even as Grant drove northward to cut the railroad linking that place with Vicksburg.

On May 12, with McClernand's advance elements only four miles from the railroad at Edwards, McPherson's corps, on the right flank, walked into an unexpected battle at Raymond. Brigadier General John Gregg's brigade, recently arrived from Port Hudson, moved out from Jackson to attack what he thought was a small detachment but which turned out to be Logan's division of McPherson's corps. Although McPherson drove back the audacious Gregg with some difficulty, the fight at Raymond alerted Grant to the imminent appearance of Confederate reinforcements on his right flank. In a daring move, Grant suspended the advance toward Edwards, turned his back on Pemberton, and shifted his main effort to the reduction of Jackson. Sherman and McPherson captured the city on 14 May, driving out a Confederate rearguard while McClernand guarded their rear. General Johnston, who had arrived in Jackson just in time to order its evacuation, led the Confederate retreat northwards.

Thus, the Union seizure of Jackson temporarily halted the convergence of Confederate forces upon that place and bought Grant time to deal unmolested with Pemberton's force around Edwards. Meanwhile, Sherman's corps remained in Jackson to finish the demolition of industrial and transportation assets while McClernand and McPherson marched west. Pemberton, bedeviled by conflicting guidance, was ill prepared to receive the Union onslaught. His own inclinations were to stand on the defensive at the Big Black and meet

Grant in prepared positions. On 14 May, his subordinates talked him into launching an offensive southeastward against Grant's line of communications. This movement had barely begun on 15 May when peremptory orders arrived from Johnston directing Pemberton to march eastward and unite forces with him. Pemberton's command had just begun to countermarch on 16 May when Grant's forces surprised the Confederates in the vicinity of Champion Hill.

Thanks to excellent intelligence (including a plant, who delivered to the Union high command a copy of Johnston's orders to Pemberton), Grant opened the battle with 32,000 troops converging from three directions upon 23,000 Confederates. His tactical control, however, did not match the operational artistry with which he had brought on the battle. Only one of the three Union columns pressed the fight. But Pemberton's generalship was no better, and at the end of the day, his army was in full retreat toward the Big Black. One of the three Confederate divisions, moreover, failed to reach the bridges leading to safety and was lost to Pemberton; it later united with Johnston.

Grant exploited the situation ruthlessly. All three corps drew up along the Big Black on 17 May. At the railroad bridge over the river, McClernand's corps crushed a Confederate rearguard that remained on the east bank. All three corps then forced crossings at separate locations. Pemberton's command, stunned by two defeats in two days, streamed back in despair and disorder to the fortifications of Vicksburg. There, the weary troops joined the two fresh divisions that Pemberton had kept near Vicksburg throughout the campaign of maneuver.

On 18 May, Grant's army advanced on Vicksburg with McClernand's corps on the left, McPherson in the center, and Sherman on the right. Grant and Sherman personally accompanied the troops that occupied Haynes' Bluff, overlooking the Yazoo River north of town. With Haynes' Bluff in Union hands, Grant had captured the decisive terrain of the campaign—an interface between navigable water and high ground. Supplies and reinforcements could now flow to Grant's army unimpeded by either geography or Confederate action.

On 19 May, Grant mounted a hasty assault against the Vicksburg fortifications, hoping to capitalize upon the disorganization that the Confederates had displayed during their retreat. However, the "loess hills" terrain, the fortifications exploiting that terrain, and a renewed resolve within the Confederate ranks, combined to defeat the attack.

Sherman's corps bore the brunt of the fighting and the casualties. Grant returned to the attack with a full-scale push by all three corps on 22 May but suffered an even bloodier repulse. (McClernand's conduct during and after the 22 May assault contributed materially to his being relieved by Major General Edward O. C. Ord on 19 June.) Recognizing that time was on his side, Grant then commenced regular siege operations.

The siege phase of the campaign lasted six weeks. Both sides conducted siege operations in the formalized European style that had remained unchanged in its essentials for two centuries. Grant's men dug fortifications facing the Confederate works and established siege batteries to batter the Confederate strong points. Porter's gunboats and mortar scows added their fire from the river. As reinforcements flowed in from other departments, Grant extended his lines until they reached the river south of the city, thus completing the investment. Other reinforcements became part of a separate maneuver force under Sherman's command that faced the Confederate army that Johnston was assembling in the interior. Within the siege lines, Union troops dug approaches and mines but undertook no general assaults after 22 May.

Pemberton's position was a strong one, with well-conceived strong points guarding the few approaches allowed by the terrain. Although essentially cut off from resupply, Vicksburg was the main storehouse for Pemberton's department, hence supplies of food and ammunition were adequate though not plentiful. From Pemberton's point of view, he was accomplishing his mission so long as the Confederate flag flew over Vicksburg. It was up to Johnston to raise the siege from without. Johnston, however, feared the campaign was lost the moment Pemberton allowed himself to be contained within the Vicksburg fortifications. Johnston eventually managed to assemble an army of 30,000, but Union strength grew even faster. Grant finished the campaign in command of 90,000 troops (over 70,000 "present for duty"). Of this force, about two-thirds stood in the siege lines, and one-third in Sherman's maneuver force.

Inside Vicksburg, Johnston's failure to appear, coupled with sickness, hunger, and resurgent suspicions about Pemberton, depressed morale to the breaking point. As June gave way to July, Pemberton grew increasingly apprehensive of his troops' ability and will to fight. Believing that Grant would mount a general assault on Independence Day and doubting that his soldiers could resist,

Pemberton opened negotiations with Grant on 3 July. Grant, eager to conclude the siege before Johnston put in an appearance, and unwilling to encumber his lines of communications with 30,000 prisoners of war, agreed to parole the Vicksburg garrison. The Confederates stacked their arms on 4 July, one day after the repulse of Pickett's charge won the battle of Gettysburg for the Union. Five days later, the Confederate garrison at Port Hudson capitulated to Major General Nathaniel P. Banks, thus opening the Mississippi River to Union traffic from source to mouth.

Grant's victory at Vicksburg is generally counted as one of the decisive moments in the Civil War. Opening the Mississippi constituted a significant political victory for the Lincoln administration and was a humiliating and irretrievable setback for the Confederate cause. After Vicksburg fell, any status quo peace settlement would leave the Confederacy a bisected nation, excluded from one of the greatest transportation arteries on the continent. On an emotional level, the simultaneous defeats at Gettysburg and Vicksburg constituted a serious blow to Southern morale. July 1863 marks the point at which many citizens of the Confederacy despaired of winning peace on terms other than national extinction.

Militarily, the significance of Vicksburg is somewhat less pronounced. With the Mississippi secured, the city of Vicksburg proved to be an operational dead end for Grant's Army of the Tennessee. The victors suddenly found themselves on the remote periphery of the war with no significant objectives within reach. Moreover, while the damage done to the Confederate war effort was serious, it was far from decisive. Many of Pemberton's paroled troops would return to the war. Moreover, the interdiction of communications and trade with the Trans-Mississippi was not a fatal blow to Confederates on either side of the river.

Eventually, many of the combatants at Vicksburg, both Union and Confederate, would join the struggle for Chattanooga. Grant's victory there, building upon the renown he won at Vicksburg, propelled him to the position of commanding general in 1864. Grant's accession to the Army's highest command, plus the constriction of the active theater of war to the Eastern seaboard, were two of the most important legacies of the Vicksburg campaign. Vicksburg demonstrated that when "Sam" Grant set himself a goal, he would eventually attain it. The grim determination displayed by Union forces at Vicksburg was the attribute that would eventually win them the war.

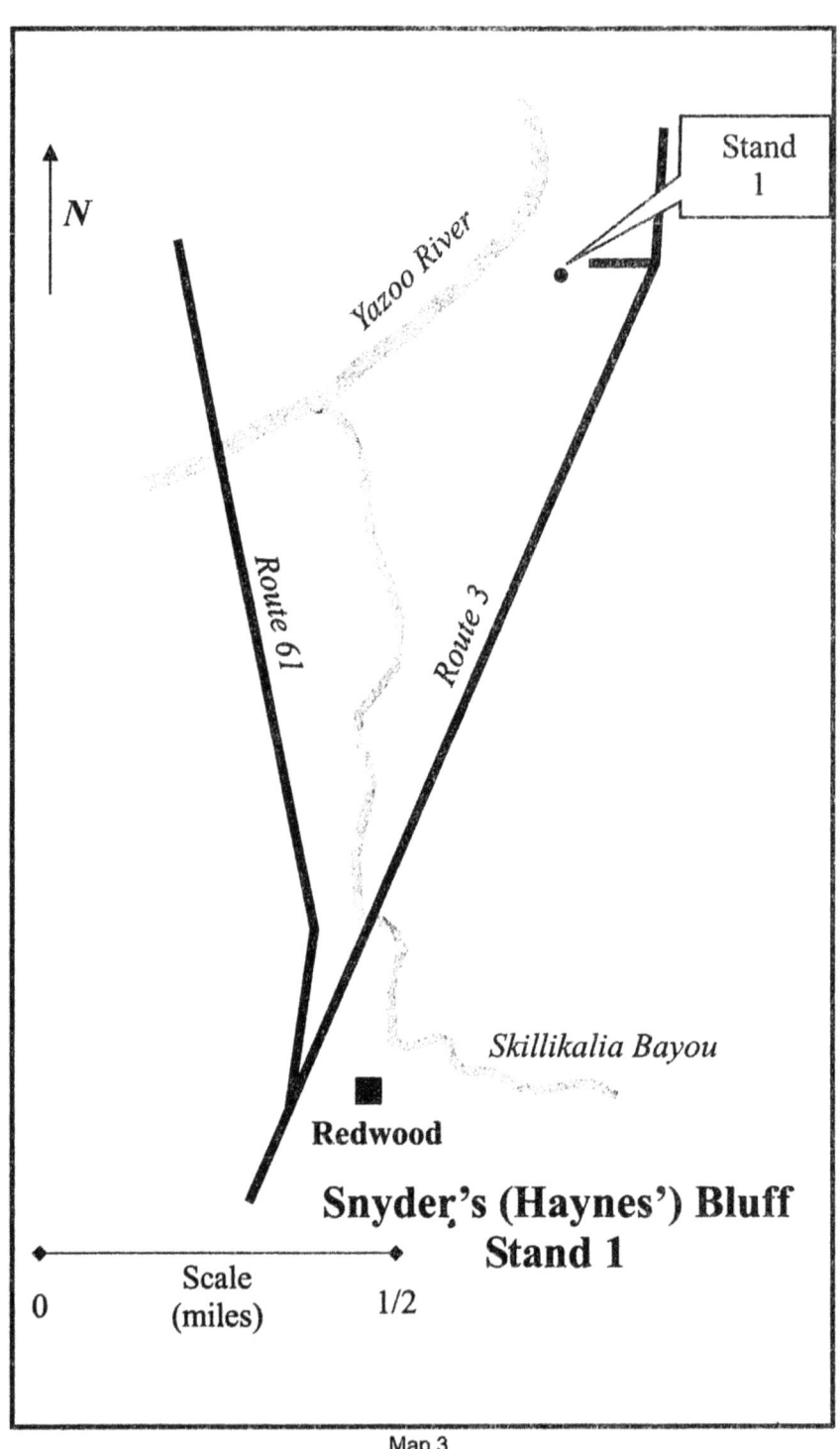

III. SUGGESTED ROUTE AND VIGNETTES

Introduction

During the course of the Civil War, the struggle for control of Vicksburg spanned about a year and involved operations separated by hundreds of miles. Because of the wide chronological and geographical span of the campaign, it has been necessary to exercise selectivity in packaging a staff ride that can be executed within a reasonable amount of time. Actions at outlying places, such as the raid on Holly Springs, Grierson's raid, the battle of Jackson, and the siege of Port Hudson have been omitted here to save travel time, even though they were significant elements of the overall campaign.

The resulting itinerary involves considerable driving time. The full itinerary, with discussions at each stand, will absorb approximately three days. Individual groups can tailor this schedule to accommodate the time available to them or to focus upon aspects of the campaign that are of particular interest to them.

In following this itinerary, be aware that not all of the stands are designated by signs or monuments. For this reason, directions are as specific as possible in terms of mileages, road names, and landmarks. Even so, roads and landmarks may change over time, and mileages are no more accurate than the odometer of the vehicle. A set of topographic maps (see bibliography) and route advice from park personnel will help prevent unintentional detours.

DAY 1

Stand 1
Snyder's ("Haynes") Bluff

Directions: To reach Snyder's Bluff from Vicksburg, go east on I-20 to exit 5A, then north on U.S. Route 61 to Redwood. At Redwood, turn on State Route 3 north. Approximately 1.1 miles north of Redwood, on the left, there is a pull-off and a historical marker. Park here and find a spot where the Yazoo River is visible through the vegetation (see map 3 on page 82).

Orientation: Snyder's Bluff is one of those key places where navigable water runs along the foot of a bluff. In this case, the water happens to be the Yazoo River, which in the 1860s emptied into the Mississippi a few miles upstream from Vicksburg (about fourteen miles south and west from here). This bluff, as well as the hills traversed while driving north from Vicksburg, are part of the Walnut Hills, a section of the north-south bluff line that marks the eastern edge of the Mississippi floodplain.

Situation 1: Confederate Defenses, December 1862-May 1863. The U.S. Navy's victory at Memphis, on 6 June 1862, exposed the Mississippi River between Memphis and Vicksburg to attack by Union gunboats since there was no defensible terrain between those two points. Also vulnerable were the tributaries, such as the Yazoo, flowing into that section of the Mississippi. Following the Union expedition to Vicksburg in the summer of 1862, the Confederates fortified this spot, which is the first high ground encountered when coming upstream on the Yazoo. Although the purpose of this fortified complex was to block Union gunboats from raiding the fertile Yazoo River valley, it also constituted an outpost of the main Vicksburg fortifications, which were located twelve miles to the south. Any river-borne Union force seeking to bypass the Vicksburg defenses by sailing up the Yazoo could be blocked here.

In December 1862, the Snyder's Bluff defensive position, which was anchored on this hill and extended approximately two miles southward, was commanded by Colonel Edward Higgins. His force consisted of nine large guns and two regiments, the 22d Louisiana and the 3d Mississippi, for a total garrison of approximately 1,300. The guns were positioned in earthworks here on the bluffs, while the infantry was sheltered in rifle pits located among the guns and down near the riverbank. The batteries at this particular spot commanded the entire stretch of river to the left as far as the next bend downstream. Union vessels coming up this stretch not only presented an easy target, but also had to sail single file and could fight back with only their bow guns. Moreover, the Confederates obstructed the channel with "torpedoes," or mines, and a floating log barricade, referred to as a "raft," that blocked the river from bank to bank immediately in front of this stand. Viewed from above, this raft was shaped like the letter "W" (see map 4).

The Confederates generally referred to this formidable defensive position as "Snyder's Mill," or "Snyder's Bluff," which is the name of the hill upon which you are now standing. The U.S. Navy referred to it as "Drumgould's Bluff," which is the next hill to the south, where the left wing of the position rested. The U.S. Army usually called the position "Haynes' Bluff," which is actually the name of the next hill to

Official Records of the Union and Confederate Navies in the War of Rebellion, Vol. 24, p. 591.

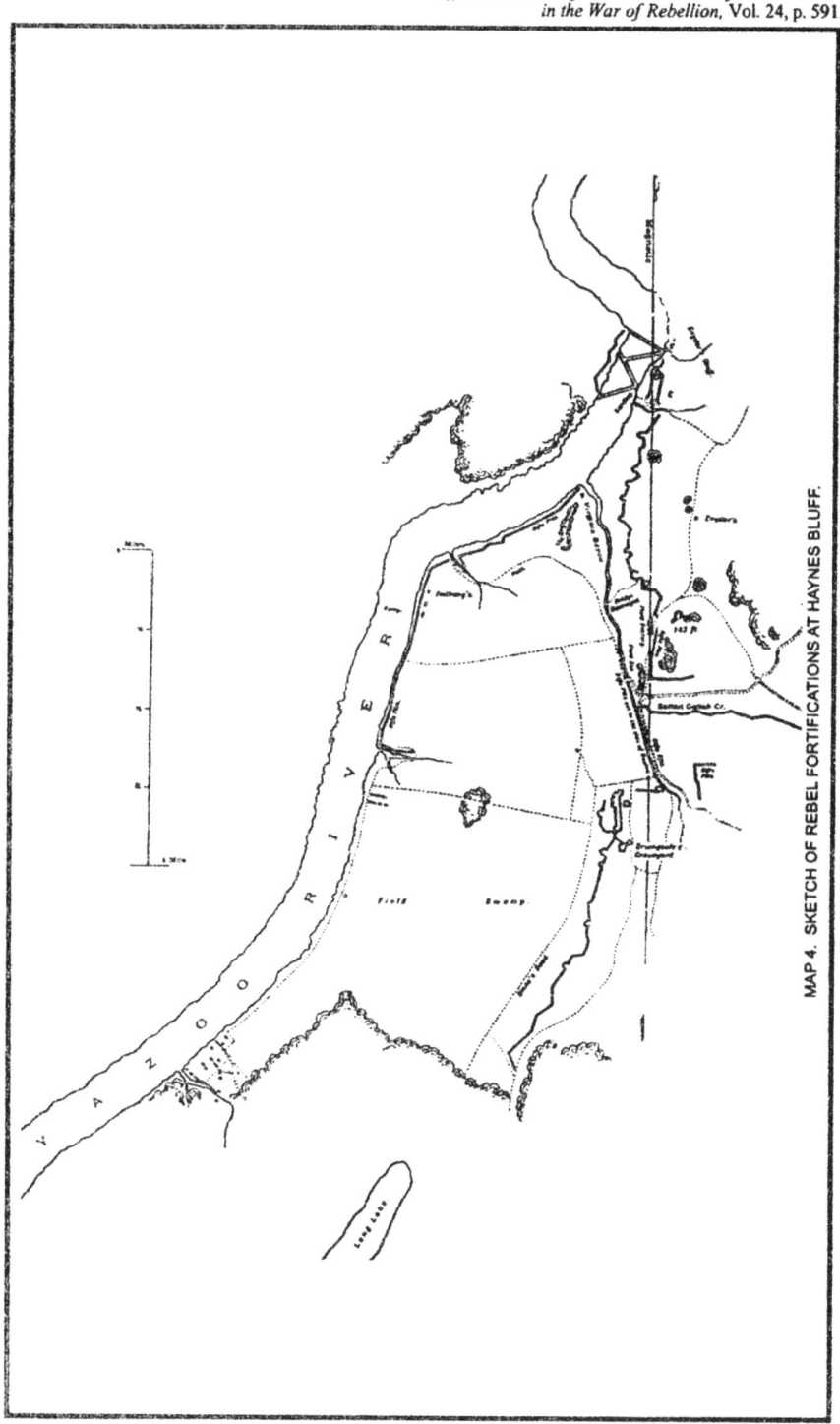

MAP 4. SKETCH OF REBEL FORTIFICATIONS AT HAYNES BLUFF.

the north and which was not part of the main defensive works. Nonetheless, the name "Haynes' Bluff" is the term used by most historians to designate this fortified position, which actually occupied Drumgould's and Snyder's bluffs. By any name, this piece of ground and the defensive works located here constituted some of the most important terrain in the campaign for Vicksburg.

War came to the Yazoo River in December 1862 when a Union naval force arrived to reconnoiter the river in anticipation of an eventual Army landing. Commanded by Captain Henry Walke, the force consisted of two tinclads, a ram, and two ironclads. The reconnaissance came to an abrupt halt on 12 December, approximately three miles downstream from Snyder's Bluff, when the ironclad *Cairo* struck a "torpedo" and sank. This setback meant that the Army's landings would have to take place even farther downstream, well short of the river-bluff interface.

Two weeks later, Major General William T. Sherman's troops landed at Chickasaw Bayou, approximately six miles downstream from Snyder's Bluff. To support the landings, Rear Admiral David D. Porter personally led another expedition up the Yazoo. Four ironclads (led by the huge *Benton*), two timberclads, four tinclads, and two rams cleared "torpedoes" and tried to divert attention from the Army landings. When Porter's vessels reached the bend about one mile downstream from here, they opened fire on these bluffs. The ensuing artillery duel lasted about ninety minutes, with the *Benton* bearing the brunt of the action. (Since the channel was too narrow to bring vessels abreast, the other gunboats remained downstream from the bend and lobbed their shells over the point.) Because of their elevation, the Confederate batteries delivered a plunging fire that could smash through unarmored decks, even if it could not penetrate armored casemates. The *Benton* received more than twenty hits and sustained about a dozen casualties, including her commander, Lieutenant Commander William Gwin, who was mortally wounded when a large-caliber rifled shot struck him in the chest and arm. The Confederate batteries were undamaged, and casualties amounted to only one killed and two wounded.

Three days later, when it was clear that Sherman's Chickasaw Bayou operation had failed, Sherman and Porter devised a plan for a nighttime amphibious assault against Snyder's Bluff. Under the plan, a ram fitted with a rake-like mine-clearing device would lead a force of seven ironclads, two timberclads, and two tinclads that would cover the landing of 10,000 picked assault troops. The infantry, consisting of Brigadier General Frederick Steele's division and Colonel Giles A. Smith's brigade, was to land between Drumgould's and Snyder's Bluffs and then storm the heights. Scheduled to take place in the early morning hours of 31 December, this ambitious operation was called off due to heavy fog.

The idea of mounting a direct assault on these bluffs resurfaced three months later. By the end of March, Grant's "bayou expeditions" had come to naught, and he was casting about for some way to get a toehold on the east side of the Mississippi. On 2 April, Porter, Grant, and Sherman reconnoitered the position by boat but decided that an assault landing would incur prohibitive casualties. Nonetheless, on 30 April, Sherman returned here with ten transports, each carrying a regiment. Sherman's purpose, however, was not to assault but to divert Confederate attention from Grant's force, which was about to cross the Mississippi near Grand Gulf, forty miles to the south. Accompanying the transports was a naval force under Lieutenant Commander K. Randolph Breese that included three ironclads, a timberclad, four tinclads, and three mortar boats. Sherman's troops disembarked downstream from here and formed for an assault, while Breese's gunboats engaged the Confederate batteries. The Union forces repeated the performance on 31 April, then departed. Thus ended the last Union challenge to the Snyder's Bluff fortified position.

Teaching Points: Decisive terrain, placement of defenses, riverine operations.

Situation 2: Union Defenses. Following the Union victories at Champion Hill and Big Black River, the Confederates at Snyder's Bluff evacuated their positions and withdrew into the Vicksburg stronghold. On 18 May, the same day that the first Union troops reached the fortifications of Vicksburg, the 4th Iowa Cavalry of Sherman's corps reached the Yazoo River at Snyder's Bluff and captured thirteen heavy guns abandoned there by the Confederates. On the riverbank below, the Union troopers met the ironclad *De Kalb*. Grant and Sherman arrived in person shortly thereafter to inspect the key terrain that they had struggled so long to attain.

Union logisticians selected the W. A. Johnson plantation, located on Chickasaw Bayou several miles downstream from Snyder's Bluff, to serve as the logistics base for Grant's army during the siege of

Vicksburg. The first supplies moved through on 21 May. Thereafter, Union forces were assured of a steady flow of supply.

To protect the Johnson's Plantation depot and to guard the rear of Union forces besieging Vicksburg, Grant posted a covering force on a line running from Haynes' Bluff to the Big Black River. Union troops erected new fortifications, facing north along that line. By the end of the siege, three divisions occupied the Haynes' Bluff-Big Black River line: Brigadier General Thomas Welsh's and Brigadier General Robert B. Potter's divisions from IX Corps and Brigadier General William "Sooey" Smith's division from XVI Corps. Confederate forces never attacked this line.

Teaching Points: Logistics base, covering force.

Stand 2
Boat Slough

Directions: From Snyder's Bluff, backtrack south on State Route 3, then merge with U.S. Route 61 South toward Vicksburg. Turn right on Business Route 61, which marks the approximate trace of the Confederate positions during the Chickasaw Bayou battle. Travel 4.1 miles on Business Route 61 to the first traffic light. Then, turn right at the light, in the direction of the Port of Vicksburg. After 0.6 mile, turn right on Long Lake Road. After 4.6 miles, turn right at the T intersection and travel one mile. Park near the white church (see map 5.

Orientation: The last mile on the route to this stand passes along the section of the Yazoo River bank that Sherman used to land his force on 26-27 December. In 1862, this was the only useable landing site between the mouth of the Yazoo and Haynes' Bluff. This stand is on the ground occupied by Morgan's division. The body of water beside the church is Boat Slough (pronounced "slew").

Situation: The 30,000 Union troops that Sherman landed here in December 1862 represented one arm of a Union pincer movement directed against Mississippi. Grant's force, advancing overland from Tennessee, was the other. Union strategy was predicated on the assumption that Pemberton could not counter both threats, thus either Grant or Sherman would be free to move virtually unopposed against the interior of Mississippi. Moreover, it was expected that Sherman's lodgment on the Yazoo would become Grant's logistical depot when Grant reached the Vicksburg vicinity.

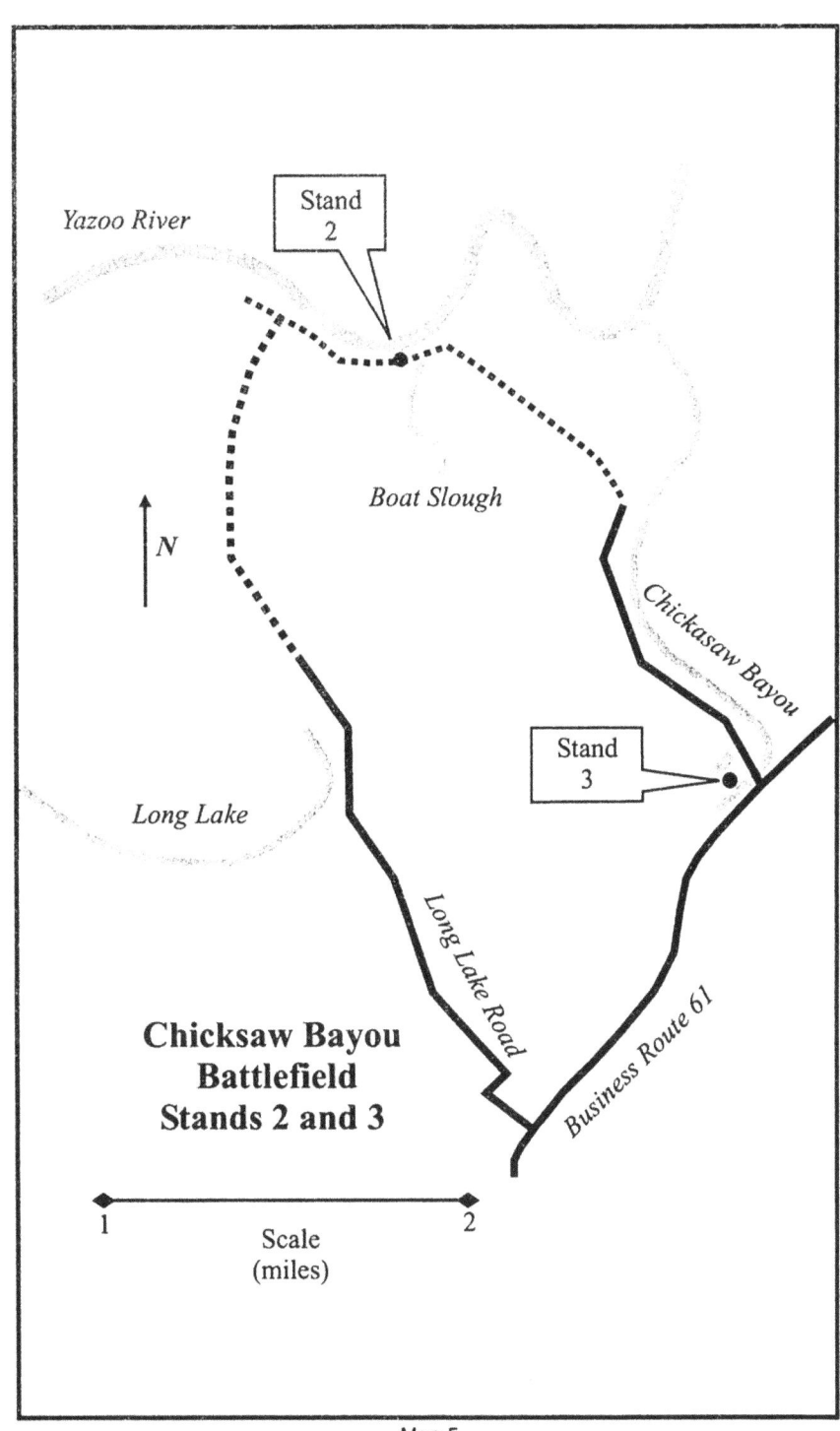

Sherman's force consisted of four divisions, three of which had been assembled in Memphis, the fourth coming from Helena, Arkansas. The Memphis divisions consisted of veteran troops jumbled together with new recruits that had been raised by Major General John C. McClernand, the political general from Illinois. In his haste to get underway before McClernand arrived in Memphis to reclaim his troops, Sherman rushed the embarkation process, which resulted in confusion and disorder. There was no attempt at combat loading; rather, men, animals, and equipment were tumbled on to any available vessel. Finally, on 20 December, forty-one transports, escorted by twelve gunboats, sailed south from Memphis. Another nineteen transports, carrying the division from Arkansas joined en route. Sherman's armada reached the mouth of the Yazoo on 26 December.

In ascending the Yazoo, Sherman intended to turn the flank of Vicksburg's main defenses, which faced the Mississippi. Sherman was compelled to find a landing site somewhere between the mouth of the Yazoo and Haynes' Bluff, where Confederate works blocked the river. His only real option was to land at the plantations that lined the riverbank near Chickasaw Bayou. Brigadier General George W. Morgan's division came ashore on the left, near Boat Slough. Brigadier General Frederick Steele's division constituted the Union center, and Brigadier General Morgan L. Smith's division the right. Brigadier General Andrew J. Smith came ashore with his division the following day. The Union landings occupied about two miles of riverbank in all.

The confusion and disorder of disembarkation were as great as the chaos of embarkation had been at Memphis. Moreover, Sherman's men were three miles away from their immediate objective—the line of bluffs that would put them on high, dry ground. Between the Yazoo and the bluffs were fields, trees, swamps, and bayous. In fact, the ground that Sherman had landed upon was virtually an island.

The Union landing force made only limited advances on the 26th. Owing to the chaos of unloading, most units bivouacked near the boats. Just a few Confederate skirmishers were on hand to harass the landing force. Major General Martin L. Smith, the Confederate commander at Vicksburg, possessed only 6,500 troops with which to counter Sherman's 30,000. However, help was on the way because Grant's advance into northern Mississippi had been turned back by the 20 December raid upon his supply lines. This allowed the Confederates to shift troops by rail from northern Mississippi to Vicksburg.

Vignette (Grant's orders to Sherman): "You will proceed with as little delay as possible to Memphis, Tenn., taking with you one division of your present command. On your arrival at Memphis you will assume command of all the troops there, and that portion of General Curtis' forces at present east of the Mississippi River, and organize them into brigades and divisions in your own way. As soon as possible move with them down the river to the vicinity of Vicksburg, and with the co-operation of the gunboat fleet under command of [Rear Admiral] Porter proceed to the reduction of that place, in such manner as circumstances [and] your own judgement may dictate." (Grant to Sherman, 8 December 1862, in *O.R.*, vol. 17, pt. 1, 601.)

Teaching Points: Consequences of inadequate planning, logistics preparation of the battlefield.

Stand 3
Chickasaw Bayou

Directions: Continue along the gravel road that approximates the route of Morgan's division toward Chickasaw Bayou. Travel 3.3 miles to a point short of Business Route 61 where two small bodies of water lie to the right of the road. The easternmost body (a brush-filled depression in dry weather) is what is left of Chickasaw Bayou (see map 5 on page 89).

Orientation: Chickasaw Bayou flowed northeast along the foot of the bluffs, then curved left (west) to empty into the Yazoo. In 1863, the road traveled by Morgan's division crossed Chickasaw bayou on a bridge approximately one hundred yards downstream (northeast) of this stand. De Courcy's attack came in the vicinity of that bridge. Thayer's attack occurred near the site of this stand.

The Confederate main line of resistance in this particular area was located several hundred yards beyond the bayou, on the slopes leading up to the bluffs.

Situation: The Union advance inland from the Yazoo landing sites was impeded by the terrain as much as by Confederate action. It took two days, 27 and 28 December, for Sherman's entire force to close on the enemy's main line of resistance. Swamps and woods constrained the Union troops to a few restricted avenues of approach. Artillery had poor fields of fire, and the gunboats back on the Yazoo were of little help. In an effort to broaden the advance, Sherman shifted Steele's division farther upstream to Blake's Levee on 27 December but recalled it on 28 December when the route proved to be constricted and stoutly defended.

The Confederates capitalized on the abundance of natural obstacles to conduct a masterful delaying action. While a handful of regiments held back Sherman, Martin L. Smith and his subordinate on the scene at Chickasaw Bayou, Brigadier General Stephen D. Lee, assembled an ad hoc force that numbered about 15,000 by 29 December. These troops prepared a defensive position at the base of the bluffs, placing Chickasaw Bayou between themselves and the advancing Union forces. They dug rifle pits, chopped down trees to form abatis, and cleared fields of fire at the few places where Chickasaw Bayou could readily be crossed. The defenders enjoyed excellent lateral communications along the road that paralleled their works. Thus, the Confederates were well-established in their defenses by 29 December when Sherman's men were finally in position to launch a concerted attack. Three days had elapsed since the Union force landed on the banks of the Yazoo.

Sherman's plan for the 29 December attack designated Morgan's division as the main effort. Morgan was to cross Chickasaw Bayou in the vicinity of a corduroy bridge, then storm the heights beyond. His attack would come up against Lee's Confederate brigade. To Morgan's left, Brigadier General Frank P. Blair's brigade of Steele's division was to make a supporting attack. Off to the right, the divisions of Morgan L. Smith and A.J. Smith likewise were to pin down the defenders in their front (Brigadier General Seth M. Barton's brigade).

Things began to go wrong even before the attack started. Engineers who were supposed to emplace a pontoon bridge across Chickasaw Bayou under cover of darkness discovered that certain components had been left behind in Memphis. Then, they mistakenly inserted the bridge on the wrong stream. It was daylight before work began at the proper site, by which time Confederate marksmen were able to prevent completion of the bridge. Without this bridge, two of Morgan's three brigades would be unable to participate in the assault.

Thus, when the time came to attack, Morgan led off with just one reinforced brigade, commanded by Colonel John F. DeCourcy. DeCourcy's men succeeded in crossing the bayou and entering the Confederate positions, but obstacles disrupted their assault, and Confederate fire finally stopped it. Brigadier General John M. Thayer's brigade of Steele's division attempted to attack in support of

De Courcy, but due to a mix-up, only one regiment reached the far bank of the bayou. A Confederate counterattack drove DeCourcy back in confusion.

To the left, Blair's supporting attack fared no better. His brigade found itself struggling through obstacles and raked by enfilading fire from both flanks. Blair's men retreated across the same bridge that DeCourcy used in his attack.

To the right, just one brigade became decisively engaged. Elements of Colonel Giles A. Smith's brigade succeeded in crossing the bayou at the Indian Mound but were immediately pinned down under the shelter of the far bank. Some of the survivors did not escape until nightfall; others were captured.

Unwilling to force another frontal assault at Chickasaw Bayou, Sherman and Porter laid plans for an Army-Navy night assault farther upstream, at the foot of Snyder's Bluff. Heavy fog on the morning of 31 December forced Sherman to call off the operation. On 2 January, Sherman gave up the campaign. His forces evacuated the Chickasaw Bayou landing and sailed back down the Yazoo.

The Chickasaw Bayou battle cost the Union 208 killed, 1,005 wounded, and 563 missing. Confederate casualties totaled fifty-seven killed, 120 wounded, and ten missing.

Vignette 1 (DeCourcy's 29 December attack across Chickasaw Bayou): "At ten minutes before 12 o'clock the order to advance was given and the Twenty-second and Forty-second Regiments found themselves immediately engaged under a hot fire in the toils of a nearly impassable abatis of heavy timber... By this time the Sixteenth Ohio, Fifty-fourth Indiana, and a part of the Twenty-second Kentucky, having a much easier and less encumbered ground to march over, had dashed across the bayou on their front, and by a road had marched up to and deployed on the open ground which sloped up to the works which they were to attack. This attack they began immediately, in splendid style, and nearly accomplished their object, notwithstanding the immense and fearfully-destructive fire which poured in from front, left, right, and even rear, for as soon as these regiments had advanced a few hundred yards toward the works the enemy opened with a battery in rear of the left of their advance... [T]he brave men composing these [regiments] had nearly crossed the large and open space of more than half a mile which lay stretched out before them glacis fashion, when the enemy increased his fire of small-arms and grape to such a degree as to render a farther advance impossible." (Report of Col. John F. De Courcy, 29 December 1862, in *O.R.*, vol. 17, pt. 1, 649-50.)

Vignette 2 (Thayer's brigade in support of De Courcy): "By the advice of General Morgan I dismounted and directed all officers mounted to do the same, as we would be sure to draw the fire of the enemy's sharpshooters if mounted. The Fourth Iowa, Col. J. A. Williamson, was on the right. I took my place at the head of the column and moved forward by the right flank. We crossed the bayou and went over the enemy's outside works. I then directed Colonel Williamson to deploy his regiment to the right and extend them as skirmishers. We were still advancing in front of the enemy's rifle-pits and batteries and crossed over a high rail fence. On seeing the ground I at once formed my plan to move up the hill, when, looking back for my other regiments, to my amazement none were to be seen and none coming, for I could see back to the point from which I had started. I could not account for it. I had supposed that five regiments were following me. I found myself within the enemy's works with but one regiment.

" . . . I observed [de Courcy's brigade], which had entered the works away to my left, retiring, which of course added to our extreme peril. The Fourth Iowa was then drawing the concentrated fire of all the enemy's batteries and rifle-pits . . . It was nothing but slaughter for it to remain. During the half-hour it was there 7 men were killed and 104 wounded [out of 480 engaged]." (Report of Brig. Gen. John M. Thayer, 31 December 1862, in *O.R.*, vol. 17, pt. 1, 658-59.)

Vignette 3 (Confederate perspective): "At daylight on the 29th the attack commenced with renewed fury and soon the appearance of a largely-increased force in front indicated an intention to assault, which was attempted almost simultaneously along the whole line. In front of General Lee the attack was the most formidable, as owing to the ground, they could deploy on a greater front, thus taking advantage of their superiority of numbers. The assaulting force—estimated at 6,000—moved from their concealed position in the woods, advanced rapidly on an open space of say 400 yards, and made a determined attack upon his entrenched position. Taken in flank by the artillery and met in front by a withering sheet of musketry fire, the enemy struggled up to within a short distance of our line, when he wavered, stopped, and soon fled in irretrievable panic and confusion, strewing the ground with his dead and wounded, leaving in our possession 4 regimental colors, over 300 prisoners, and 500 stands of arms." (Report of Maj. Gen. Martin L. Smith, [?] January 1863, in *O.R.*, vol. 17, pt. 1, 671-74.)

Teaching Points: Use of terrain in defense, problems of attack in constricting terrain.

Stand 4
Grant's Canal

Directions: Continue along the road to Business Route 61 and turn right. Follow Route 61 through downtown Vicksburg, where it becomes Washington Street. South of town, take Interstate 20 West across the Mississippi into Louisiana. Take Exit 186, turn right, and then right again on the old highway, Louisiana Route 3218. After two miles, turn right and cross the railroad tracks. Bear right and go under the interstate overpass. Historical markers on the left side of the road mark the site of Grant's Canal (see map 6 on page 96).

Orientation: This stand is near the southern (downstream) end of the canal. In 1863, the river channel was several hundred yards nearer to this spot than it is today.

Situation 1: Weather and the River. In January 1863, Grant reorganized his army and moved it to camps at Milliken's Bend and Young's Point on the Mississippi. His objective was to reach the high ground east of the Mississippi floodplain. The greatest obstacle to his continuation of operations against Vicksburg was high water. Although conditions had been a little drier than normal during Sherman's Chickasaw Bayou operations, the deluge came in January. By 20 January, the swamps on the floodplain were full, and still the rains fell. The river rose higher and higher through mid-March. By then, virtually the only dry ground on the floodplain was the top of the river's natural levees. Not until April did the floodwaters abate. By mid-April, the river stages were dropping precipitately until normal levels were at last attained. While it lasted, the flood placed serious constraints upon military operations and adversely affected the health and morale of the Union troops.

Situation 2: Grant's Canal (see map 7 on page 97). Grant's first attempt to find a water route bypassing the defenses of Vicksburg involved digging a canal across De Soto peninsula, in the expectation that the river would scour the canal into a new channel. Union troops had begun work on such a canal during Farragut's 1862 expedition to Vicksburg. Grant resumed the enterprise in late January 1863, utilizing troops from Sherman's corps, runaway slaves, and, eventually, several dipper dredges (floating steam shovels). Plans called for a canal sixty

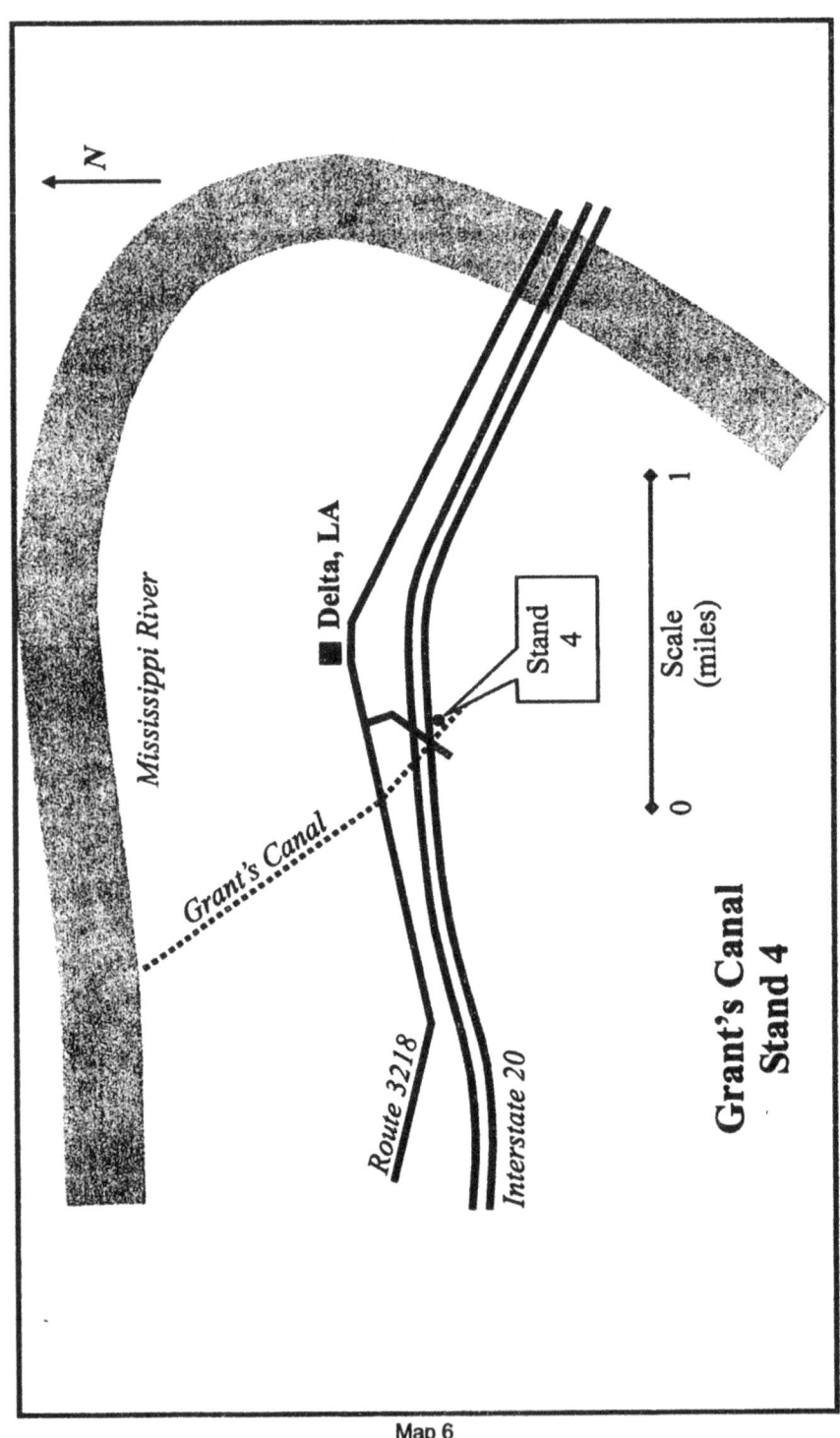

Map 6

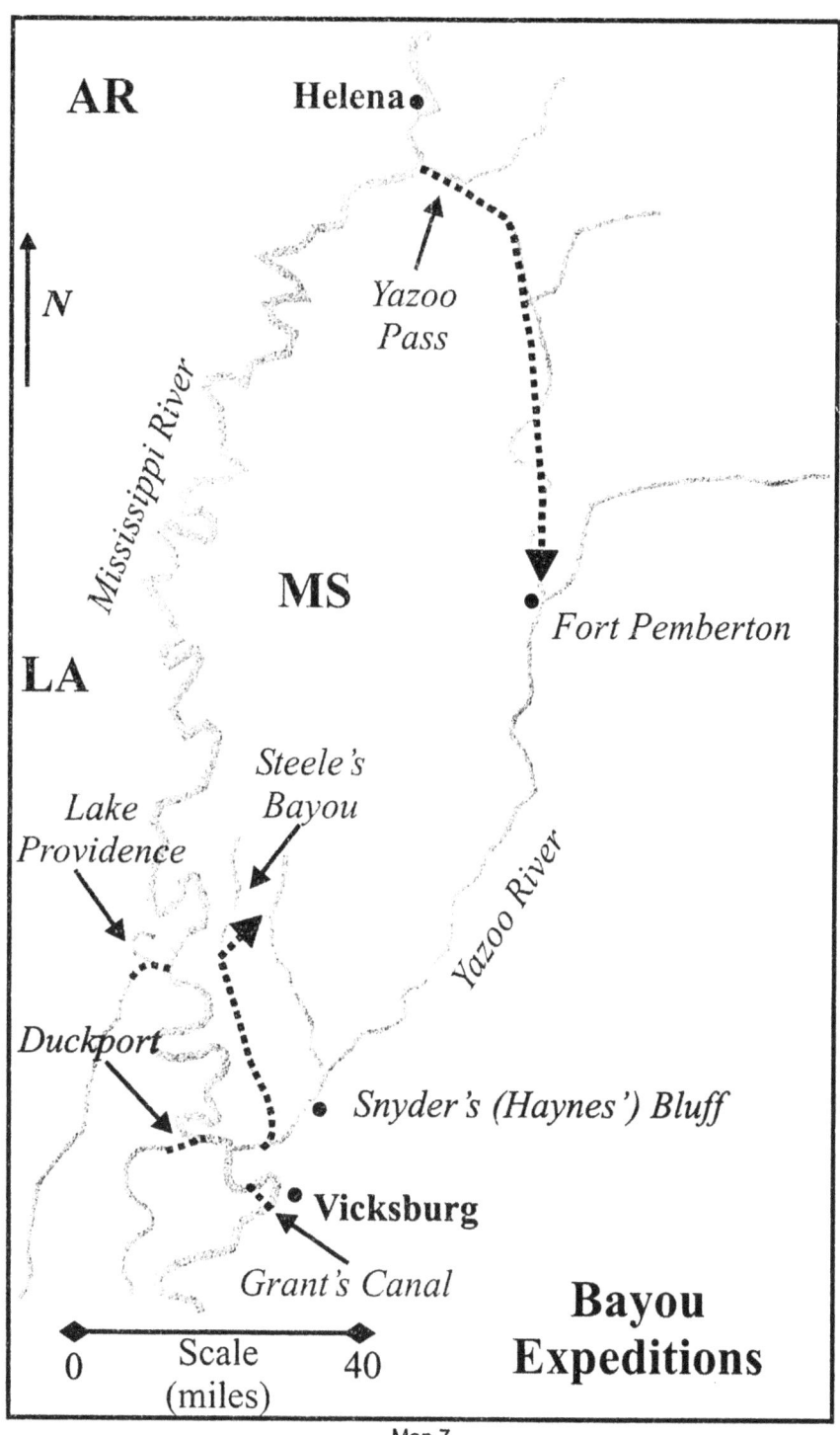

Map 7

Grant's Canal as it appears today.

feet wide, six feet deep, and about one mile long. Ironically, high waters hindered the digging and made living conditions miserable for the men. Meanwhile, the Confederates erected batteries that commanded the length of the canal and eventually drove out the dredges. Work on the canal essentially stopped on 24 March. When the river level receded in April, the canal drained out. By 4 May, it was dry.

Situation 3: Lake Providence. Grant had allowed work on the canal to go on even after he shifted his attention to other enterprises. About 3 February, Union troops cut a short canal from the Mississippi to Lake Providence, an oxbow lake more than forty miles upstream from Vicksburg that was once part of the Mississippi. Lake Providence emptied into a watery maze of bayous and rivers that eventually joined the Red River and ultimately the Mississippi, far south of Vicksburg. Troops from Major General James B. McPherson's corps labored to clear obstacles on what Grant at first considered to be the "most practicable route for turning Vicksburg." By mid-March, however, it was clear that the Lake Providence route was unlikely to succeed. Meanwhile, Grant had already initiated yet another experiment.

Situation 4: Yazoo Pass. On 3 February, Union engineers blasted a hole in the levee that separated the Mississippi from the headwaters of the Yazoo River, approximately ten miles below Helena, Arkansas. A major expedition, consisting of two ironclads, six tinclads, two rams, a mortar boat, and thirteen transports carrying Brigadier General Leonard F. Ross's division, sailed through the gap on 24 February. Grant's plan, ultimately, was to place an entire corps on the east bank of the Yazoo River upstream from Haynes' Bluff as part of a coordinated attack involving the entire army. But as the flotilla crept downstream on the Yazoo's tributaries, Confederate Major General William W. Loring established a defensive position, named Fort Pemberton, to block the Union advance. Union gunboats engaged the fort on 11, 13, and 16 March but failed to silence the Confederate guns. Although Union forces lingered in the area until early April, they made no further attempts against Fort Pemberton.

Situation 5: Steele's Bayou. Meanwhile, Rear Admiral Porter found another route to the upper Yazoo through the tangled waterways of the Delta. On 14 March, with Porter in command, five ironclads and one ram started up Steele's Bayou on a circuitous route that would bring them back to the Yazoo upstream of Haynes' Bluff. Brigadier General David Stuart's division of Sherman's corps followed the flotilla to secure its communications and to establish a bridgehead on the east bank of the Yazoo from which operations could be mounted against Haynes' Bluff. But Porter's expedition never reached the Yazoo, owing to Confederate obstructions and sniper fire. In fact, Porter required assistance from Sherman's infantry to extricate his vessels from a potential trap.

With the failure of this last expedition, Grant faced the prospect of having to attempt another assault at Chickasaw Bayou. He conducted a reconnaissance by boat on 1 April and concluded that such an assault would meet the same fate as had Sherman's operation the preceding December. "This, then, closes out the last hope of turning the enemy by the right," Grant wrote to Porter.

Vignette 1 (Advice to Grant from the General in Chief): "Direct your attention particularly to the canal proposed across the point. The President attaches much importance to this." (Halleck to Grant, 25 January 1863, in *O.R.*, vol. 24, pt. 1, 10.)

Vignette 2 (Sherman's opinion of the various experiments): "Our canal here don't amount to much. It is full of water, but manifests no disposition to change the channel. It is a very small affair, and we can hardly work a barge through it for stumps. Even if it succeeds,

Warrenton Bluff lies below, next Grand Gulf, next Rodney, and so on... But Grant is on two other projects: to turn some of the waters of the Mississippi through Old Yazoo Pass into the Yazoo, above the forts at Haynes' Bluff, so that our gunboats may reach the Yazoo fleet above Yazoo City; and to turn the main river into Lake Providence, when its waters would follow the Tensas to the Black River, then the Red and Atchafalaya, thus actually reaching the sea without approaching any bluff or ground easy of defense. This is a magnificent scheme, and, if successful, will be a grand achievement. A glance at the map will show it at least probable." (Sherman to Curtis, 7 February 1863, in *O.R.*, vol. 24, pt. 3, 37-38.)

Vignette 3 (Grant expresses disappointment over the failure of the bayou expeditions): "I regret that the chances look so gloomy for getting through to the Yazoo by that route [Steele's Bayou]. I had made so much calculation upon the expedition down Yazoo Pass, and now again by the route proposed by Admiral Porter, that I have really made but little calculation upon reaching Vicksburg by any other than Haynes' Bluff." (Grant to Sherman, 22 March 1863, in *O.R. Navies*, vol. 24, 489.)

Teaching Points: Effect of weather on terrain, mobility operations, joint operations, innovation and perseverance in operational planning.

Stand 5
U.S.S. *Cairo*

Directions: Retrace your route to Interstate 20 East, and recross the Mississippi to Vicksburg. Take Exit 1C and turn left on Hall's Ferry Road. Hall's Ferry Road joins with Cherry Street, which in turn becomes Fort Hill Street on the north side of town. After passing the park entry station, turn left to the *Cairo* museum (see map 8 on page 102).

Situation: The U.S.S. *Cairo* is the only surviving example of the gunboats designed specifically for combat upon the western rivers. She was much broader for her length than an ocean-going vessel would be and much shallower in draft. Her odd assortment of guns represent the ordnance that happened to be available in the western theater when she was completed in early 1862. Although an imposing instrument of war, the *Cairo* was almost too "hi-tech" for the western theater in that she burned coal (nearly one ton per hour), which was not available locally.

The U.S.S. *Cairo*

In addition to her military functions, the *Cairo* served as a rather uncomfortable home for 175 officers and men. The relics and exhibits inside the *Cairo* museum help to remind us not only of the military technology but also the human dimension of the war on the rivers.

Vignette (The sinking of the Cairo, *12 December 1862, as recounted by her captain):* "In the meanwhile, the head of the *Cairo* having got in toward the shore, I backed out to straighten upstream, and ordered *Marmora* to go ahead slow. I had made but half a dozen revolutions of the wheel and had gone ahead perhaps half a length, the *Marmora* a little ahead, leading, when two sudden explosions in quick succession occurred, one close to my port quarter, the other apparently under my port bow, the latter so severe as to raise the guns under it some distance from the deck.

"She commenced to fill so rapidly that in two or three minutes the water was over her forecastle. I shoved her immediately for the bank, but a few yards distant, got out a hawser to a tree, hoping to keep her from sliding off into deep water. The pumps, steam and hand, were immediately manned and everything done that could be.

"Her whole frame was so completely shattered that I found immediately that nothing more could be effected than to move the sick and the arms. I ordered the *Queen of the West* alongside and passed

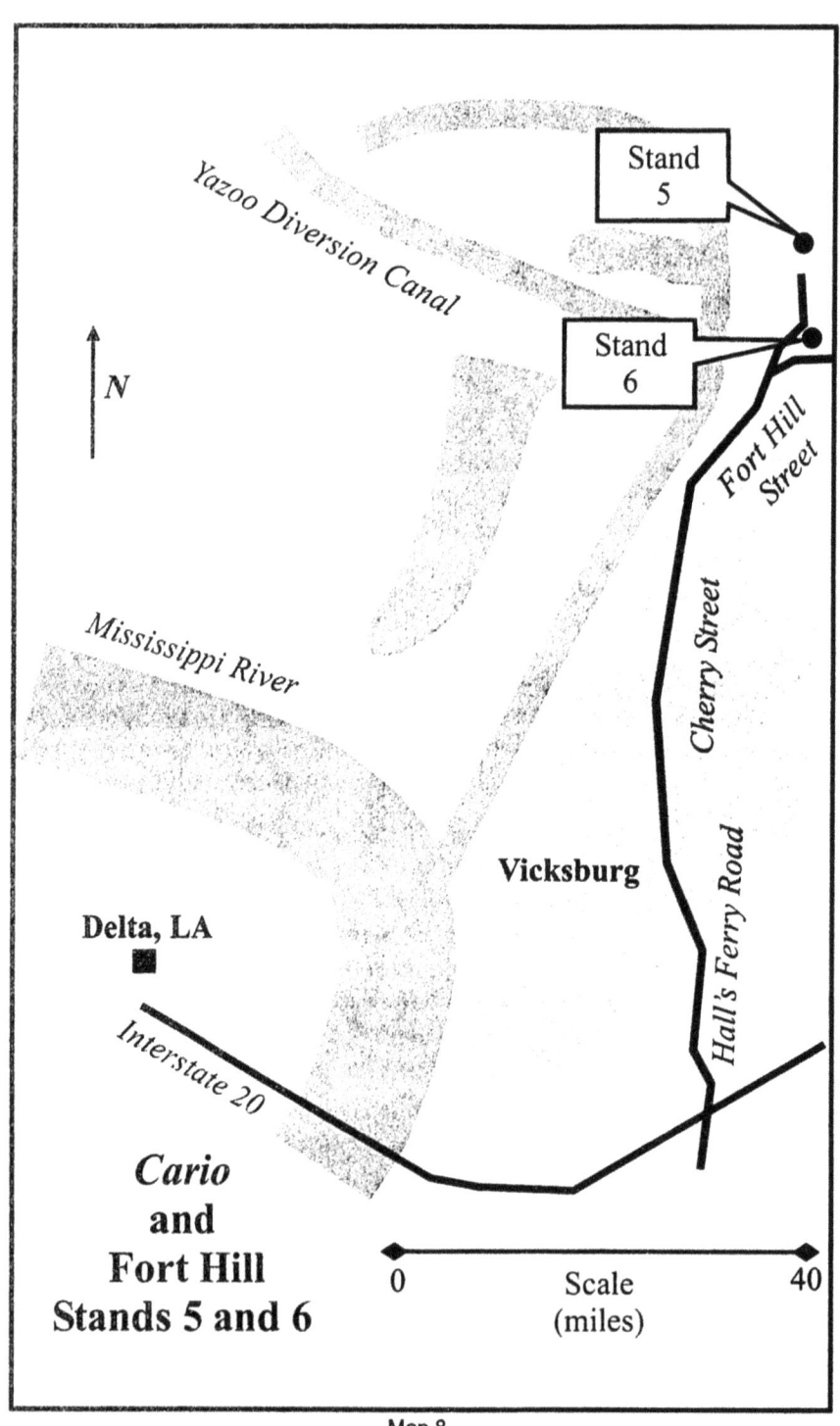

Map 8

what articles I could get at into her, with a portion of the crew, the remainder taking to our boats. The *Cairo* sunk in about twelve minutes after the explosion, going totally out of sight, except the top of her chimneys, in 6 fathoms of water. I am happy to say that, though some half a dozen men were injured, no lives were lost." (Report of Lieutenant Commander Thomas O. Selfridge, 13 December 1862, in *O.R. Navies*, vol. 23, 548-550.)

Teaching Points: Naval technology in 1863, Navy as a combat multiplier.

Stand 6
Fort Hill

Directions: Exit the *Cairo* museum area, and turn left at the gatehouse. Ascend the hill to the first parking area (stop 9 on the battlefield tour route) (see map 8).

Orientation: Fort Hill anchored the northwest corner of the Vicksburg defenses. Landward defenses follow the ridge that runs east from this stand. The river batteries extend south from this location. The waterway at the base of the bluff today is not the Mississippi River; it is the outflow of the Yazoo Diversionary Canal, which occupies part of the old Mississippi riverbed. The crescent-shaped Vicksburg harbor area to the northwest approximates the river's hairpin bend around De Soto Point, as it would have appeared in 1863.

The view from Fort Hill during high water. The curving waterway in the upper right is the remnant of the hairpin bend in the Mississippi (1997).

The mounted artillery pieces visible near the highway at the foot of Fort Hill indicate the site of Water Battery.

Situation 1: River Batteries. The Confederate river defenses at Vicksburg, commanded by Colonel Edward Higgins, consisted of thirty-seven large-caliber antiship guns, plus thirteen field artillery pieces, distributed in thirteen batteries covering three miles of waterfront. Three of these batteries, Marine Hospital Battery, Wyman's Hill Battery, and Water Battery, were particularly significant. All three stood thirty to forty feet above river level, which gave them the benefits of some plunging fire, without the drawbacks of depressing the gun muzzles too far. (The projectiles of muzzleloading artillery pieces had a tendency to shift forward, or "start," when the muzzle was depressed, with adverse effects on ballistics.) The guns of these three batteries were also close to the river, which simplified aiming and ensured high projectile velocity at the target. Marine Hospital Battery, located south of downtown Vicksburg, contained three 42-pounder smoothbores, two 32-pounder smoothbores, and two 32-pounder rifles. Wyman's Hill Battery, located on the northern outskirts of Vicksburg, held three 10-inch Columbiads, one 8-inch Columbiad, one 32-pounder rifle, one 2.71-inch Whitworth rifle, and one 3-inch Armstrong rifle. The most important of these batteries was Water Battery. Water Battery commanded the hairpin turn in the river, where vessels had enough trouble navigating without the added burden of combating

The "Widow Blakely," one of Vickburg's river defense guns.

Confederate firepower. In April 1863, Water Battery mounted three 32-pounder rifles, one 32-pounder smoothbore, and one 10-inch Columbiad.

The high velocity of the Mississippi at Vicksburg was both good and bad for the Confederate defenders. The river ran too fast for them to emplace barrier rafts or torpedoes, as they had done on the Yazoo. On the other hand, the current made it extremely dangerous for Union vessels to attempt an upstream passage of the Vicksburg position. Racing downstream, a Union vessel might get through the danger zone in front of the batteries in as little as twenty minutes. Clawing her way upstream, the same vessel would be under fire for ninety minutes. In effect, Union boats running downriver past Vicksburg were making a one-way trip so long as the river batteries remained in Confederate hands.

Teaching Points: Terrain analysis, placement of defenses.

Situation 2: Running the Batteries. On the night of 16-17 April, Rear Admiral Porter led a portion of his squadron downriver in a dash past the Vicksburg batteries. In the lead were six ironclads: the *Benton*, which bore Porter's flag and which had the tug *Ivy* lashed to its starboard side; *Lafayette*, with the ram *General Price* lashed alongside; *Louisville; Mound City; Pittsburg; and Carondelet*. Next came three transports, the *Silver Wave, Henry Clay*, and *Forest Queen*. Bringing up the rear was the misbegotten ironclad *Tuscumbia*. All the vessels had one or more barges lashed alongside, which carried coal for the ironclads and supplies for Grant's army. One barge loaded with ammunition floated downstream by itself.

Porter's flotilla left its anchorage at the mouth of the Yazoo at 2115. As the vessels neared Vicksburg, their captains reduced steam so as to avoid alerting the Confederates with the sound of churning pistons. At 2310, *Benton* drifted around the hairpin bend and received a spattering of musket fire from sentinels along the shore. It took another six minutes for the Confederate artillery to open. *Benton* ran close in to the Mississippi shore and, at 2323, began blasting away with her guns in the general direction of the Confederate batteries.

For the next two hours, the Vicksburg waterfront was transformed into a surreal scene. One after the other, Union vessels swept around the treacherous bend. Ironclads and shore batteries filled the air with shot and shell as the Union boats groped their way downstream. Dazzled by the light of fires set by the Confederates to illuminate the river, confused by smoke, and buffeted by eddies, several pilots lost control of their vessels, some of which spun completely around before facing downstream again. Collisions occurred as the formation fell apart. One of the transports, *Silver Wave*, sought safety in speed. She left her place in line and raced ahead among the ironclads, ultimately to emerge unscathed from the gauntlet. The other two transports, *Henry Clay* and *Forest Queen*, apparently sought safety in retreat. In any event, their bows were pointed upstream when *Tuscumbia*, bringing up the rear, herded them back downriver. *Tuscumbia* took *Forest Queen* under tow when a Confederate shot severed the transport's steam line. *Henry Clay* was not so fortunate. Disabled and set afire by Confederate shells, she was abandoned by her crew and burned to the waterline.

By 0200, the Confederate guns had fallen silent, and in the predawn hours, Union vessels straggled in to the rendezvous point at New Carthage, some twenty-five miles below Vicksburg. Although every vessel had sustained hits, the only losses were *Henry Clay* and one coal barge. Incredibly, personnel losses totaled twelve wounded and no fatalities.

Back in Vicksburg, there was consternation over the poor showing of the river batteries. On the average, each gun had fired only seven rounds during the entire engagement. The gunners did better on 22 April, when six unarmed and unarmored Union transports, manned largely by Army volunteers, ran the Vicksburg batteries. This time, the Confederates were fully alert. Moreover, there was no return fire to interfere with their gunnery. Each gun fired an average of fourteen rounds on this occasion, sinking one transport and six of the twelve barges.

The presence of Union ironclads below Vicksburg did little to clarify the strategic picture for Pemberton, who remained at his headquarters in Jackson. There were still Union ironclads and troops above Vicksburg, which meant that he could not rule out the possibility of a direct attack on Vicksburg. Moreover, with Union troops, transports, and ironclads below Vicksburg, the entire eastern riverbank from Vicksburg to Port Hudson was vulnerable to assault.

Vignette 1 (excerpt from the log of the gunboat Benton*, 16 April):* "At 8:45 P.M. the admiral and staff came on board. 9 o'clock hoisted signals for fleet to get underway [from anchorage at the mouth of the Yazoo]. 9:15 got underway, with the tug *Ivy* lashed to the starboard quarter, and steamed down slowly toward Vicksburg, the other vessels taking their places in line astern of us. 9:50 stopped the engines and drifted slowly down, waiting for the other boats . . . 10:30 started ahead very slowly, the lights of Vicksburg plainly in sight. 11 o'clock rounded the point. 11:10 the enemy's musketry opened upon us; they also beat the long roll [summoning troops to their posts]. [11:16] the enemy's batteries opened upon us, slowly at first, but afterwards quite rapidly. 11:23 opened fire on batteries and town with forward and port batteries and went ahead at full speed. The rebels built fires to light up the batteries, which showed our vessels very plainly. The enemy now firing very rapidly. 12:29 arrived opposite Biggs plantation (below the canal). General Sherman and Mr. Bridgman came on board, conversed, and went on shore. 1:15 passed Warrenton; not a shot fired at us . . . Eighty-one shot fired from this vessel, viz, three IX-inch shrapnel, five-second [fuse]; eighteen IX-inch shell, five-second; sixteen 42-pounder shell, five-second; twenty-one 32-pounder shell, five-second; twenty-three 32-pounder stand grape . . . Were struck six times; but one shot passing through casemate. Casualties, 5 wounded . . . (Abstract log of the *Benton*, in *O.R. Navies*, vol. 24, 681-85.)

Vignette 2 (from Charles A. Dana's report to the Secretary of War): " . . . for an hour and a half the cannonade was terrific, raging incessantly along the line of about 4 miles in extent. I counted five hundred and twenty-five discharges . . . " (Dana to Stanton, 17 April 1863, in *O.R.*, vol. 24, pt. 1, 76.)

Vignette 3 (Pemberton's reaction to news of Porter running the batteries): "I regard the navigation of the Mississippi River shut out from us now. No more supplies can be gotten from the Trans-Mississippi Department." (Pemberton to Chalmers, 18 April 1863, in *O.R.*, vol. 24, pt. 1, 313.)

Teaching Points: Joint planning and risk assessment, defense plan, engagement area.

DAY 2

Stand 7
Grand Gulf: Fort Cobun

Directions: To reach Grand Gulf from Vicksburg, take Interstate 20 to Exit 1B. Travel south twenty-two miles on US Route 61. Turn right at the sign for Grand Gulf State Park, and drive approximately 8.1 miles, past the park headquarters, and through what is left of Grand Gulf (bear left at the ruins of the old schoolhouse), until the road ends in a cul-de-sac (see map 9).

Orientation: This is the site of Fort Cobun. In 1863, the Mississippi River flowed in from the west to the foot of this bluff, where it made a bend to the south. This is the first place south of Vicksburg where the river met the bluffs. The Big Black River emptied into the Mississippi just a few hundred yards north of this spot.

Situation 1: The March Down-River. On 29 March, Grant ordered McClernand to move his corps from Milliken's Bend to New Carthage, which is south of Vicksburg on the Louisiana side of the Mississippi River. When Grant issued this order, he had not yet given up all hopes of outflanking Vicksburg from the north. Union elements of the Yazoo Pass expedition still lingered near Fort Pemberton. Grant still toyed with the idea of assaulting again at Chickasaw Bayou. However, with the floodwaters receding at last, maneuver on land became a possibility once more. On 31 March, Brigadier General Peter J. Osterhaus led his division from Milliken's Bend to Richmond, Louisiana, the first leg of a march that would outflank Vicksburg from the south. The remainder of McClernand's corps followed.

Largely, the terrain of the Mississippi floodplain dictated the Union army's route of march. Much of the route to New Carthage followed the levees along Roundaway Bayou, which was once the main channel of the Mississippi. Although the route required extensive improvement, at least the levees were above the still-inundated swamps.

On the same day that Osterhaus moved out from Milliken's Bend, engineers began work on yet another experiment to open a navigable water route around Vicksburg. Near Grant's headquarters at Young's Point, work began on the Duckport Canal, which was intended to link Roundaway Bayou to the Mississippi. This would open a water route to New Carthage that could supplement the march route along the levees. Ironically, this was one experiment that would have worked - were it not for the falling river levels, which eventually left the canal high and dry.

By 17 April, McClernand's corps had reached the vicinity of the Smith plantation, called Pointe Clear, just north of New Carthage. Porter's flotilla had run the Vicksburg batteries the night before and was gathered in the river near New Carthage. On 18 May, Grant ordered McPherson to follow McClernand's route. With both his

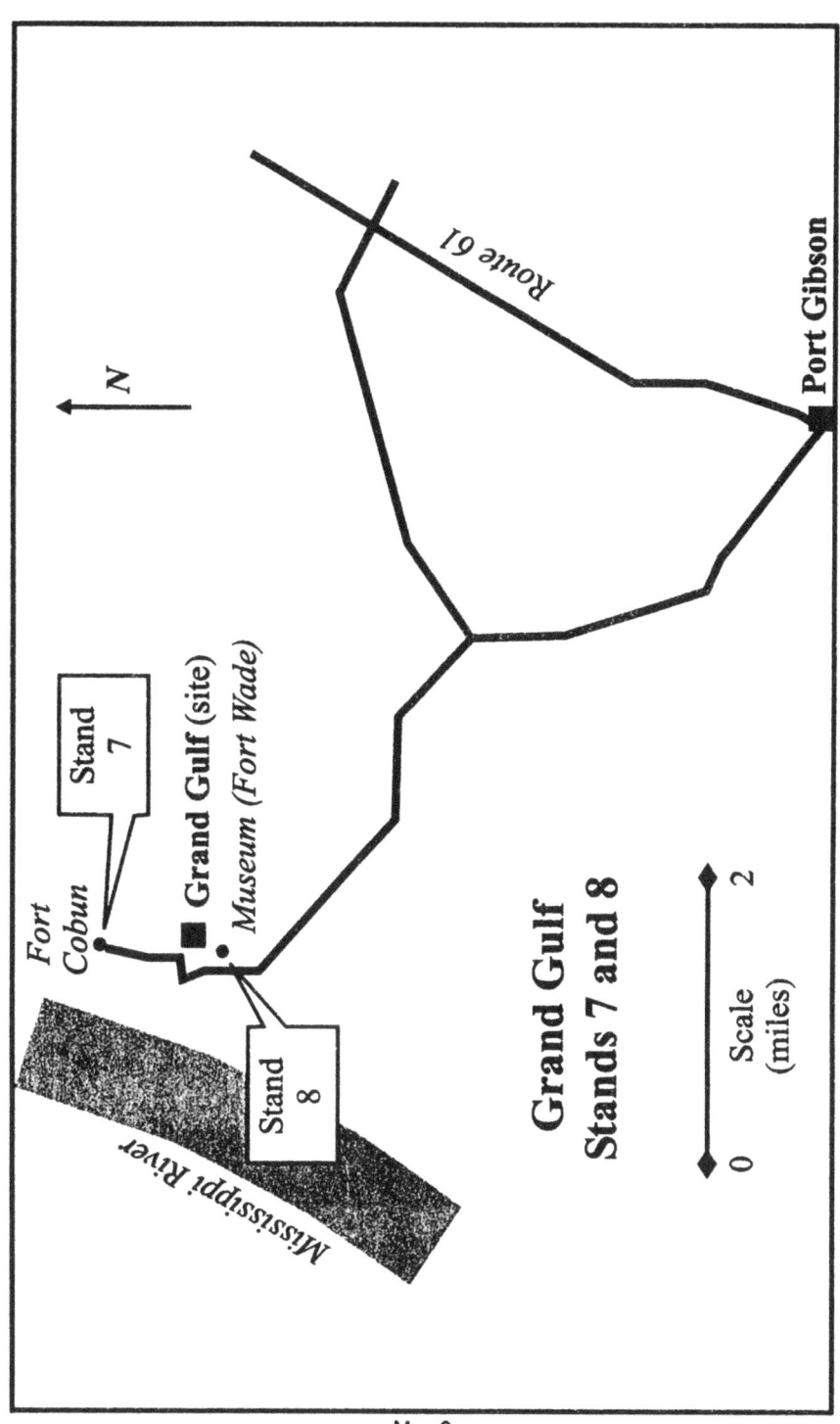

Map 9

troops and river transport below Vicksburg, Grant had, for all practical purposes, outflanked the "Gibraltar of the West."

In Pemberton's headquarters at Jackson, these developments received little attention, despite the fact that Confederate troops operating out of Grand Gulf skirmished repeatedly with McClernand's advance elements and reported regularly on Union progress. Brigadier General John S. Bowen, the commander at Grand Gulf, believed this to be the Union main effort and told Pemberton as much. However, during the first ten days of McClernand's movement toward New Carthage, Pemberton actually believed that Grant was withdrawing to Memphis. He even designated two of his brigades to be sent off as reinforcements for the Army of Tennessee. Porter's running of the batteries refocused Pemberton's attention upon the Mississippi and prompted him to recall the two detached brigades. One day later, Union Colonel Benjamin H. Grierson embarked upon a spectacular cavalry raid that cut a swath through central Mississippi, drawing Pemberton's attention away from Grant once again.

Grant, however, did not yet make his move to cross the river. When he directed McClernand to march to New Carthage, Grant had not yet decided whether he would cross to the east bank at Warrenton, ten miles below Vicksburg, or at Grand Gulf, thirty air miles below Vicksburg. By 26 April, he had decided on Grand Gulf. On that date, he ordered McClernand to move south to Hard Times, just upstream and opposite from Grand Gulf. Three of McClernand's divisions traveled by boat, but elements of the fourth division (Osterhaus), followed by two divisions of McPherson's corps, moved overland. Osterhaus opened a road to Hard Times that ran along Bayou Vidal and Lake Saint Joseph. Sherman's corps remained at Young's Point to protect the line of communication.

Vignette 1 (Grant's orders for the march down river): "The following orders are published for the information and guidance of the army in the field in the present movement to obtain a foothold on the east bank of the Mississippi River, from which Vicksburg can be approached by practicable roads . . .

"6. Troops will be required to bivouac until proper facilities can be afforded for the transportation of camp equipage . . .

"9. As fast as the Thirteenth Army Corps [McClernand] advances, the Seventeenth Army Corps [McPherson] will take its place, and in its turn will be followed in like manner by the Fifteenth Army Corps [Sherman] . . .

"12. The movement of troops from Milliken's Bend to New Carthage will be so conducted as to allow the transportation of ten days' supply of rations and half the allowance of ordnance required by previous orders.

"13. Commanders are authorized and enjoined to collect all the beef-cattle, corn, and other supplies necessary for the army on the line of march, but wanton destruction of property, taking of articles, unless for military purposes, insulting civilians, going into and searching houses without proper orders from division commanders, are positively prohibited. All such irregularities must be summarily punished." (Headquarters, Department of the Tennessee, Special Orders No. 110, 20 April 1863, in *O.R.*, vol. 24, pt. 3, 212-14.)

Vignette 2 (Pemberton's initial response to news of the Union movement): "Also reported, but not yet confirmed, movement under McClernand, in large force, by land west of river and southward. Much doubt it." (Pemberton to Cooper, 9 April 1863, in *O.R.*, vol. 24, pt. 3, 729-30.)

Vignette 3 (Confederate commander at Grand Gulf on the day before the bombardment): "Reports indicate an immense force opposite me. Harrison is fighting them now." (Bowen to Pemberton, 28 April 1863, in *O.R.*, vol. 24, pt. 3, 797.)

(Pemberton replies): "Have you force enough to hold your position? If not, give me the smallest additional force with which you can." (Pemberton to Bowen, 28 April 1863, in *O.R.*, vol. 24, pt. 3, 797.)

(Bowen responds): "I advise that every man and gun that can be spared from other points be sent here." (Bowen to Pemberton, 28 April 1863, in *O.R.*, vol. 24, pt. 3, 797.)

Teaching Points: Operational decision-making, mobility operations, austere logistics plan, interpreting intelligence.

Situation 2: Bombardment of Grand Gulf. Grand Gulf was once an important river landing, but floods and disease had ravaged the town by the time the Civil War began. Then in 1862, Farragut's flotilla burned the town during its expedition up to Vicksburg. On 12 March 1863, the Confederate brigade commanded by Brigadier General John S. Bowen began building fortifications at Grand Gulf, which would be the first defensible spot downstream from Vicksburg in the event that Grant's Canal succeeded.

Bowen's men established two fortified batteries, approximately 1,000 yards apart, on either side of Grand Gulf's ruins (see map 10). Just upstream of the town was Fort Cobun, which they created by cutting a notch into the face of the bluff forty feet above river level, and piling the spoil to form a parapet forty feet thick. Fort Cobun mounted one 8-inch Dahlgren, one 30-pounder Parrott, and two-32 pounders. Downstream was Fort Wade, which stood about twenty feet above river level and approximately 300 yards back from the river. Fort Wade boasted one 100-pounder Blakeley rifle, one 8-inch Dahlgren, and two 32-pounder rifles. In addition, several field pieces stood within and between the fortified places. A portion of Bowen's infantry manned a line of rifle pits that connected the forts, but Bowen kept the bulk of his command behind the crests of the hills.

At 0730 on 29 April, the seven Union ironclads that had run the Vicksburg batteries cast off from Hard Times. Their mission was to silence the guns of Grand Gulf so that Grant's army could force a landing. Six transports carrying 10,000 men of McClernand's corps followed the ironclads. Grant himself would observe the action from aboard the tug *Ivy*.

Leading the way downstream were the *Pittsburg, Louisville, Mound City*, and *Carondelet*. These four City-Class gunboats steamed past Fort Cobun at 0800, firing volleys as they passed, and proceeded to Fort Wade. There, they came about, bows pointing back upstream, close in to the Mississippi bank, wheels churning just fast enough to hold them stationary in the current. Then, there ensued a brutal, close-range duel with the Confederate shore batteries. Meanwhile, the three larger ironclads began trading blows with Fort Cobun. *Benton* and *Tuscumbia* ran in close, while *Lafayette* stood off and fired from a distance.

Of the two actions, the Union bombardment of Fort Wade was the more successful. With some help from *Lafayette*, sent downstream by Porter, the City-Class boats succeeded in demolishing Fort Wade's parapet and dismounting two of the four Confederate guns. After several hours of pounding, Fort Wade fell silent, whereupon all of the ironclads massed against Fort Cobun.

Fort Cobun proved to be a tougher objective. Higher than Fort Wade, its fire was more effective, and it was better protected from the

Official Records of the Union and Confederate Navies in the War of Rebellion, Vol. 25, p. 628.

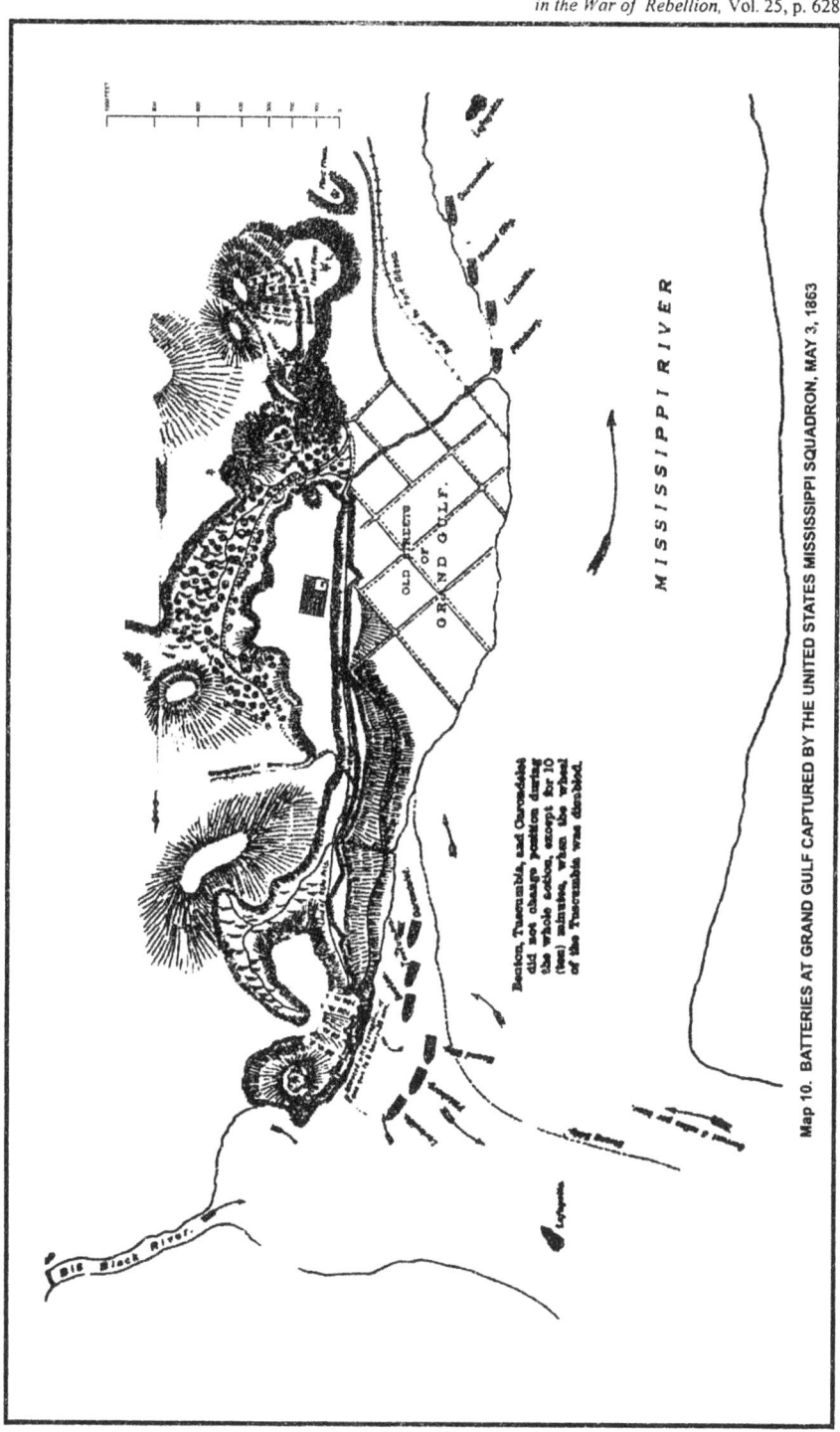

Map 10. BATTERIES AT GRAND GULF CAPTURED BY THE UNITED STATES MISSISSIPPI SQUADRON, MAY 3, 1863

gunboats. Moreover, the fort was a more stable firing platform than were the Union gunboats, which struggled to hold their positions in the treacherous eddies that swept the river. The *Benton* took forty-seven hits, one demolishing the pilothouse and wounding the pilot and Rear Admiral Porter. Temporarily disabled, the *Benton* drifted out of the battle until new steering apparatus could be rigged. The *Tuscumbia* shuddered under the impact of no fewer than eighty-one Confederate projectiles. Several of her armor plates fractured, and others came loose. Finally, she lost power in one engine and floated helplessly downstream. The *Tuscumbia* would require major repairs before returning to service.

Porter called off the bombardment at 1300. His ships, mounting eighty-one large guns, had fired 2,500 rounds at the Confederate forts but had failed to destroy them. The Confederates, with just eight large-caliber guns, had scored over 200 hits on the ironclads, killing eighteen and wounding fifty-six Union personnel. Confederate casualties were three killed and nineteen wounded. Obviously, it would have been suicide to send in the unarmored troop transports. Grant, consequently, canceled the landing operation.

Later that evening, the Union gunboats returned to Grand Gulf and resumed their artillery duel with the Confederate batteries. Behind the ironclads, the Union transports and barges slipped by in the darkness, heading farther downstream.

Vignette 1 (Confederate commander's perspective): "Six gunboats, averaging ten guns, have been bombarding my batteries terrifically since 7 A.M. They pass and repass the batteries at the closest ranges. I cannot tell the effect of our shots. Six transports in sight, loaded with troops, but stationary. My loss as yet only 2 killed. The batteries, especially the lower ones, are badly torn to pieces. I cannot tell the result, but think that re-enforcements would hardly reach me in time to aid in the defense if they attempt to land." (Bowen to Pemberton, 29 April 1863, in *O.R.*, vol. 24, pt. 1, 575).

Vignette 2 (account from the commander of the gunboat Benton*):* "After getting the fleet in line, we, at 7:30, slowly steamed down[stream] toward the batteries at Grand Gulf. At 7:55 the enemy opened fire on the leading vessels; at 8:13 we opened fire from the forward battery upon the guns on the bluff [Fort Cobun], rounded to[,] with head upstream, and kept firing whenever a gun would bear, the enemy responding; while near the shore the enemy fired upon us with musketry. At 9 a shell penetrated the thin iron on our starboard quarter and exploded in a stateroom, setting it on fire; it was speedily extinguished. At 9:05 a shell from No. 5 gun carried away the enemy's flagstaff; it was soon replaced. At 10:10, having gotten into an eddy, were obliged to round out [turn around]; did so, and fired with our port and stern guns when they would bear. We, in turning round, dropped downstream 1,500 yards and ran into the bank, to aid us in turning round. We then steamed up to the batteries on the bluff again and continued the engagement. At 12:25 rounded out and stood upstream to communicate with General Grant, who was on a tug. While going up used our stern guns. At 12:50 the enemy ceased firing at us, this vessel having been under fire four hours and eleven minutes . . . The following ammunition was expended: 70 9-inch 5-second shell; 40 9-inch 5-second shrapnel; 29 9-inch grape; 7 9-inch canister; 45 5-second 42-pounder rifle shell; 1 10-second 42 pounder rifle shell; 69 5-second 32-pounder shell; 30 10-second 32-pounder shell; 5 32-pounder solid shot; 11 32-pounder canister; 23 32-pounder grape; 9 50-pounder rifle shell; 8 50-pounder solid shot; a total of 347 fires. We were struck 47 times . . . The casualties were 7 men killed and 19 persons wounded..." (Report of Lieutenant Commander Greer, 30 April 1863, in *O.R.Navies,* vol. 24, 613-14.)

Vignette 3 (Porter's congratulatory order to his men reveals some impatience with the Army): "Those who have shared in the engagement of the 29th of April may always speak of it with honest pride. It is not our fault that the enemy's guns and munitions of war are not in our hands. Ours is the duty to silence batteries; it cannot be expected that we shall land and take possession." (General Order of Acting Rear Admiral Porter, 2 May 1863, in *O.R. Navies,* vol. 24, 626.)

Teaching Points: Terrain analysis, placement of defenses, naval gunfire in support of joint operations.

Stand 8
Grand Gulf: Fort Wade

Directions: Backtrack through Grand Gulf to the park headquarters and museum. There is a nominal admission charge. Ask the park personnel about conditions on the road to the Shaifer House (stand 10) (see map 9 on page 109).

Orientation: Fort Wade is located on the hill behind (north of) the museum buildings. It was the lower (downstream), fortified battery at

Grand Gulf. In 1863, the Mississippi came within three hundred yards of Fort Wade.

Teaching Points: Terrain analysis, placement of defenses.

Stand 9
Windsor (Bruinsburg)

Directions: Turn left upon leaving the Grand Gulf museum. After 4.1 miles, bear right at the "Y" intersection. This road becomes Anthony Street in Port Gibson. Turn right on Flower Street (3.3 miles from the "Y" intersection), then right on Rodney Road (Route 552) 0.1 mile later. Travel approximately ten miles. Turn left at the sign marking the Windsor House (see map 11).

Orientation: Windsor House, once one of the most elegant residences in the South, was a landmark to riverboat pilots on the Mississippi. It survived the war, only to be destroyed by fire in 1890. The cotton field that was once Bruinsburg is approximately two miles west of Windsor. A road ran from Bruinsburg to the top of the bluff not far from Windsor.

Situation: With the Union failure to silence the guns of Grand Gulf, Grant decided to proceed downstream and stage his crossing of the Mississippi at Rodney. Gunboats and transports ran past Grand Gulf

The ruins of Windsor, near Bruinsburg (1997)

117

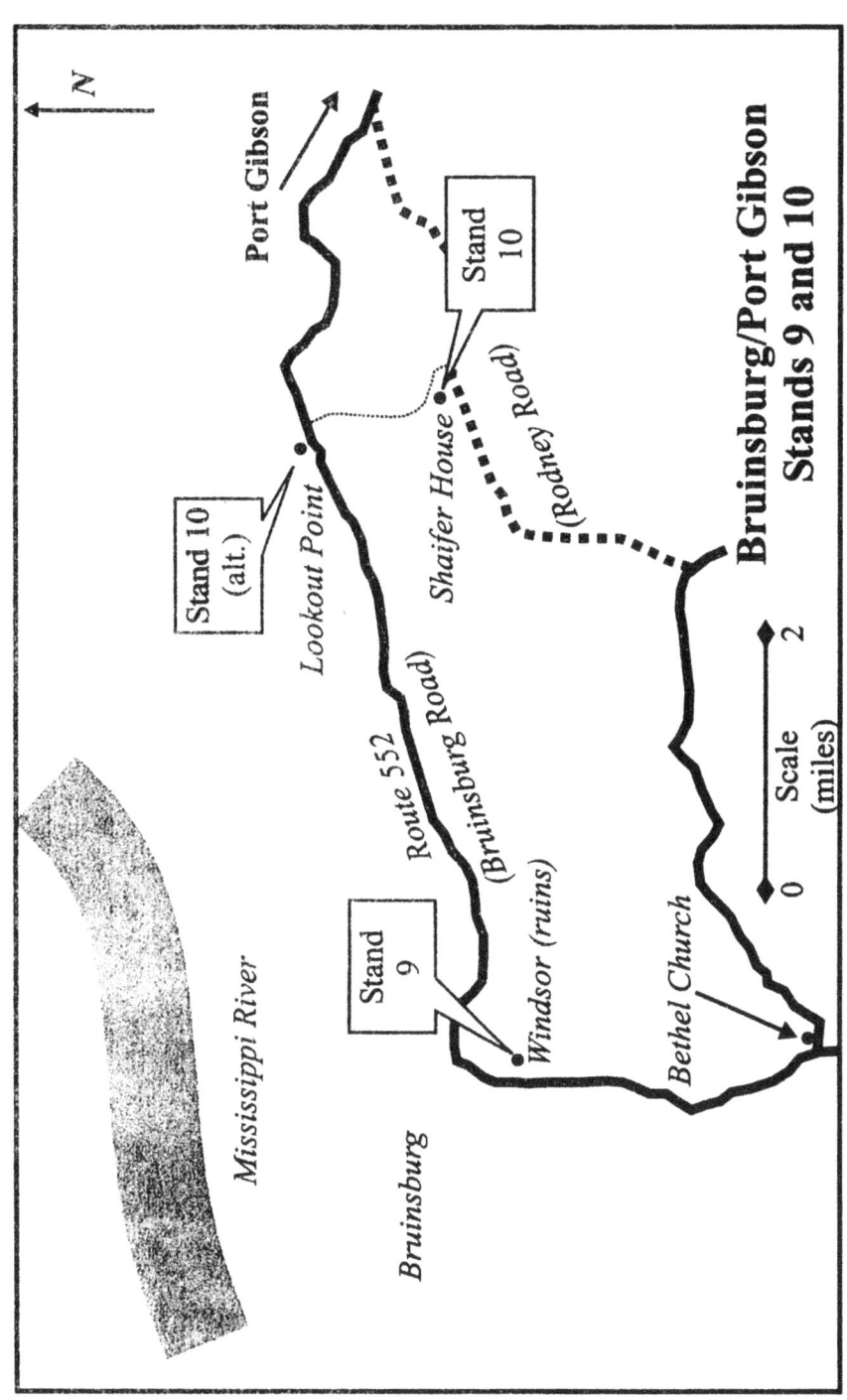

Map 11

on the night of 29-30 April. McClernand's corps marched across the neck of land opposite Grand Gulf and bivouacked downstream from the Confederate stronghold. Union reconnaissance parties crossed to the eastern bank of the river seeking information on landing sites and roads running inland. One of these returned with a slave, who informed Grant of a plantation landing known as Bruinsburg, roughly halfway between Grand Gulf and Rodney. Grant quickly decided to land at Bruinsburg rather than farther downstream at Rodney.

Early on the morning of 30 April, McClernand's corps boarded Porter's ironclads and transports and steamed downstream to Bruinsburg. Union landings began without opposition. However, the bluff line that represented high, dry ground was about a mile inland from the Bruinsburg landings. If the Confederates should establish defensive positions at the bluffs before Grant pushed inland, it could be Chickasaw Bayou all over again. Heightening the tension was the fact that McClernand had neglected to issue rations to his troops before they had embarked that morning, so there was a four-hour delay while the disembarking troops drew supplies.

McClernand had all 17,000 troops ashore by 1600, when the advance inland finally began. No Confederate opposition materialized as McClernand's troops climbed the bluffs near Windsor and moved out on the southernmost of the two roads leading to Port Gibson. Brigadier General Eugene A. Carr's division led the way, followed by those of Brigadier General Peter J. Osterhaus, Brigadier General Alvin P. Hovey, and A.J. Smith. Meanwhile, the boats that had landed McClernand in the morning were already crossing the lead elements of McPherson's corps. McPherson would have 4,500 men on the road to Port Gibson by nightfall.

Thus, the Battle of Bruinsburg, potentially the most important engagement of the Vicksburg campaign, never took place. The Confederates had badly misjudged Union intentions. Pemberton, distracted by Union operations in the Delta (north of Vicksburg) and by Grierson's raid into eastern Mississippi, had not fully discerned Grant's intentions. Conflicting advice from his subordinates compounded Pemberton's indecision. Major General Carter L. Stevenson, in Vicksburg, argued against any detachments from his command at the same time that Bowen, in Grand Gulf, had warned that the Union main effort was heading his way. Not until the Union bombardment of Grand Gulf on 29 April had Pemberton realized that Bowen was right. Belatedly, he had ordered Stevenson to send two brigades to Bowen, but these were still on the road when Grant came ashore at Bruinsburg on the 30th. (Brigadier General Edward D. Tracy's brigade marched from Warrenton, and Brigadier General William E. Baldwin's brigade marched from camps north of Vicksburg late on 29 April.) Pemberton further ordered a concentration at Jackson of those troops that had been chasing Grierson's raiders. Significantly, when Pemberton learned that Grant was ashore in force, he moved his headquarters from Jackson to Vicksburg—he did not come to Port Gibson to direct operations in person.

Vignette 1 (Two days before *the bombardment of Grand Gulf, Bowen recognized the danger of a Union landing downstream from his post):* "I have the honor to report that all the movements of the enemy during the last twenty-four hours seem to indicate an intention on their part to march their army still lower down in Louisiana, perhaps to Saint Joseph, and then to run their steamers by me and cross to Rodney. In view of this, and from the fact that Port Gibson is almost essential to this position [Grand Gulf], I have examined myself and now have the engineers on a reconnaissance selecting a line of battle south of Port Gibson." (Bowen to assistant adjutant general, 27 April 1863, in *O.R.,* vol. 24, pt. 3, 792-93.)

Vignette 2 (On 30 April, Bowen's concern proves justified): "Six gunboats, with two transports lashed to them, passed my batteries [last night] between 9 and 10 o'clock. Enemy on Louisiana shore, below. Hurry up reinforcements." (Bowen to Pemberton, 30 April 1863, in *O.R.,* vol. 24, pt. 1, 657.)

(Later that day): "Three thousand Federals were at Bethel Church, 10 miles from Port Gibson, at 3 P.M., advancing. They are still landing at Bruinsburg." (Bowen to Pemberton, 30 April 1863, in *O.R.,* vol. 24, pt. 1, 658.)

Vignette 3 (Grant's reaction to the landings): ". . . I felt a degree of relief scarcely ever equalled since. Vicksburg was not yet taken it is true, nor were its defenders demoralized by any of our previous moves. I was now in the enemy's country, with a vast river and the stronghold of Vicksburg between me and my base of supplies. But I was on dry ground on the same side of the river with the enemy. All the campaigns, labors, hardships and exposures from the month of December previous to this time that had been made and endured, were for the accomplishment of this one object." (U.S. Grant, *Personal Memoirs,* vol. 1 [New York: Charles L. Webster, 1885], 480-81.)

Teaching Points: Operational decision making, seizing the initiative.

Stand 10
A. K. Shaifer House (Battle of Port Gibson)

Directions: (This route involves travel on some narrow, rough, unpaved roads. It should not be attempted by bus. If you are not confident that your vehicle is capable of negotiating this route, backtrack 6.1 miles to Lookout Point and conduct stand 10 there. Afterwards, proceed to Port Gibson and on to stand 11.)

Turn left on Route 552. After traveling 1.3 miles, bear left at the "Y" intersection. Turn left after 1.2 miles, just beyond Bethel Presbyterian Church. Go 4.7 miles and turn left on a gravel road. The Shaifer House is about 3.2 miles up this road. Be alert for washouts, debris on the road, and overhanging branches (see map 11 on page 117).

Orientation: This route to the Shaifer House is the old Rodney Road, the southernmost of two routes leading from Bruinsburg to Port Gibson. Grant's army took this road on 30 April. The northern route, once called the Bruinsburg road, is today Route 552. A few yards east of the Shaifer House is the old farm road that links the two routes. The Magnolia Church site is about one-half mile farther east along this road.

In 1863, the ridge tops in this area were cleared and cultivated. The ravines looked much as they do today. Thus, one could see from one ridgecrest to another. Moving troops through the steep, vine-choked ravines, however, was a diffucult proposition.

Situation 1: Rodney Road Battle. Bowen's reaction to the Union landing at Bruinsburg was to mount a delaying action that would give Pemberton time to assemble field forces for a meaningful counterstroke. The ground that Bowen selected for his battle was in the "loess hills" country between Bruinsburg and Port Gibson, Grant's probable objective. With off-road movement almost impossible, the loess hills made it feasible for a small force to delay a much stronger opponent.

On the evening of 30 April, Bowen had two brigades in position. Brigadier General Martin E. Green's brigade straddled the Rodney

The old Rodney Road, west of the Shaifer House (1997)

Road at Magnolia Church ridge, with pickets advanced to the A. K. Shaifer house. Farther north, Tracy's brigade, having completed a forty-mile, 27-hour march from Warrenton, took up positions along the Bruinsburg Road near Lookout Point. Baldwin's brigade, also detached from the Vicksburg defenses, camped north of Port Gibson. Colonel Francis M. Cockrell's Missouri brigade remained in reserve at Grand Gulf. Bowen's forces at this point totaled about 8,000. Marching toward him through the darkness were 26,000 Union troops: the four divisions of McClernand's corps and Major General John A. Logan's division of McPherson's corps.

Shortly after midnight on 1 May, McClernand's advance force encountered and exchanged volleys with Green's pickets near the Shaifer house. After ascertaining that the Confederates were present in force, McClernand chose to gather up his corps and await daylight before pressing the fight. When morning came, McClernand deployed two divisions (Carr and Hovey), with a third (A.J. Smith) in reserve. He initially intended to work around Green's left flank, but a Confederate attack against the center of his line changed his mind. McClernand proceeded to mass his forces along and on both sides of the Rodney Road. There was not much room on the ridge tops in which to deploy. Regiments stacked up two, three, and four deep on the ridges around the Shaifer House. At 1000, the blue juggernaut rolled forward

The Shaifer House (1997).

and, after some bitter fighting, broke Green's brigade and drove it from the field in disarray. McClernand's troops occupied Magnolia Church ridge and halted.

On the Confederate side, Bowen recognized that Green's troops had done all the fighting that they could for the time being. He permitted Green to retreat all the way to the intersection of the Rodney and Bruinsburg roads, reconstituting his force on the march. To take Green's place on the Rodney Road, Bowen brought up Baldwin's brigade and two of Cockrell's regiments. Rather than deploying these troops on the open ground of the next ridge top where they would be vulnerable to Union firepower, Bowen set them in the low ground along Willow Creek—Baldwin astride the Rodney Road, with Cockrell covering his left flank.

Following a pause on Magnolia Church ridge, during which time McClernand and the governor of Illinois delivered patriotic speeches, McClernand's troops resumed their advance. When they crested the ridge overlooking Willow Creek, they met renewed Confederate resistance. Sensing trouble ahead, McClernand asked for and received reinforcements—one brigade of Logan's division (McPherson's corps). This gave McClernand four brigades on line, and three in reserve, on a 2,000-yard front. When this force failed to dislodge

Baldwin's Confederates from Willow Creek, McClernand opted for even greater density. He packed twenty-one regiments on a front of 800 yards against the Confederate center. Still Baldwin's brigade held its ground.

At this point in the battle, Cockrell's depleted brigade launched an audacious counterattack against the right flank of McClernand's massive force. Cockrell succeeded in driving off two Union regiments, but Hovey, whose division received the attack, had seen Cockrell coming and had already positioned artillery and infantry to protect the threatened flank. After hard fighting, Cockrell's men fell back. Not long thereafter, Baldwin also retreated in the face of overwhelming Union pressure.

Vignette 1 (Stone's brigade of Carr's division, McClernand's corps, reports on the nighttime march along Rodney Road and the morning's fighting at Magnolia Church): "The road over which we marched passed through a country much broken by gorges and ravines, and thickly covered with tall timber, underbrush, and cane, so peculiar to the Southern country. While moving forward in this order, and about three-quarters of a mile from Magnolia Church, our skirmishers were fired upon by a heavy picket force of the enemy, posted in an angle of the road . . . We then moved forward in column . . . and as our skirmishers reached the head of the lane in front of Magnolia Church they received a tremendous volley of musketry from the enemy, strongly posted on the right and left of the church. I . . . formed the advance companies into line, and sent an order back for the entire brigade to move forward into line . . .

"Soon after sunrise the battle was renewed by the enemy, who held their position during the night . . . About 10 o'clock it became evident that the enemy were massing their forces upon our immediate front, as their musketry was increasing in volume and rapidly advancing toward us. At this juncture I moved my brigade forward in double lines of battalions, for the purpose of charging upon the advancing columns of the enemy. We were compelled to cross a deep hollow, thickly covered on both slopes with underbrush and cane, but my men moved forward with the spirit and steadiness of veteran troops, and with unbroken lines. When the thicket was passed, and as we advanced into the open field close to the enemy's lines, we opened our fire upon them with such rapidity and precision that, unable to resist it, they soon broke and retreated in utter confusion. This ended the battle of the morning."

(Report of Col. William N. Stone, 2 May 1863, in *O.R.*, vol. 24, pt. 1, 628-31.)

Vignette 2 (Cockrell's account of his attack against the Union right flank during the afternoon battle along Willow Creek): "The Third [Missouri] and Fifth [Missouri] Infantry were moved, by the order and under the personal direction of General Bowen, to the extreme right of the enemy, and forming in order of battle—the Fifth in front and the Third in its immediate rear—charged upon the enemy in large force (outnumbering these two regiments at least five to one), supported by a battery of six to eight guns. The enemy immediately began to change their lines so as to meet our troops, and the Third moving to the left to unmask the Fifth, these regiments dashed upon and engaged the enemy at very close range for some forty minutes and drove back in confusion the line first engaging us. As often as one line was driven back, another of fresh troops was thrown in our front. When it became manifest that a continuance of the engagement could result in no advantage to us, these two regiments fell back and took their original position on the extreme left, having inflicted on the enemy an heavy blow which deterred him from attempting to pursue." (Report of Col. Francis M. Cockrell, 22 June 1863, in *O.R.*, vol. 24, pt. 1, 668-70.)

Vignette 3 (Cockrell's attack, as perceived by Slack's brigade of Hovey's division, McClernand's corps): "These lines had not more than been formed when three rebel regiments—two Missouri and one Louisiana—came down at a charge, with terrific yells, and could not be seen, because of the very thick growth of cane, until they reached a point within 30 yards of my line.

"The Fifty-sixth Ohio and Forty-seventh Indiana opened upon their line in front, and the Twenty-fourth Indiana on their flank, a most terrific and jarring fire, which arrested their charge and threw them into some confusion, but they soon recovered, and returned our fire with great spirit and pertinacity for about two hours, when the rebel survivors fled in utter confusion, leaving their dead and wounded upon the ground." (Report of Col. James R. Slack, 5 May 1863, in *O.R.*, vol. 24, pt. 1, 610-12.)

Teaching Points: Use of terrain in defense, attack over difficult terrain.

Situation 2: Bruinsburg Road Battle. Meanwhile, a separate fight took place along the Bruinsburg road. During the predawn hours, Tracy formed his brigade parallel to and south of the road, with its right flank on Bayou Pierre and its front towards the Shaifer House, where musket fire could be heard. Unknown to Tracy, there was a farm path that ran from the Shaifer house to his position along the Bruinsburg road. McClernand's fourth division (Osterhaus), later reinforced by one brigade from McPherson's corps, formed up near the Shaifer house and attacked northwards, guiding on this farm path. Tracy's skirmishers—and the terrain—quickly disordered the Union advance. Units lost their alignments and wandered off their axes of advance, creating gaps in the line and causing instances of friendly fire as Union formations crossed in front of each other. When Osterhaus' men finally reached Tracy's battle line south of the Bruinsburg Road, they attempted an assault, which fell apart in the bullet-swept jungle.

Bad as it was for the Union troops, things were little better for the Confederates, who stood on open ridge tops raked by fire coming from opponents concealed in the ravines below. Tracy was killed early in the action. His successor, Colonel Isham W. Garrott, knew little about the disposition of friendly forces and nothing about Tracy's concept of operation.

There came a pause in the action, during which Osterhaus sorted out his intermingled units. Then, the Union attack resumed. Osterhaus anchored his right and advanced his left, which crossed Bruinsburg Road and broke Garrott's hold on Bayou Pierre. With their right flank in danger of being turned, Garrott's men fell back, fighting stubbornly along the Bruinsburg Road. To reinforce Garrott, Bowen sent Green's brigade, which had reassembled after its defeat on Magnolia Church ridge. But Green tied in on the wrong flank—Garrott's left, not his hard-pressed right.

At about 1730, Bowen recognized that he had done all he could to delay Grant, short of sacrificing his little force altogether. He ordered all his troops to break contact and retreat. On the Union side, McClernand's soldiers were too fatigued and disoriented to pursue. Bowen made good his escape, having obstructed the Union campaign for a full day. What use did Pemberton make of this time? When he learned by telegraph of the fighting in progress, Pemberton realized for the first time the full significance of Union moves during the preceding month. He sent a telegram to Jefferson Davis asking for reinforcements from other departments. Within his own department, Pemberton ordered Major General William W. Loring to move his division from Jackson toward Port Gibson and to take command of all the Confederate troops confronting Grant. Pemberton himself remained in Vicksburg.

Grant's forces lost 131 killed, 719 wounded, and twenty-five missing in the Battle of Port Gibson. Bowen's casualties were numerically fewer—Confederate returns were incomplete—but as a proportion of his total force, his loss was much more severe.

Vignette 1 (Bowen informs Pemberton of the battle by telegraph at 1320): "We have been engaged in a furious battle ever since daylight; losses very heavy. General Tracy is killed . . . We are out of ammunition for cannon and small arms, the ordnance trains of the re-enforcements not being here. They outnumber us trebly. There are three divisions against us. My whole force is engaged, except three regiments on Big Black, Bayou Pierre, and Grand Gulf. The men act nobly, but the odds are overpowering." (Bowen to Pemberton, 1 May 1863, in *O.R.,* vol. 24, pt. 1, 659.)

Vignette 2 (Pemberton calls on President Davis for help): "Enemy can cross all his army from Hard Times to Bruinsburg, below Bayou Pierre. Large reinforcements should be sent me from other departments. Enemy's movement threatens Jackson, and, if successful, cuts off Vicksburg and Port Hudson from the east. Am hurrying all re-enforcements I possibly can to Bowen. Enemy's success in passing our batteries has completely changed character of defense." (Pemberton to Davis, 1 May 1863, in *O.R.,* vol. 24, pt. 3, 807.)

Teaching Points: Use of terrain in defense, attack over difficult terrain, loss of commander, contrasting command styles.

Stand 11
Willows (Willow Springs)

Directions: Continue east on the Shaifer House road and return to Port Gibson. In Port Gibson, bear right at the Y intersection, go two blocks, then turn left on Church Street (Route 61). Approximately 3.5 miles north of town, turn right on State Route 462. Go 4.5 miles to a five-way intersection (see map 12).

Orientation: The section of Route 462 leading to this stand was not a Civil War-era road. Facing north, the road to the right and rear was the road from Port Gibson, via Grindstone Ford. The road to the left ran to Ingleside and Grand Gulf. The road straight ahead connected with routes to Hankinson's Ferry and Rocky Springs.

127

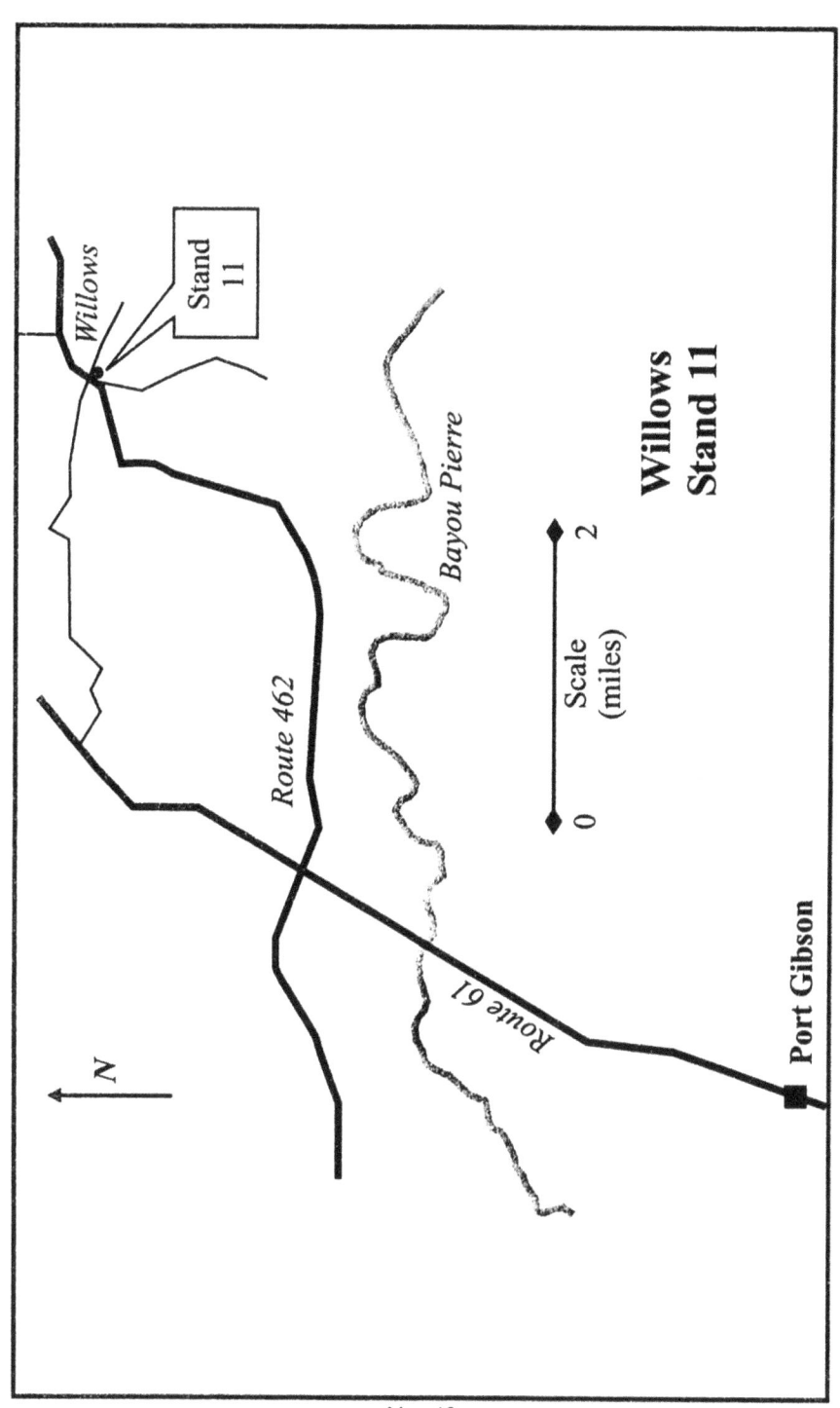

Map 12

Situation 1: Operational Pause. On 2 May, elements of McPherson's corps pushed on into Port Gibson while McClernand's corps policed the battlefield. McPherson found that the retreating Confederates had destroyed the Little Bayou Pierre bridge just north of town. Tearing materials from nearby buildings, Union work parties constructed a 166-foot-long floating raft-bridge in just four hours. The next day, McPherson's troops repaired a bridge over Big Bayou Pierre at Grindstone Ford. McPherson promptly sent one division (Logan) west toward Ingleside and the other (Brigadier General Marcellus M. Crocker) north toward Hankinson's Ferry on the Big Black River. The crossroads at Willow Springs was a busy place on 3 May.

McPherson's advance toward the Big Black threatened to cut off Bowen and the 7,000 Confederates who had fallen back to Grand Gulf. On 3 May, Bowen evacuated Grand Gulf and barely escaped to the north bank of the Big Black. Grant rode into Grand Gulf that day, where he found that Porter's ironclads had already secured the landing. Grand Gulf became Grant's base of operations for the next two weeks.

From 3 to 9 May, Grant's army paused in the general vicinity of Willow Springs, while Sherman's corps made the long march from Milliken's Bend to join the main body. Grant used the time to bring up supplies and to weigh his options for continuing the campaign. Messages he received from downriver revealed that Major General Nathaniel P. Banks, commander of the Department of the Gulf, expected Grant to detach a portion of his force to aid Banks in the reduction of Port Hudson. Banks would then support Grant in an operation against Vicksburg. Grant dismissed this course of action because it would yield the initiative to Pemberton for a period of several weeks.

Alternatively, Grant could mount an immediate advance directly toward Vicksburg. To test this option, McPherson sent a small force to reconnoiter the route from Hankinson's Ferry toward Warrenton. Not only did the reconnaissance force encounter Confederate defenses at Redbone Church, but also an advance on this axis would compel Grant to struggle through "loess hills" terrain all the way to Vicksburg.

A third option, and the one that Grant selected on 7 May, was to advance inland, along the watershed of the Big Black and Big Bayou Pierre. This course of action would allow him to cut off Vicksburg from the rest of the Confederacy before turning west to deal with Pemberton's army. Accordingly, on 9 May, McPherson's corps moved off to Utica, where it constituted the right flank of the advance. On 10 May McClernand's corps advanced with its left flank protected by the Big Black River. Sherman's corps, which had crossed from Hard Times to Grand Gulf on 6 and 7 May, assumed the center position in the Union advance on 11 May. The army's objective was the Vicksburg-Jackson railroad in the vicinity of Edwards. Grant timed the advance so that all three corps reached Fourteen Mile Creek, a natural defensive line for the enemy, on 12 May.

Pemberton's response to Grant's pause and march inland was essentially passive. Aside from some minor raids, the Confederates did nothing to interfere with Grant's forces during the pause. Reinforcements that Pemberton had started toward Port Gibson pulled back when Bowen retreated across the Big Black. Believing that Grant was about to drive directly toward Vicksburg, Pemberton set up a defensive line running from Warrenton to the Big Black River railroad bridge near Edwards. As Grant's army moved steadily inland along the Big Black, Pemberton correctly deduced that Grant's objective was the railroad, specifically, the Edwards bridge. On 11 May, he shifted Loring's and Stevenson's divisions from the defenses near Warrenton to a position nearer Bowen's division at Edwards. Two other divisions remained close to the Vicksburg fortifications. Pemberton himself finally joined his army in the field on 12 May, moving his headquarters from Vicksburg to Bovina. However, he rejected all suggestions that the Confederates attempt to seize the initiative.

Vignette 1 (Grant decides not to send aid to Banks): "It was my intention, on gaining a foothold at Grand Gulf, to have sent a sufficient force to Port Hudson to have insured the fall of that place with your cooperation, or rather to have co-operated with you to secure that end.

"Meeting the enemy, however, as I did, south of Port Gibson, I followed him to the Big Black, and could not afford to retrace my steps . . .

"Many days cannot elapse before the battle will begin which is to decide the fate of Vicksburg, but it is impossible to predict how long it may last. I would urgently request, therefore, that you join me or send all the force you can spare to co-operate in the great struggle for opening the Mississippi River." (Grant to Banks, 10 May 1863, in *O.R.,* vol. 24, pt. 3, 288-89.)

Vignette 2 (One of Pemberton's division commanders proposes that the Confederates seize the initiative): "The enemy are reported fortifying positions along the road leading to the railroad and toward Jackson. They will not attempt to pass the Big Black or move upon the railroad until this is done. Is it not, then, our policy to take the offensive before they can make themselves secure and move either way as it may suit them? . . . I believe if a well-concerted plan be adopted, we can drive the enemy into the Mississippi, if it is done in time. They don't expect anything of the kind; they think we are on the defensive." (Loring to Assistant Adjutant General, 9 May 1863, in *O.R.*, vol. 24, pt. 3, 849.)

Teaching Points: Turning tactical success into operational advantage, operational pause, operational decision making.

Situation 2: Union Logistics. In his memoirs, Grant wrote that his army cut itself off from the base at Grand Gulf and marched into Mississippi without maintaining a line of communications. It is true that the Union soldiers relied heavily on local food and forage during their march inland and that Grant made no attempt to garrison the roads reaching back to Grand Gulf as his army advanced. However, Grant continued to receive supplies from the rear throughout the campaign of maneuver. His line of communications ran by boat from Memphis to Milliken's Bend, then overland to Perkins' Plantation (later, Bower's Landing), by boat again to Grand Gulf, then by heavily-escorted wagon train to the troops. Two divisions, one from McPherson (Brigadier General John McArthur) and one from Sherman (Blair), remained temporarily west of the river to guard the line of communications and provide escorts for the wagon trains.

Vignette (Grant's logistics plan): "I do not calculate upon the possibility of supplying the army with full rations from Grand Gulf. I know it will be impossible without constructing additional roads. What I do expect, however, is to get up what rations of hard bread, coffee, and salt we can, and make the country furnish the balance. We started from Bruinsburg with an average of about two days' rations, and received no more from our own supplies for some days. Abundance was found in the mean time. Some corn meal, bacon, and vegetables were found, and an abundance of beef and mutton.

"A delay would give the enemy time to re-enforce and fortify. If Blair were up now, I believe we could be in Vicksburg in seven days." (Grant to Sherman, 9 May 1863, in *O.R.*, vol. 24, pt. 3, 285-86.)

Teaching Points: Austere logistics plan.

Stand 12
Raymond

Directions: Continue north on State Route 462 for 12.5 miles. Turn right at the four-way stop onto Fisher Ferry Road. After approximately ten miles, this road becomes Main Street in Utica. Turn right where the road ends on the far side of town, then left onto State Route 18 toward Jackson. After thirteen miles turn right onto Cidero Road. Stop where there is a good view to the north (see map 13 on page 132).

Orientation: Fourteen Mile Creek is in the tree line approximately one-half mile to the north. Gregg's Confederate brigade formed on the ridges behind Fourteen Mile Creek. McPherson's corps approached from Utica on what is now State Route 18. The Confederate artillery position was near the site of the Raymond water tower, visible in the distance. Union artillery deployed along the slope behind (south of) this stand.

Situation: Confederate reinforcements had begun flowing toward Vicksburg ever since Grant crossed the Mississippi River. Jackson, Mississippi, was the point of convergence as forces arrived from other parts of Pemberton's department and from other departments within the Confederacy.

One of the first reinforcements to reach Jackson was Brigadier General John Gregg's brigade, which came from Port Hudson. On 10 May, Pemberton ordered Gregg to advance from Jackson to Raymond, which placed Gregg in the path of McPherson's two-division corps. Pemberton intended for Gregg to attack the Union right rear, but not until Grant swung his army west toward Vicksburg. Gregg, however, decided to pick a fight with the Union force bearing down on him from Utica, believing it to be no larger than his own. Gregg's 3,000-man brigade proceeded to lay a trap for McPherson's 11,000-man corps. For the battleground, Gregg selected Fourteen Mile Creek, just south of Raymond.

May 12 dawned hot, dry, and still. McPherson's corps, advancing along the Utica-Jackson road, had been skirmishing with Confederate cavalry since the predawn hours when the march began. The Union column was an attenuated one, due to the dusty conditions, and this caused units to allow unusually long intervals. In the morning light, McPherson's cavalry patrols discovered Confederate infantry skirmishers along Fourteen Mile Creek and spotted Gregg's line of battle on the slopes beyond. At 1000, McPherson began to commit the

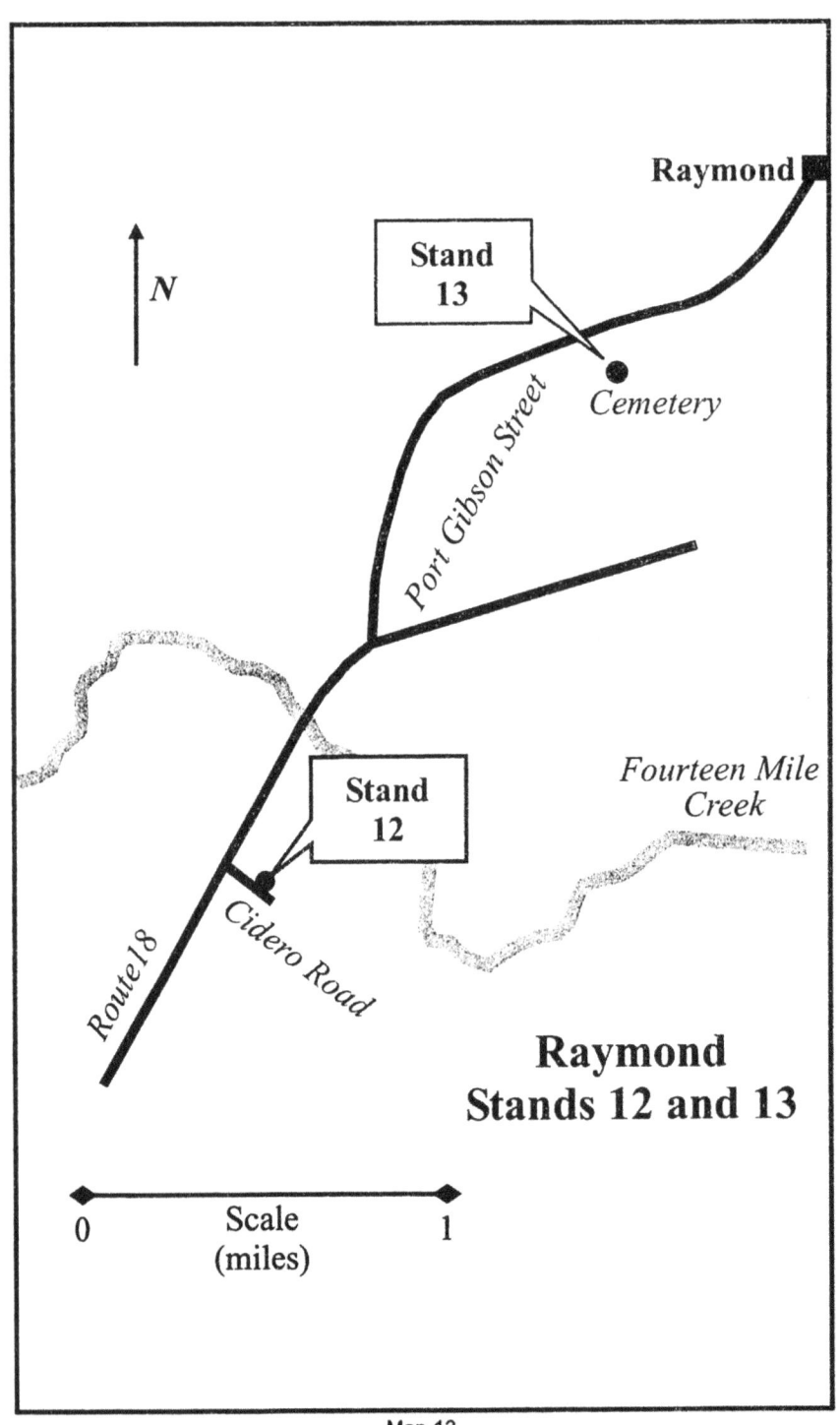

regiments of Logan's division to the task of forcing a crossing of the creek.

Gregg, still unaware of the Union strength, attempted an envelopment of the oncoming Union force. Two regiments, the 7th Texas and the 3d Tennessee, attacked Brigadier General John E. Smith's brigade of Logan's division in the creek bottom, while three other regiments marched off to the east to strike the Union right flank. The Confederate flanking force, its vision unobscured by the smoke and dust rising from the battle in the creek bottom, discovered that the Federals were already present in division strength, with more regiments arriving on the Utica road. Union artillery, deploying on the forward slope, already outnumbered Gregg's three guns. Eventually twenty-two Union guns would be in action. The Confederate flanking force wisely declined to press its attack.

Meanwhile, McPherson fed regiments into the battle as they arrived, thus making his effort piecemeal. Neither he nor Gregg exercised effective control, due perhaps to the choking dust and the jungle-like vegetation in the creek bottom. Regiments fought their own battles.

Eventually, McPherson's disorganized forces pushed across the creek and began driving the Confederates up the slopes toward Raymond. At about 1600, Gregg succeeded in disengaging his badly outnumbered brigade and making good his escape toward Jackson. Casualties in the hard-fought battle totaled 73 killed, 252 wounded, and 190 missing for the Confederates. Union losses, almost all incurred by Logan's division, came to 66 killed, 339 wounded, and 37 missing.

Vignette 1 (Grant's instructions to McPherson): "Move your command to-night to the next cross-roads if there is water, and to-morrow with all activity into Raymond. At the latter place you will use your utmost exertions to secure all the subsistence stores that may be there, as well as in the vicinity. We must fight the enemy before our rations fail, and we are equally bound to make our rations last as long as possible. Upon one occasion you made two days' rations last seven. We may have to do the same thing again . . .

"One train of wagons is now arriving, and another will come with Blair, but withal there remains the necessity of economy in the use of the rations we have, and activity in getting others from the country." (Grant to McPherson, 11 May 1863, in *O.R.,* vol. 24, pt. 3, 297.)

Vignette 2 (Pemberton's instructions to Gregg): "Do not attack the enemy until he is engaged at Edwards or Big Black Bridge. Be ready to fall on his rear or flank at any moment. Do not allow yourself to be flanked or taken in the rear. Be careful that you do not lose your command." (Pemberton to Gregg, 12 May 1863, in *O.R.*, vol. 24, pt. 3, 862.)

Vignette 3 (the battle along Fourteen Mile Creek, J. E. Smith's Union brigade): "In compliance with orders, when about 3 miles from Raymond, about 10 a.m. of the 12th, I formed in line on the right of the road . . . The enemy's advance were discovered posted in a ravine, protected by the dense timber and undergrowth, and also by a branch of Fourteen-Mile Creek—at times a considerable stream with steep banks—but now with only about 2 ½ feet of water, and affording an excellent cover for the enemy. With all these advantages of position in his favor, our skirmishers advanced steadily to the attack, the line also advancing . . . The Twenty-Third Indiana, being in advance of the line, were suddenly attacked by an unseen foe.

"Lieutenant-Colonel Davis, finding his command exposed without support, withdrew, and formed on the right of the Twentieth Illinois. The enemy, rushing forward, encountered the Forty-fifth Illinois, thinking they were alone, and attempted to cut them off, but Colonel McCook, of the Thirty-first, had, unperceived by the enemy, moved upon their flank, and opened fire on them with such effect that they were driven from the right, and massed their forces in the center, evidently endeavoring to cut through, but here they were opposed by the Twentieth Illinois . . . on the left of the brigade, and the Twentieth Ohio . . . on the right of the Second, who maintained their positions under a galling fire nearly two hours." (Report of Brig. Gen. John E. Smith, 23 June 1863, in *O.R.*, vol. 24, pt. 1, 706-11.)

Vignette 4 (the battle along Fourteen Mile Creek, Confederate 7th Texas Regiment): "As my skirmishers neared the wood on the brow of the hill, the enemy commenced firing from their first line of infantry, posted near the base of the hill. I ordered my regiment to advance in double-quick time. The men obeyed with alacrity, and, when in view of the enemy, rushed forward with a shout. So near were the enemy and so impetuous the charge, that my regiment could have blooded a hundred bayonets had the men been supplied with that weapon. As it was, the enemy fled after firing one volley, leaving a number of prisoners, among them Captain Tubbs, Twenty-third Indiana Infantry.

"The enemy made a stand of some ten minutes at the creek, when we took position just beyond the run of the creek, using the bluff as a breastwork. After holding this position an hour and a half (during which time the firing was uninterrupted and terrific), I received word... that the enemy were outflanking [us] on the left... I held the position on the bluff of the creek until the men had exhausted their own ammunition, and emptied the cartridge-boxes of the dead of the enemy and of our own killed and wounded... [T]he Third Tennessee [to our left] having previously withdrawn, the enemy had doubled round my left flank, and were pouring a murderous enfilading fire along my already shattered ranks. I then ordered a retreat." (Report of H. B. Granbury, 7th Texas Regiment, 15 May 1863, in *O.R.,* vol. 24, pt. 1, 747-48.)

Teaching Points: Situational awareness, failure to mass.

Stand 13
Raymond Cemetery (Battle of Jackson)

Directions: Resume travel north on Route 18. Go 0.7 mile and turn left toward Raymond (Port Gibson Street). Approximately 1.3 miles beyond the turn, on the right-hand side of the road, is Raymond's Civil War cemetery (see map 13 on page 132).

Orientation: Jackson is located about fifteen miles northeast of Raymond. Urban development has obliterated most of the landmarks associated with the engagements of 14 May 1863.

Situation 1: Battle Deaths. The citizens of Raymond collected the Confederate dead from the battle of 12 May, interred them here, and have tended the graves ever since. Approximately 130 of Gregg's soldiers are buried in this place. To find a Civil War cemetery near the site of a relatively minor battle is unusual. Most Civil War dead were either collected in centralized cemeteries (such as the one at Vicksburg), returned to their families, or lost forever. These headstones serve to remind us that the soldiers who fell in "minor" battles made the same supreme sacrifice as those killed in the Shilohs and Gettysburgs of the Civil War.

Teaching Points: Cost of battle.

Situation 2: The Battle of Jackson. The bloody little battle at Raymond had a profound impact upon Grant's campaign plan. On the day of the battle, McClernand, commanding the westernmost of the three Union corps, had pushed his patrols to within a few miles of the Vicksburg-Jackson railroad at Edwards Station. Sherman's corps was nearby in support at Dillon's plantation. When Grant learned of the hard fight at Raymond, he immediately gave orders to orient his army toward the east. He directed McPherson and Sherman to capture the city of Jackson. McClernand moved his corps eastward to protect their rear. Thus, Grant intended to clear the threat on his right flank before he dealt with Pemberton and the railroad bridge at Edwards.

Jackson was not just the capital of Mississippi but also a manufacturing and commercial center of some importance. Most significant to the Vicksburg campaign were the railroads intersecting there. With the Mississippi River under the control of the Union navy, virtually all of the supplies and reinforcements intended for Pemberton's army would have to pass through Jackson by rail. On 12 May, approximately 10,000 Confederate troops were on board trains bound for Jackson. They came from other parts of Mississippi, from Tennessee, and even South Carolina. These reinforcements might have given Pemberton the strength to both garrison Vicksburg and challenge Grant in open battle.

Pemberton, however, would not be involved directly in the defense of Jackson. On 9 May, the Confederate government directed General Joseph E. Johnston, Pemberton's superior, to leave his headquarters in Tullahoma, Tennessee, and take direct command in Mississippi. Johnston arrived in Jackson on 13 May and found the place defended by only 6,000 Confederate troops (including Gregg's bloodied brigade), some state troops, and an assortment of civilian volunteers. A hastily constructed line of trenches, forming a semicircle on the western outskirts of the city, was the only prepared defensive position. Upon surveying the situation, Johnston sent a telegraph message to the Confederate government, saying, "I am too late." He promptly ordered the evacuation of the city, even though Grant's army had not yet arrived. Gregg's brigade (reinforced) would conduct a delaying action while military supplies were evacuated. Additionally, Johnston ordered Pemberton to advance from Edwards and attack the Union rear at Clinton, west of Jackson, while the Jackson garrison retreated northward.

Pemberton, however, stayed in his defensive positions near Edwards. Grant proceeded to turn his back on Pemberton and concentrate the Union army against Jackson. On 13 May, McPherson's corps marched north from Raymond to Clinton, where his engineers cut the Vicksburg-Jackson railroad. Meanwhile, Sherman's corps marched from Dillon's plantation through Raymond (crossing behind McPherson's corps) to Mississippi Springs, which positioned it southwest of Jackson. McClernand's corps feinted toward Edwards to hold Pemberton there, then moved east to Raymond.

On 14 May, in the midst of a driving rainstorm, McPherson and Sherman launched a converging attack on Jackson, with McClernand guarding their rear. McPherson's corps, Crocker's division in the lead, advanced on Jackson from the west. Crocker came under artillery fire while still well forward of the Jackson fortifications, whereupon McPherson called a halt to organize a deliberate attack. The Confederate force confronting him, however, was only a rearguard consisting of some 900 men. When it came, McPherson's assault drove the Confederates back upon their trenches. McPherson paused again. When the Union advance resumed, the Confederates were gone.

In the meantime, Sherman's corps advanced from the southwest with Brigadier General James M. Tuttle's division leading. Tuttle encountered a hastily assembled Confederate force that he overwhelmed with artillery and then pushed back to the Jackson trench line. Confederate artillery fire held Tuttle at bay until a Union patrol discovered that the trenches on the Union right were unoccupied. Tuttle quickly swept up the guns confronting him, which were manned by only a handful of Confederate volunteers. Sherman's corps then advanced into Jackson and linked up with McPherson. While McPherson's quartermasters foraged for much-needed supplies, Sherman commenced the destruction of manufacturing and railroad facilities. It would take weeks for the Confederates to reopen the rail lines into Jackson.

Union losses in the Jackson engagements totaled 42 killed, 251 wounded, and seven missing. Confederate losses are not known. However, the low casualty count belies the significance of this affair. In fact, the capture of Jackson held enormous implications for Grant's campaign against Vicksburg because it temporarily reversed the convergence of Confederate reinforcements toward Pemberton. Johnston, along with the Jackson garrison, retreated north to Canton. Those forces that were converging on Jackson stopped where they were when they learned of the city's fall. Had Johnston retained Jackson, he would have had 13,000 troops poised on Grant's flank within a day or two. But with Jackson temporarily neutralized as a transportation center, Grant was free to turn his full attention upon Pemberton.

Vignette 1 (Sherman's account of the destruction in Jackson): " ... on the morning of May 15, Steele's division was set to work to destroy the railroad and property to the south and east, including the Pearl River Bridge, and Tuttle's division that to the north and west. This work of destruction was well accomplished, and Jackson, as a railroad center or Government depot of stores and military factories, can be of little use to the enemy for six months.

"The railroads were destroyed by burning the ties and warping the iron. I estimate the destruction of the roads 4 miles east of Jackson, 3 south, 3 north, and 10 west.

"In Jackson the arsenal buildings, the Government foundry, the gun-carriage establishment, including the carriages for two complete six-gun batteries, stable, carpenter and paint shops were destroyed. The penitentiary was burned, I think, by some convicts who had been set free by the Confederate authorities; also a very valuable cotton factory." (Report of Maj. Gen. William T. Sherman, 24 May 1863, In *O.R.,* vol. 24, pt. 1, 751-58.)

Vignette 2 (Grant's orders to McClernand after the capture of Jackson): "Our troops carried this place about 3 o'clock this p.m., after a brisk fight of about three hours. The enemy retreated north toward Canton; Johnston was in command. It is evidently the design of the enemy to get north of us, and cross the Black River and beat us into Vicksburg. We must not allow them to do this. Turn all your forces toward Bolton Station, and make all dispatch in getting there ...

"Sherman and McPherson will immediately retrace their steps, only detaining a force to destroy the railroads north and east." (Grant to McClernand, 14 May 1863, in *O.R.,* vol. 24, pt. 3, 310.)

Teaching Points: Impact of tactical engagement upon campaign plan, initiative, delaying action.

DAY 3

Stand 14
Coker House

Directions: The Coker House is approximately 3.5 miles east of Edwards on State Route 467. To pick up the campaign where Day 2 of

The Coker House (1997)

the staff ride ended, start from the square in the middle of Raymond. Take Main Street west, which becomes State Route 467. Proceed west for 9.1 miles. Just beyond Military Road, on the south side of the highway, is the Coker House. Turn left at the large Cal-Maine Foods sign (see map 14 on page 143).

Orientation: The Coker House is the only building on the Champion Hill battlefield that dates from the Civil War. It is located on the southern edge of the battle area. The Raymond Road (State Route 467) is the southernmost of the three routes by which Grant's army converged on Pemberton. In Civil War times, there was a farm path (the Ratliff Road) that ran north from this vicinity to the crossroads just south of Champion Hill where the Jackson Road and the Middle Road met. The Ellison House site is approximately 1.5 miles east of the Coker House.

Situation 1: Confederate Movements. Grant's capture of Jackson on 14 May cut off Pemberton from any hope of speedy reinforcement. He would be compelled to defend Vicksburg with the forces already at hand: three divisions (23,000) at Edwards and two divisions (13,000) near Vicksburg. If combined, these forces would number about the same as the Union army in and around Jackson. But Pemberton steadfastly refused to bring out the garrison of Vicksburg, even temporarily. President Jefferson Davis of the Confederacy had instructed Pemberton to defend Vicksburg, and Pemberton was inclined to interpret that guidance quite literally. Pemberton's plan was to stay in his defensive position on the Big Black, maul Grant's army in a defensive battle, and only then to take the offensive to drive the Federals from Mississippi.

On 14 May, however, Pemberton received the message that Johnston had sent from Jackson the day before instructing Pemberton to march east and attack the Union forces at Clinton. Unhappy at the prospect of moving his field army farther away from Vicksburg, Pemberton convened a council of war (composed of all general officers present) to help him out of his dilemma. Loring proposed that the Confederates mount an attack but that they strike Grant's line of communications rather than the Union field forces. Pemberton reluctantly agreed with Loring and gave orders for an attack the next day against the Union supply depot at Dillon's Plantation.

Pemberton's halfhearted offensive of 15 May never got off the ground. Owing to bad staff work, the march from Edwards to Dillon did not even begin until 1300. Then, it was discovered that the bridge over Baker's Creek on the Raymond Road had washed out, necessitating a lengthy detour over Champion Hill. Pemberton was still well short of Dillon when darkness fell. Loring's division, in the lead, camped near the Ellison house on the Raymond Road. Behind Loring were Bowen's and Stevenson's divisions, which pitched camp along the Ratliff Road. Pemberton established his headquarters at the Ellison House.

At 0800 on the morning of 16 May, Pemberton received a message from Johnston, dated 15 May, informing him that Jackson was in Union hands and ordering Pemberton to unite his army with Johnston's force north of Jackson. This time, Pemberton obeyed, even though his reconnaissance elements reported sizable Union forces nearby. (A serious shortage of cavalry in the Confederate force prevented Pemberton from learning any details about Union dispositions.) He issued orders for his army to reverse course and return to Edwards, from where it would march east and north to join Johnston. The sudden onset of battle prevented these orders from being carried out.

As if he did not have problems enough, Pemberton carried an additional handicap into the forthcoming battle. He was losing the confidence of his army. His apparent reluctance to give battle, coupled with his Northern birth and abrasive command style, evoked dislike and distrust among officers and men alike. Foremost among Pemberton's detractors was William W. Loring.

Teaching Points: Command climate, fog and friction of war.

Situation 2: Union Movements. On 14 May, shortly after occupying Jackson, Grant received an important document from a Union agent who had infiltrated the Confederate command. It was a copy of the 13 May message from Johnston to Pemberton ordering the latter to attack Grant at Clinton. Thus alerted that Pemberton might soon be marching east, Grant resolved to intercept and defeat him before he could unite with Johnston. On 15 May, while Pemberton spent most of the day finding a way across Baker's Creek, Grant skillfully faced his army about to the west. McClernand's corps, which had been the rearguard while Grant captured Jackson, became the advance, with one division on the Jackson Road, two on the Middle Road, and one on the Raymond Road. McPherson marched his two divisions from Jackson to Bolton, where they linked up with McClernand's right-flank division. Sherman remained in Jackson with two divisions to complete his work of destruction, while his third division, just arrived from Grand Gulf, joined McClernand's left flank division on the Raymond Road. McClernand commanded the Middle Road and Raymond Road forces, while McPherson and Grant eventually assumed control over the Jackson Road axis. By nightfall on 15 May, Grant had seven divisions, totaling 32,000 men, poised on the line Raymond-Bolton and facing west.

At 0500 on 16 May, two railroad workers made their way to Grant's headquarters with the information that Pemberton had indeed marched east from Edwards. Grant promptly ordered Sherman to finish his business in Jackson and come west to join the main force. He then directed McClernand and McPherson to advance cautiously and locate the enemy.

First contact occurred on the Raymond Road about 0700, when Union cavalry ran up against a Confederate roadblock. Soon after, A. J. Smith's division of McClernand's corps encountered Loring's division drawn up for battle in the vicinity of the Coker House. Confederate and Union artillery dueled vigorously, but there was no assault. The battle of Champion Hill had begun.

Vignette 1 (President Davis reminds Pemberton of the importance of holding Vicksburg): "To hold both Vicksburg and Port Hudson is necessary to a connection with Trans-Mississippi. You may expect whatever is in my power to do." (Davis to Pemberton, 7 May 1863, in *O.R.*, vol. 24, pt. 3, 842.)

Vignette 2 (Johnston's 13 May message urges Pemberton to mass forces against Grant's army): "It is important to re-establish communications, that you may be reinforced. If practicable, come up on [the enemy] rear [at Clinton] at once . . . All the strength you can quickly assemble should be brought." (Johnston to Pemberton, 13 May 1863, in *O.R.*, vol. 24, pt. 3, 870.)

Vignette 3 (Johnston's 15 May message disapproves Pemberton's expedition to Dillon's): "Our being compelled to leave Jackson makes your plan impracticable. The only mode by which we can unite is by your moving directly to Clinton . . ." (Johnston to Pemberton, 15 May 1863, in *O.R.*, vol. 24, pt. 3, 882.)

Vignette 4 (McClernand's orders to his corps for 16 May): "The movement will be toward Edwards Station, with the purpose to feel the enemy and to engage him if it be found expedient to do so. Let each division keep up communication with that or those next to it, and all move on parallel with each other as near as may be." (McClernand to Carr, Smith, Hovey, and Osterhaus, 15 May 1863, in *O.R.*, vol. 24, pt. 3, 314.)

Vignette 5 (At 0530 on 16 May, Grant calls up part of Sherman's force in Jackson): "Start one of your divisions on the road at once, with their ammunition wagons, and direct the general commanding the division to move with all possible speed until he comes up with our rear beyond Bolton. It is important that the greatest celerity should be shown in carrying out this movement, as I have evidence that the entire force of the enemy was at Edwards Depot at 7 p.m. last night, and was still advancing. The fight may, therefore, be brought on at any moment. We should have every man in the field." (Grant to Sherman, 16 May 1863, in *O.R.*, vol. 24, pt. 3, 319.

Teaching Points: Operational decision making, tempo of operations, flexibility.

Stand 15
Champion House

Directions: Proceed west on Route 467 for 1.4 miles, crossing Baker's Creek. Turn right on Buck Reed Road. Go 1.5 miles, then turn right on

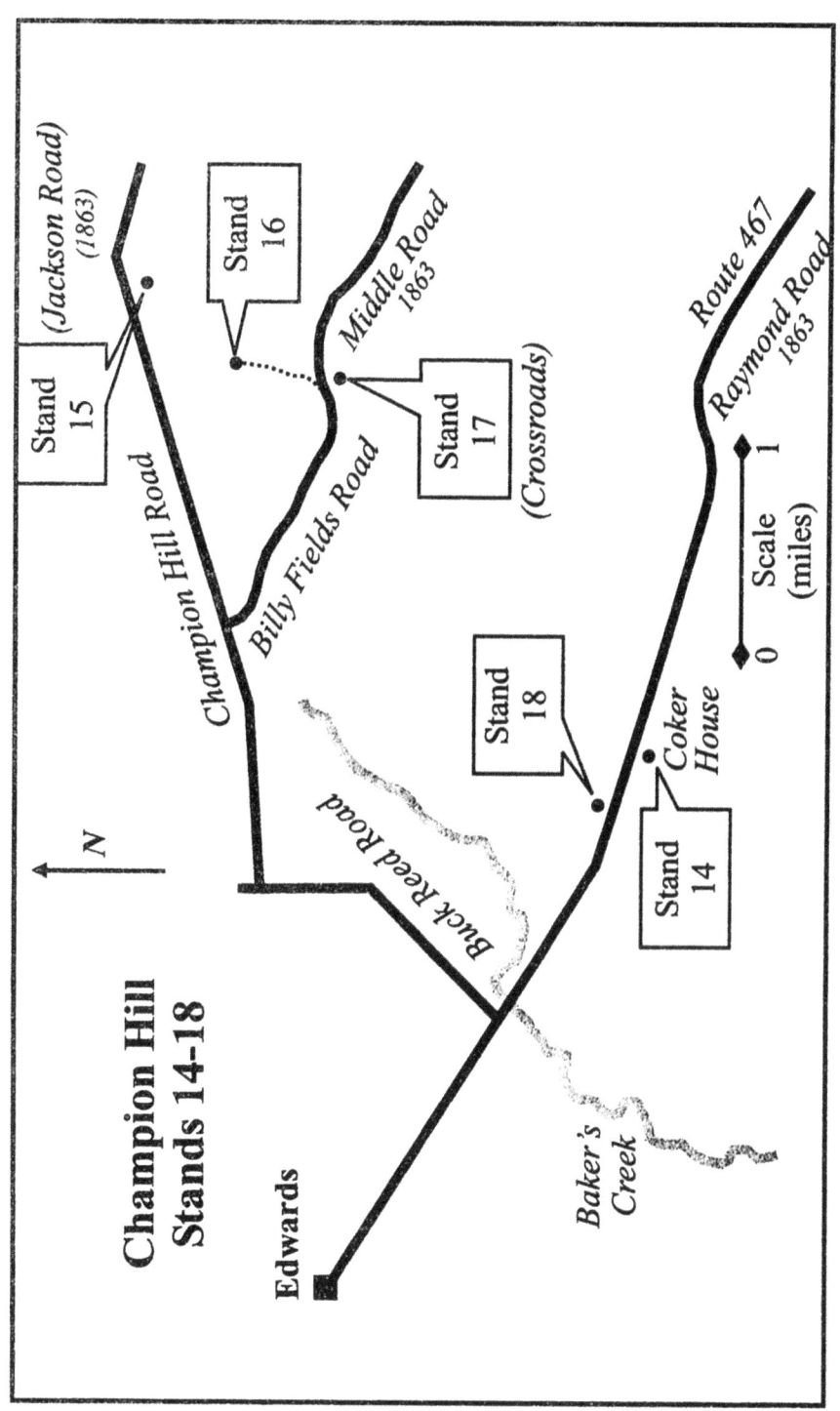

Champion Hill Road. After 3.1 miles stop at the driveway of the Champion Hill MBC Church (see map 14 on page 143).

Orientation: The Champion Hill MBC Church occupies the approximate site of the Champion House, which served as Grant's headquarters during the battle. In 1863, the road from Jackson came in from the east, turned south here, and climbed Champion Hill, which is the high ground to the south. Beyond the crest of Champion Hill is the crossroads where the Jackson Road met the Middle Road and the Ratliff Road. Beyond the crossroads, about four miles south of here, stands the Coker House.

In 1863, much of the land in this vicinity was under cultivation. Fields and woods flanked the Jackson road where it ascended Champion Hill, and the top of the hill was cleared.

(The segment of Champion Hill Road between Billy Fields Road and the Champion Hill MBC did not exist during the Civil War. To get from here to Edwards in 1863, it would have been necessary to climb the hill and turn right at the crossroads.)

Situation 1: Confederate Dispositions. Stevenson's division, which at 11,000 strong was by far the largest of Pemberton's divisions, constituted the rear of the 15 May advance from Edwards toward Dillon's. Stevenson's men spent the night of 15-16 May in the vicinity of the crossroads on the south flank of Champion Hill. When Pemberton gave orders the next morning to countermarch to Edwards, Stevenson became the lead division. The nearest Union forces were thought to be those menacing the Coker House and the Ratliff Road, where Loring and Bowen stood prepared to shield the Confederate withdrawal.

At about 0900, while Stevenson's division was preoccupied with the task of turning around for the return to Edwards, a patrol from one of its brigades pushed north to the crest of Champion Hill. From there, the startled Confederates could see swarms of Union troops deploying into line of battle near the Champion House. Stevenson quickly began pulling regiments from his right and feeding them into a defensive line facing north, protecting the crossroads that constituted the only Confederate line of retreat. Stevenson's new line stood at right angles to the line occupied by Bowen and Loring along the Ratliff Road. Thus, the Confederate battle line assumed the shape of a large "V." The apex of the "V" rested on the crest of Champion Hill.

Vignette (Lee's Brigade, Stevenson's division, establishes a new defensive line facing north): "At about 9 o'clock it was discovered that the enemy was massing troops on the left, evidently for the purpose of turning our left flank and getting between our army and Edwards Depot. My brigade was at once marched (under fire) by the left flank for the purpose of checking the enemy . . .

"As early as 10 o'clock in the morning it became evident that the enemy was in heavy force and determined on battle, as his skirmishers were bold and aggressive, and several divisions of his troops were visible in front of our left." (Report of Brig. Gen. S. D. Lee, 25 July 1863, in *O.R.,* vol. 24, pt. 2, 101-3.)

Teaching Points: Failure of reconnaissance, hasty defensive line.

Situation 2: Union Dispositions. By midmorning, Grant's three columns were ideally situated to deliver a concentric attack upon the Confederates. McClernand's command, two divisions each on the Raymond and Middle Roads, had made contact with the enemy and compelled him to form for battle. On the Jackson Road, McPherson (accompanied by Grant in person) deployed two divisions for an assault up Champion Hill. Hovey's division (which belonged to McClernand's corps but fought with McPherson on this day) formed up on the left side of the road near the Champion House. Logan's division lined up on Hovey's right. McPherson's other division (Crocker) was still coming forward from Bolton.

At about 0945, McClernand, who was with Osterhaus' division on the Middle Road, dispatched a message to Grant inquiring if it was time to bring on a general engagement. Apparently, McClernand's courier traveled by the roads instead of across country, thus turning a three-mile trip into a twelve-mile journey each way. (Grant later dispatched a courier of his own, who made the trip in thirty minutes.) More than four hours would elapse before McClernand received the order to attack.

Vignette (Hovey's deployment near the Champion House): "On arriving near Champion's Hill, about 10 a. m., [we] discovered the enemy posted on the crest of the hill, with a battery of four guns in the woods near the road, and on the highest point for many miles around . . . I immediately rode forward and ordered General McGinnis to form his brigade in two lines, three regiments being in the advance and two in the reserve . . .

"The Second Brigade, Col. James R. Slack commanding, was immediately formed on the left of the First Brigade, two regiments in advance and two in reserve. Skirmishers were at once sent forward, covering my entire front, and had advanced to within sight of the enemy's battery. They were directed not to bring on the action until we were entirely ready . . . In the mean time Major-General Grant had arrived, and with him Major-General McPherson, with his command." (Report of Brig. Gen. Alvin P. Hovey, 25 May 1863, in *O.R.*, vol. 24, pt. 2, 40-46.)

Teaching Points: Meeting engagement, battlefield communication, synchronization.

Stand 16
Champion Hill

Directions: Backtrack 1.7 miles on Champion Hill Road, and turn left on Billy Fields Road. After traveling 1.3 miles, pull off at the intersection with D. J. Johnson Road. Opposite from Johnson Road is a path leading north. Walk this path to the top of the hill (see map 14). (The path lies on private property. If you have not coordinated trespass permission through Vicksburg National Military Park headquarters, conduct stand 16 at the intersection of Billy Fields Road and D. J. Johnson Road.)

Orientation: In 1863, the intersection of Billy Fields Road and Johnson Road was the all-important crossroads. The Middle Road (Billy Fields Road) came in from the east to join the Jackson Road (the trail you are on) as it descended Champion Hill and turned west toward Edwards. Johnson Road represents the Ratliff Road but no longer goes through to the Coker House. From the top of the hill, the Champion House is approximately one mile down the slope to your north.

Part of Champion Hill has been quarried out for gravel since 1863. Lumbering activities have further reconfigured the landscape, which was more open and trafficable than it is today.

Situation 1 (McPherson's attack): The Union advance up Champion Hill began at about 1030. An hour later, Hovey and Logan had pushed in the Confederate pickets and were poised to assault Stevenson's main line. McPherson ordered the assault at 1130. Hovey's division, on the left of the assault, struck the apex of the Confederate salient and broke it. Union troops faced right and left, enfilading nearby Confederate brigades.

Logan's division on the right of the assault encountered more difficult terrain and more effective Confederate fire. Seeking a weak spot in the Confederate line, Logan sent a brigade around his right flank and found that the Confederate left was open. This brigade pressed forward and eventually reached the Jackson Road, effectively severing the Confederate escape route.

Carter Stevenson, confronted with the specter of double envelopment, had no option but to withdraw his division and form a new line. After falling back some 400 yards, he established his right flank at the crossroads and ran his new battle line westward along the Jackson Road. The Union divisions followed up and maintained their pressure. Soon, the crossroads was in the hands of Hovey's Union troops.

Vignette (McGinnis' brigade, Hovey's division, in the assault on Champion Hill): "The whole line moved forward, with bayonets fixed, slowly, cautiously, and in excellent order, and when within about 75 yards of the [Confederate] battery every gun was opened upon us and every man went to the ground. As soon as the volley of grape and canister had passed over us, the order was given to charge, when the whole line moved forward as one man, and so suddenly and apparently so unexpected to the rebels was the movement, that, after a desperate conflict of five minutes, in which bayonets and butts of muskets were freely used, the battery of four guns was in our possession, and a whole brigade in support was fleeing before us, and a large number of them taken prisoners . . . The rebels were driven about 600 yards . . . " (Report of Brig. Gen. George F. McGinnis, 19 May 1863, in *O.R.,* Vol. 24, pt. 2, 48-52.)

Teaching points: Assault tactics, key terrain, face of battle.

Situation 2 (Bowen's counterattack): By the time Hovey's men fought their way to the crossroads, it was about 1400, and Stevenson's division had borne the brunt of the battle unassisted for four hours. Curiously, Pemberton seems to have been more worried about a potential battle on his quiet right flank than he was about the real crisis on his left. Finally, he peremptorily ordered Bowen to pull his division out of the Ratliff Road line and to go help Stevenson. Bowen was reluctant to abandon his position in the face of McClernand's four divisions, but he obeyed. Loring's division shifted left to cover Bowen's sector. At 1430, Bowen launched a counterattack that routed Hovey's tired troops, drove them back from the crossroads, over the crest of Champion Hill, and back to the vicinity of the Champion House—some three-quarters of a mile in all.

The crisis was now on the Union side, as Bowen threatened to rupture the Union front and break into the Union wagon train. Grant himself got involved in rallying Hovey's shaken troops to stem the Confederate advance, but other help was at hand. Sixteen Union artillery pieces enfiladed Bowen's right-hand brigade and halted it. Moreover, Crocker's division had arrived and was able to deploy in time to arrest the last of Bowen's momentum. Soon Crocker was advancing steadily back up Champion Hill, driving Bowen's tired soldiers before him. The crest of Champion Hill came under Union control yet again.

(In his memoirs, Grant stated that Bowen's counterattack caused him to pull back the brigade of Logan's division that had cut the Jackson Road on the Confederate left, inadvertently opening the route by which Pemberton's army eventually escaped. In reality, Logan returned the brigade to its position once Bowen had been repulsed. Moreover, as we shall see, most of Pemberton's army withdrew by another route altogether when the Confederate retreat took place that evening.)

Vignette (Cockrell's brigade, in Bowen's counterattack): "...I ordered the brigade to charge the heavy, strong lines of the enemy, rapidly advancing and cheering, flushed with their success and the capture of our guns; and in the most gallant, dashing, fearless manner, officers and men with loud cheers threw themselves forward at a run against the enemy's hitherto victorious lines ... Soon the enemy's lines in front of this brigade were checked, and after a very stubborn resistance and a very destructive fire from my whole line, firing continuously in its rapid advance, they were severely repulsed and driven back ...

"Fresh troops of the enemy were rapidly thrown in front of our lines, and were immediately engaged and repulsed. This fearful strife was kept up uninterruptedly for two and a half hours. The soldiers of this brigade fired away the 40 rounds of ammunition in their cartridge-boxes, and instead of abandoning the field took from the cartridge-boxes of their fallen and wounded soldiers, and even stripped the slain and wounded of the enemy, with whom the ground was thickly strewn, of all their cartridges, many of them firing 75 to 90 rounds . . . When all the ammunition in cartridge-boxes and that gathered from the slain and wounded of friend and foe was exhausted, the troops gradually began to fall back.

"In the early part of the engagement, I sent two of my staff officers for ammunition, but the ordnance train could not be found." (Report of Col. Francis M. Cockrell, 4 August 1863, in *O.R.*, vol. 24, pt. 2, 109-14.)

Teaching points: Culminating point, unsupported counterattack, leadership in battle, face of battle.

Stand 17
The Crossroads

Directions: Walk back out to the crossroads (see map 14, on page 143).

Orientation: By the later stages of the battle, Logan's division had reestablished itself on the Jackson Road (Billy Fields Road), approximately one thousand yards west of the crossroads, facing south. Osterhaus' division held a position about the same distance east of the crossroads, facing west. Pemberton's headquarters (the Roberts House) stood about five hundred yards south of the crossroads on the Ratliff Road (D. J. Johnson Road).

Situation: McClernand's four divisions stood virtually inactive on the Middle and Raymond Roads during the seesaw battle for control of Champion Hill. At 1400, McClernand finally received Grant's message, written at 1235, instructing him to attack "if an opportunity occurs." McClernand promptly ordered Osterhaus and A. J. Smith to attack "vigorously." Osterhaus' division crushed a regiment of Stevenson's division blocking the Middle Road and advanced to within six hundred yards of the crossroads. There, he stopped to await reinforcements. However, the mere presence of a Union force so close to the crossroads was sufficient to accelerate Bowen's retreat from Champion Hill and to preclude the establishment of a new defensive line in this vicinity. Crocker and Hovey, advancing from the north, drove Bowen beyond the crossroads and then stopped to rest. To their right, Logan renewed his attacks against Stevenson.

Stevenson's Confederate division, which had been heavily engaged all day, came apart under the strain. Soon his men were streaming to the rear. Two brigades of Loring's division tried to form a new line, but the battle was essentially over. With the crossroads in Union hands once again and with two of his three divisions badly battered in the day's fighting, Pemberton decided that the Confederate position was untenable. At approximately 1600, he ordered a retreat.

Vignette 1 (Grant's original instructions to McClernand, issued at 1015, restrained the otherwise-aggressive political general): "Close up all your forces as expeditiously as possible, but cautiously. The enemy must not be allowed to get to our rear." (Grant to McClernand, 16 May 1863, in *O.R.*, vol. 24, pt. 3, 317-18.)

Vignette 2 (The message Grant sent at 1235, which McClernand received at 1400): "As soon as your command is all in hand, throw forward skirmishers and feel the enemy, and attack him in force if an opportunity occurs. I am with Hovey and McPherson, and will see that they fully co-operate." (Grant to McClernand, 16 May 1863, in *O.R.*, vol. 24, pt. 3, 318.)

Vignette 3 (The commander of a Confederate regiment, posted near the crossroads, describes the collapse of Stevenson's division): "At this time our friends gave way and came rushing to the rear panic-stricken. I rushed to the front, and ordered them to halt, but they heeded neither my orders nor those of their commanders. I brought my regiment to the charge bayonets, but even this could not check them in their flight. The colors of three regiments passed through the Thirty-fifth. Both my officers and my men, undismayed, united with me in trying to cause them to rally. We collared them, begged them, and abused them in vain . . . " (Report of Col. Edward Goodwin, 28 May 1863, in *O.R.*, vol. 24, pt. 2, 87-88.)

Teaching Points: Synchronization failure, breaking point of troops, face of battle.

Stand 18
Tilghman Monument

Directions: Backtrack west on Billy Fields Road. Turn left on Champion Hill Road, and left again on Buck Reed Road. Turn left (east) onto Route 467, and travel 1.1 miles to the Tilghman monument, which is located in a small clump of trees on the north side of the road, opposite the Pilgrim Rest MBC Church (see map 14, on page 143).

Orientation: This is the old Raymond Road. The Coker House is approximately five hundred yards to the east. The bridge over Baker's Creek is about one mile to the west. The Crossroads is 2.5 miles to the northeast. Tilghman's brigade of Loring's division conducted a rearguard action here during the Confederate withdrawal.

Situation 1: Loring's Detour. Although the Battle of Champion Hill had begun on the Raymond Road early on 16 May, little subsequent fighting took place there. The Union divisions of A. J. Smith and Blair kept up an intermittent artillery duel with Loring's Confederates but never mounted an assault, not even when McClernand ordered Smith to attack "vigorously."

As for the Confederates, when Bowen's division marched north to counter the initial Union assault upon Champion Hill, Loring extended to the left to cover the sector vacated by Bowen. But Loring failed to acknowledge repeated orders to march his own division to the sound of the guns. He contended that the powerful Union force along the Raymond Road could not be left unopposed. Only after repeated urgings did Loring send one brigade (Brigadier General Abraham Buford's) to the vicinity of the crossroads, when it seemed that Osterhaus was about to cut behind the retreating Bowen. Later still, Loring committed Brigadier General Winfield S. Featherston's brigade to a position on Buford's left. This left only Brigadier General Lloyd Tilghman's brigade to face two Union divisions on the Raymond Road. To buy some time, Tilghman fell back from the Coker House to the next high ground westward. It was here that Tilghman was mortally wounded while directing artillery fire.

Meanwhile, Confederate engineers rebuilt the bridge over Baker's Creek. Stevenson's and Bowen's Divisions streamed southwestward from the crossroads along a farm path, entered the Raymond Road west of Tilghman's position, and crossed the rebuilt bridge. From Baker's Creek, the line of retreat ran through Edwards to the shelter of the Big Black River. Pemberton directed Bowen to hold the bridge until the rest of the army had crossed, but Bowen abandoned the Baker's Creek position upon hearing artillery firing to his rear.

Loring's division constituted the rearguard. The sun was setting by the time Loring crossed Baker's Creek. Believing that Union troops had reached Edwards ahead of him, Loring swerved south in search of another escape route. Finding no suitable road to the west (and losing all of his wagons and artillery in a swamp), Loring marched off to the east and an eventual junction with Johnston. At the time, Pemberton knew nothing of Loring's detour.

Vignette (Buford's brigade, leading Loring's division, turns away from Edwards): "Finding that it was impossible to cross [Bakers] creek under the fire of the enemy and the dispositions of his infantry, [Loring] ordered me to turn my column to the left, and, by going through a plantation, seek a ford lower down . . . I turned the column to the left, passed through the plantation, and endeavored to find the ford, but could not. It was then determined to try to reach a ford still lower down, distant 2 ½ miles, and under the guidance of Dr. Williamson, whom I had secured, moved forward . . .

"As the enemy were pressing us in front, in rear, and on the flank, it became necessary to move with great caution, and only over neighborhood roads and paths long unused. It soon became evident that the artillery could not travel over the paths which necessity forced us to take. Some of the pieces were, therefore, abandoned after using all possible means of saving them which the retreat, nature of the ground, and the presence of the enemy permitted. They were abandoned, however, only after rendering them useless to the enemy.

"We moved until near the ford we sought, and to gain which we had marched 10 or 12 miles instead of 2 or 3, and to a point where we had information that we could secure a guide. From him we learned that the ford was impassible, and that he could not pilot us during the darkness of the night to the fortifications near Big Black Bridge without crossing the lines of the enemy . . .

"A consultation was called by [Loring] and the facts laid before us. I expressed the opinion that to reach Vicksburg we must cross the Big Black River at some of the lower ferries, undoubtedly in presence of the enemy, and to reach even the nearest ferry we would have to march during the entire night, and if we crossed in safety would be in danger of being cut off. Our men were somewhat demoralized, our artillery abandoned, the troops intensely fatigued; we had but a few rounds of ammunition, the greater part of which would be ruined by swimming the river, as we had no means to build a bridge or boat . . . [H]ence our only feasible way of escape and to save the division was to move to the rear of the enemy and pass on his flank in the direction of the Jackson and New Orleans Railroad." (Report of Brig. Gen. Abraham Buford, 16 June 1863, in *O.R.*, vol. 24, pt. 2, 82-87.)

Teaching Points: Delaying action, command climate.

Situation 2: Evaluation of Casualties. Although the Battle of Champion Hill may have been the decisive action of the campaign, an analysis of casualty figures suggests that neither commanding general made maximum use of the forces at his disposal. Union losses totaled 410 killed, 1,844 wounded, and 187 missing. Hovey's division alone incurred losses of 211 killed, 872 wounded, and 119 missing. The other two divisions that fought under McPherson on the Jackson Road axis suffered most of the remaining casualties. By contrast, the two divisions on the Middle Road reported a total of 18 killed, 90 wounded, and 26 missing. The two divisions on the Raymond Road lost a total of 16 wounded, none killed.

On the Confederate side, the divisions that fought against Hovey and McPherson predictably bore the heaviest casualties. Stevenson's and Bowen's divisions together accounted for over 90 percent of the Confederate's casualties, which came to 381 killed, 1,018 wounded, and 2,441 missing. These figures do not include the 7,800 men of Loring's division that never rejoined Pemberton.

Vignette (Hovey reflects upon the Champion Hill battle): "It was, after the conflict, literally the hill of death; men, horses, cannon, and the *debris* of an army lay scattered in wild confusion. Hundreds of the gallant Twelfth Division were cold in death or writhing in pain, and, with large numbers of Quinby's gallant boys, lay dead, dying, or wounded, intermixed with our fallen foe . . .

"I never saw fighting like this. The loss of my division, on this field alone, was nearly one-third of my forces engaged." (Report of Brig. Gen. Alvin P. Hovey, 25 May 1863, in *O.R.,* vol. 24, pt. 2, 40-46.)

Teaching Points: Synchronization failure, cost of battle.

Stand 19
Big Black River Bridge

Directions: Travel west on State Route 467 to Edwards. Follow 467 through Edwards to a "T" intersection with Vicksburg Street (Route 80). Turn left and travel approximately five miles to the truss bridge over the Big Black River (see map 15 on page 154).

Orientation: The Confederate bridgehead is located within a large bend of the Big Black River. The tree line one thousand yards east of the bridge marks the approximate location of the Confederate fortifications. The present-day railroad bridge stands in the same spot as the 1863 structure. However, in Civil War times, the highway crossed the river (by ferry) south of the railroad rather than north of it

154

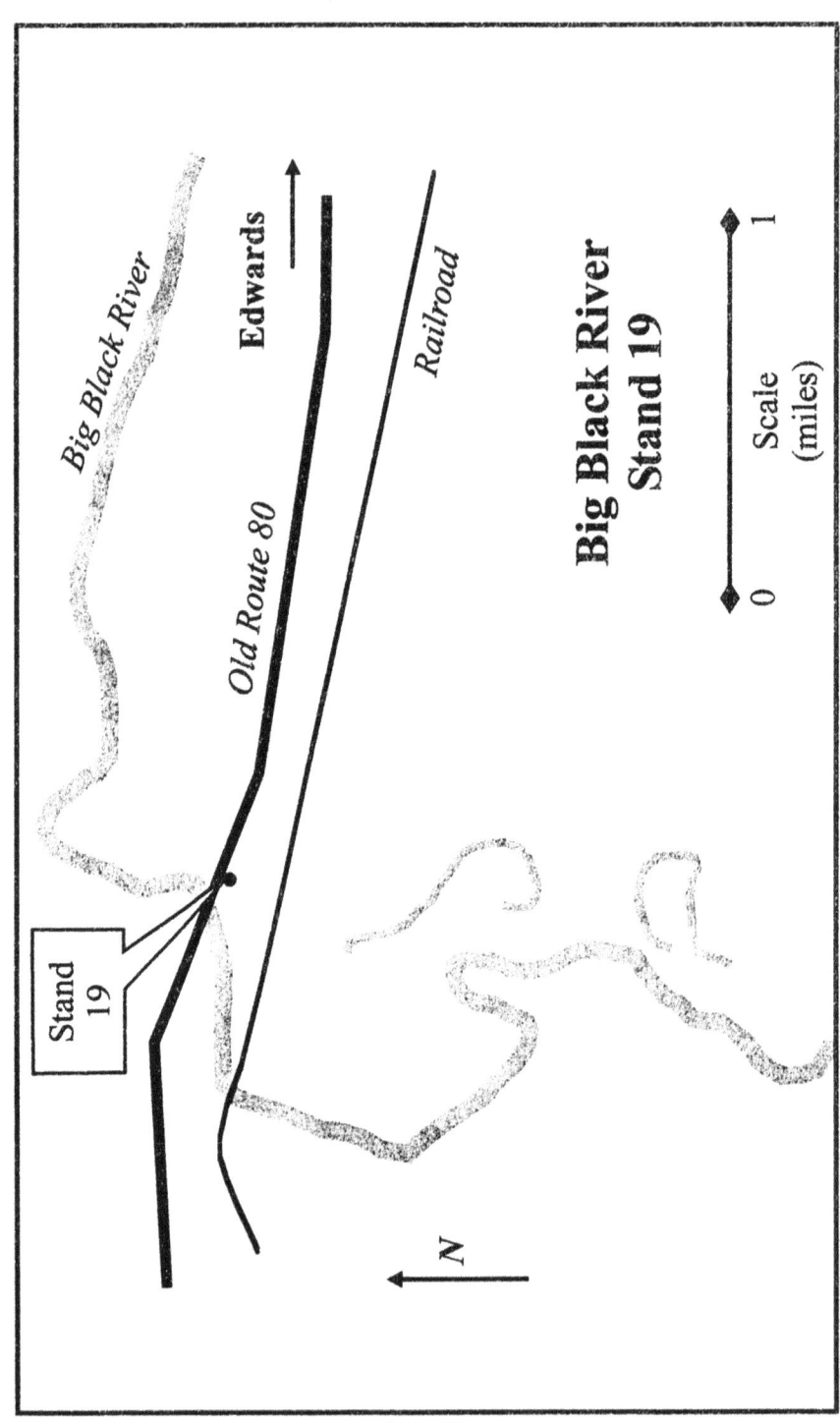

Map 15

where you are now. The bluffs on the west side of the river stand about sixty feet above the floodplain.

Situation 1: Confederate Defense. From the moment that Grant established a Union army on the east bank of the Mississippi, John Pemberton feared for the safety of the Big Black River railroad bridge. In the interval between the battles of Port Hudson and Champion Hill, Bowen's division established a fortified position to defend the bridge against an attack from the east. The Confederate works took the shape of a shallow arc, 1,800 yards in length, extending from the river on the left to Gin Lake on the right. A bayou running moat-like in front of the Confederate fortifications protected the left. Thick woods on this front afforded additional protection from deliberate assault. On the right, the approaches were open and level. The elevated embankment carrying the railroad separated left from right. To improve communications with the far river bank, Confederate work parties planked over the railroad bridge, making it passable to wagons. In addition, they made the riverboat *Dot* into a floating bridge by anchoring her crosswise in the current at the ferry landing.

On the evening of the Champion Hill battle, Pemberton directed Bowen's division to man the bridgehead fortifications while the rest of the army retreated to the west bank of the Big Black. Bowen's two brigades (Cockrell and Green) joined Brigadier General John C. Vaughn's brigade already within the position, giving Bowen three brigades and about 5,000 men to hold a 1,800-yard line. Pemberton did not intend that Bowen should fight a major battle here. Bowen was to stay only until the rearguard, Loring's division, passed through. Neither Bowen nor Pemberton knew that Loring was in fact marching away from them as fast as he could go. Bowen held his position all night and into the morning of 17 May, waiting for a division that would never come. Cockrell's brigade, along with most of the twenty available cannon, covered the right, which Bowen considered the most likely sector for a Union attack. Green's brigade manned the left, leaving the center to Vaughn's brigade of new conscripts.

Teaching Points: Terrain analysis, defense of bridgehead.

Situation 2: Lawler's Attack. McClernand's corps led the Union advance west from Edwards on 17 May. McClernand had his corps moving at 0330. The Union advance met with no opposition until McClernand's pickets encountered Bowen's bridgehead position in the early morning light. Grant, who personally accompanied

McClernand's column, had no particular need for the Big Black River bridge other than to save some time and keep the pressure on Pemberton. (McPherson's and Sherman's corps both found undefended crossing sites not far upstream.) However, Grant wanted to catch and destroy Pemberton outside of the Vicksburg fortifications, if possible. Accordingly, McClernand drew up his forces for a deliberate assault upon what seemed to be formidable works. McClernand deployed Carr's division into the woods on the Union right. Osterhaus, commanding McClernand's favorite division, formed up on the open ground to the left of the railway. Thus, McClernand's best division faced Cockrell, Bowen's best brigade, upon the best ground on the battlefield.

But far to the right, one of Carr's brigade commanders was about to preempt the battle. Brigadier General Michael K. Lawler found a covered approach in the form of a meander scar (abandoned river channel) that brought his four regiments within assaulting distance of the Confederate works. He arrayed his force into column formation (two regiments wide, two regiments deep) and launched an impetuous charge. His troops cut obliquely across the Confederate front, splashed through the moat-like bayou, and struck the Confederate works in the sector manned by Vaughn's brigade. Vaughn's troops did not wait to receive the Union attack—they broke and ran for the bridges. Lawler's assault lasted just three minutes.

Green's brigade, on Vaughn's left, watched Vaughn's collapse and saw immediately that it was in danger of being cut off from the bridges. Soon Green's troops joined the race for the safety of the bridges. Moments later, Osterhaus launched what was intended to be the Union main assault, south of the railroad embankment. His troops walked into the Confederate works without loss because Cockrell's brigade had also run for the bridges.

Confederate losses at the Big Black totaled 4 killed, 16 wounded, and 1,019 missing, most of whom were prisoners. The Confederates also left eighteen guns in the bridgehead when it collapsed. Lawler's brigade incurred most of the Union casualties, which totaled 39 killed, 237 wounded, and 3 missing. But the Confederates succeeded in firing the railroad bridge and the *Dot*, thus denying Grant a speedy crossing of the Big Black. Meanwhile, Pemberton's shattered army was able to break contact and fall back into the sanctuary of Vicksburg.

All three of Grant's corps bridged the Big Black that night. Sherman employed the army's pontoon train, while McPherson and McClernand improvised with whatever materials were at hand.

Vignette 1 (Lawler's assault, the Union perspective): " I remained [in the rear of Lawler's brigade] for some time, when General Lawler ordered me up to support a charge he was preparing to make on the enemy's works. I had not my line in position when the right regiment of his brigade charged across the open field toward the enemy. The general rode up to me and ordered me to charge at the same time, which I did, and I don't think it was anything but the daring bravery of the officers and men which ended the contest so quickly, for we had within 100 yards of the works a bayou to cross, with a heavy abatis, when the enemy commenced putting cotton on their ramrods and showed a willingness to surrender. My men charged into the bayou, and my regiment was second in the works, although they had farther to charge and deeper water to wade through than three others that started in advance of us." (Report of Col. James Keigwin, 18 May 1863, in *O.R.*, vol. 24, pt. 2, 22-23.)

Vignette 2 (Lawler's assault, as seen from the extreme left of the Confederate line): "We skirmished with the enemy for about an hour before they made the charge. They formed their men on the river in the timber where we could not see them. They brought their men out by the right flank in column of fours about 140 yards in front of my regiment at a double-quick . . . I then opened a most terrific fire upon them, and kept it up until the brigade had passed out of my sight behind a grove of timber that stood immediately on my right. They moved so as to strike the ditches occupied by General Vaughn's brigade, so I am informed . . After they had passed me, I listened for our men to open a heavy volley on my right and drive the enemy back. Upon not hearing any firing on the right, [I sent] Lieutenant-Colonel Law [to see] whether the center were holding their position or not. Colonel Law returned in a few minutes, and said that General Green ordered me to fall back. I did so at once. After I had got back below the bend in the river, I discovered that [the enemy] had crossed the ditches and were between me and the bridge . . . I told my men to swim the river . . . The officers and men who could not swim pleaded so hard for me to stay with them that I gave way to them, and we were all captured. I remained with the enemy three days and made my escape." (Report of Col. Elijah Gates, 1 August 1863, in *O.R.*, vol. 24, pt. 2, 118-20.)

Teaching Points: Subordinate initiative, use of terrain in attack, psychological effect of unexpected events.

Situation 3: Pemberton's Options. In the aftermath of Champion Hill and Big Black, Pemberton instinctively sought refuge behind the fortifications of Vicksburg. There was, however, another course of action that he might have followed, involving the abandonment of Vicksburg, an option preferred by his superior, General Johnston.

Vignette 1 (Pemberton reveals his determination to hold Vicksburg): "Every effort is now being made to reorganize the troops, and it is hoped that their numbers, although greatly diminished by [recent events], will be speedily increased.

"The army has fallen back to the line of intrenchments around Vicksburg . . . [T]his retreat will render it necessary to abandon the works at Snyder's Mill [Haynes' Bluff], which has accordingly been ordered . . . "

"I regret to say that as yet I have received no reliable information with regard to General Loring's division . . .

"I greatly regret that I felt compelled to make the advance beyond Big Black, which has proved so disastrous in its results." (Pemberton to Johnston, 17 May 1863, in *O.R.,* vol. 24, pt, 3, 887.)

Vignette 2 (Johnston insists that there is a better course of action): "If Haynes' Bluff is untenable, Vicksburg is of no value, and cannot be held. If, therefore, you are invested in Vicksburg, you must ultimately surrender. Under such circumstances, instead of losing both troops and place, we must, if possible, save the troops. If it is not too late, evacuate Vicksburg and its dependencies, and march to the northeast." (Johnston to Pemberton, 17 May 1863, in *O.R.,* vol. 24, pt. 3, 888.)

Vignette 3 (Pemberton is undeterred): "On the receipt of your communication, I immediately assembled a council of war of the general officers of this command, and having laid your instructions before them, asked the free expression of their opinions as to the practicability of carrying them out. The opinion was unanimously expressed that it was impossible to withdraw the army from this position with such *morale* and material as to be of further service to the Confederacy. While the council of war was assembled, the guns of the enemy opened upon the works . . . I have decided to hold Vicksburg as long as possible, with the firm hope that the Government may yet be able to assist me in keeping this obstruction to the enemy's free navigation of the Mississippi River. I still conceive it to be the most important point in the Confederacy." (Pemberton to Johnston, 18 May 1863, in *O.R.,* vol. 24, pt. 1, 272-73.)

Teaching Points: Operational planning.

Stand 20
Stockade Redan (19 May Assault)

Directions: Continue west on the old highway through Bovina to Vicksburg, where Route 80 becomes Clay Street. From Clay Street, turn right into the National Military Park and begin the battlefield vehicle tour. (Military groups should coordinate with park headquarters in advance and secure a waiver of the park admission fee.) Stop 5 on the tour is the Stockade Redan Attack (see map 16 on page 160).

Orientation: Seen on a map, the Confederate fortified line protecting Vicksburg resembles the numeral "7," with both ends of the figure resting on the Mississippi River. Stockade Redan constitutes the apex of the "7." On the far side of the ravine west of this stand is a large earthwork that replicates Stockade Redan. (A redan was a "V"-shaped fortification, open to the rear.) Approximately seventy-five yards south of Stockade Redan, near the Missouri monument, is Green's Lunette. (A lunette was a small outwork, sometimes crescent-shaped, usually on the flank of a larger fortification.) Approximately 150 yards west of the redan is the 27th Louisiana Lunette. The lunettes provided enfilade fire over the ground in front of the redan. The road passing from this stand to Stockade Redan is Graveyard Road.

In 1863, the ridge tops were under cultivation, while the ravines were choked with vegetation.

Situation 1: Confederate Defenses. Stockade Redan was one of nine major fortifications that anchored the Confederate defense of Vicksburg. These major works covered the roads and the railroad that constituted the best axes of advance for an attacking army. Rifle pits connecting the major works made the Confederate line more or less continuous. Artillery, totaling 102 guns, was scattered among seventy-seven positions sited to enfilade approaches to the Confederate line. (Another thirty-one heavy and thirteen light guns remained in the river batteries.) Manning the works were two divisions that had fought at Champion Hill (Stevenson's and Bowen's) plus two others that had garrisoned Vicksburg during the campaign of

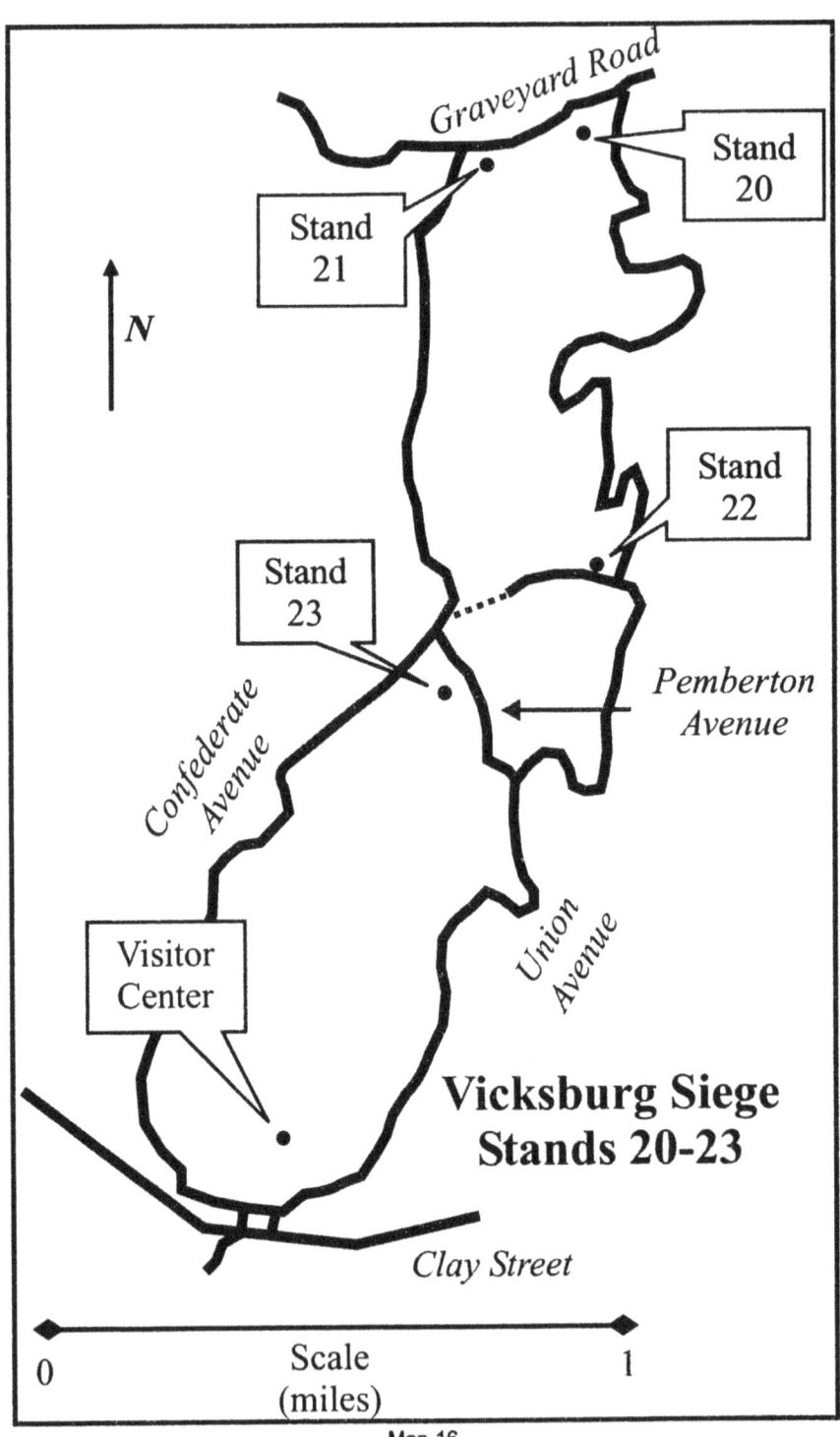

maneuver (Major General Martin L. Smith's and Major General John H. Forney's). Stevenson held the right (southern) portion of the works. Forney defended the center of the line, from the railroad to Graveyard Road. M. L. Smith's troops occupied the left (the top of the "7"), from Graveyard Road to the river. Bowen's division constituted a reserve. In total, the Confederate troops defending Vicksburg numbered about 30,000.

Stockade Redan, together with the two lunettes, guarded Graveyard Road. (The name "stockade" came from a log palisade that obstructed Graveyard Road, giving the appearance of a cattle pen.) The redan's parapet was seventeen feet high and twenty feet thick. In front of the parapet was a ditch six feet deep and eight feet wide. The defenders within Stockade Redan on 19 May consisted of the 36th Mississippi Regiment (Forney's division), who were reinforced by elements of Cockrell's brigade from Bowen's division. Man-made obstacles, not to mention dense natural vegetation, obstructed the ravine in front.

Vignette (Grant's chief engineers describe the enemy works): "Vicksburg was, then, rather an intrenched camp than a fortified place, owing much of its strength to the difficult ground, obstructed by fallen trees in its front, which rendered rapidity of movement and *ensemble* [coordination] in an assault impossible." (Report of Capts. Frederick E. Prime and Cyrus B. Comstock, 29 November 1863, in *O.R.,* vol. 24, pt. 2, 168-78.)

Teaching Points: Terrain analysis, fortified position

The V-shaped mound on the far side of the ravine is Stockade Redan, as seen from the Union line of departure for the assault of 19 May.

Situation 2: Union Assault, 19 May. On 18 May, Union forces secured Haynes' Bluff and closed on Vicksburg. Grant determined upon a hasty assault for the following day. He reasoned that the defenders would be demoralized by their recent defeats and that they might even break and run as they had at Big Black River. Sherman's corps occupied the right of the Union line, opposite the top of the "7," including Stockade Redan. McPherson's corps held the center and McClernand's the left of the line. Of the three, Sherman's corps was the only one that had worked its way close enough to the Confederate main line to launch a serious attack on 19 May. Sherman designated Blair's division as the main effort. Stockade Redan was the objective.

Blair deployed three brigades for the assault. On the left, Colonel Thomas K. Smith's brigade would attack astride Graveyard Road. Colonel Giles A. Smith's brigade, in the center, would attack through the ravine north of the road. On the right, Brigadier General Hugh Ewing's brigade would attack the 27th Louisiana Lunette.

The battle opened on 19 May, with a Union artillery prep that lasted from 0900 to 1400. At 1400, three salvoes from the artillery gave the signal for the assault. Blair's brigades, assembled behind the ridge facing Stockade Redan, passed over the crest. Assault regiments descended toward the ravine, while others remained behind to provide covering fire.

Confederate rifle and artillery fire raked the blue lines from front and flank as they plunged into the ravine—where abatis, wire entanglements, and pits covered with grass mats further broke up the Union formations. Those hardy soldiers who reached the bottom of the ravine in safety came under friendly fire from the rear when they attempted to scale the west slope. For most regiments, the assault culminated partway up the hill.

Only one regiment reached the objective. The 1/13 Infantry, part of G. A. Smith's brigade, attacked parallel to and approximately one hundred yards north of Graveyard Road. Its commander, Captain Edward C. Washington, received a fatal wound at the bottom of the ravine. A handful of men succeeded in scaling the west slope and reached the comparative safety of the ditch in front of Stockade Redan. A few men from other regiments joined them there. Sergeant Robert M. Nelson planted the regimental colors in the face of the redan, but further progress was impossible. The artillery prep had failed to break down the face of the parapet, and the men lacked scaling ladders to climb the works. Instead, they huddled in the ditch, dodging hand-grenades and artillery shells rolled down on them by the Confederates in the redan. There, they stayed throughout the afternoon and evening. Not until nightfall were they able to withdraw to Union lines. Sergeant Nelson succeeded in bringing back the regimental colors. He had four bullet holes in his clothes. There were eighteen holes in the flag and two pieces of canister and one musket ball in the staff. Private Patrick Moher dragged the national colors to safety, with the staff in three pieces and fifty-six holes in the flag. Of the 250 men that went into battle with the 1/13, 71 were casualties at the end of the day.

The assault of 19 May cost Sherman's corps 134 killed, 571 wounded, and 8 missing. Confederate casualties are not known but probably totaled less than 200 on all parts of the line. McPherson's and McClernand's corps, which launched only limited attacks that day, suffered a combined total of 23 killed and 206 wounded.

Vignette 1 (T. K. Smith's account of his brigade's attack astride Graveyard Road): "At the appointed hour the signal was given, and at the command 'forward' the troops advanced gallantly and without hesitation. It was almost vain to essay a line, owing to the nature of the ground, yet three times, under a most galling and destructive fire, did these regiments halt and dress upon their colors . . . Having advanced some 400 yards, I discovered that the men were thoroughly exhausted, and halted the left wing under the crest of a hill, from 65 to 75 yards from the ditch and parapet, and where they were comparatively sheltered from the small-arms of the enemy. Returning to reconnoiter the position of my right wing, hid from my view by the embankment of the road, I perceived their colors advanced to the very base of the parapet, and also that my brigade was alone, unsupported on the left or right, save by a portion of the Thirteenth Regulars, who had advanced to a position under the parapet . . . ordered my men to cease firing and fix bayonets, with intent to charge, when, upon closer view, I discovered the works too steep and high to scale without proper appliances . . . [T]herefore I determined to maintain the position and await developments." (Report of Col. Thomas Kilby Smith, 24 May 1863, in *O.R.,* vol. 24, pt. 2, 265-71.)

Vignette 2 (Confederate perspective): "Three regiments and one battalion of General Hébert's brigade repelled the attack of the enemy today, commencing at 2.30 p. m., advancing in three lines. They succeeded in getting immediately under the parapet of the battery, in position on the Graveyard road. Two colors were left within 10 feet of the works, but were not taken, on account of the very severe fire of the enemy's sharpshooters, and were either destroyed or taken away after dark.

"Three attacks were made. In the first they were driven back; in the second the same result, and in the third they reached the parapet, as stated above. About 50 will cover the losses in front of this position, and perhaps one-fourth of these fatally." (Report of Maj. Gen. John H. Forney, 19 May 1863, in *O.R.,* vol. 24, pt. 2, 359-60.)

Vignette 3 (General Orders No. 64, Department of the Tennessee, 15 August 1863): "The board finds the Thirteenth United States Infantry entitled to the first honor at Vicksburg, having in a body planted and maintained its colors on the parapet with a loss of 43.3/10's per cent including the gallant Commander Washington who died at the parapet. Its conduct and loss the board, after a careful examination believe unequaled in the army and respectfully ask the General commanding the department to allow it the inscription awarded 'First at Vicksburg.'" (Quoted in Terrence J. Winschel, "The First Honor at Vicksburg: The 1st Battalion, 13th U.S. Infantry," *Civil War Regiments,* vol. 2, no. 1, 1-18.)

Teaching Points: Hasty assault over difficult terrain, friendly fire, face of battle.

Stand 21
Stockade Redan: 22 May Assault

Directions: Go west along *Graveyard Road to Stockade Redan (stop 10 on the battlefield tour)* (see map 16 on page 160 mjmnnmbbbcvccbhs).

Situation 1: Sherman's Assault. Grant responded to the setback on 19 May with a decision to mount a deliberate, all-out attack using his entire army. He especially wished to finish off Pemberton and secure Vicksburg before Johnston, in central Mississippi, could organize a sizable Confederate relief force. For this operation, each of the three Union corps would attack in force. Sherman's corps would again attack Stockade Redan, because Graveyard Road afforded the only practicable axis of advance in its sector. Defending the Stockade Redan area were three Confederate brigades: Brigadier General Louis Hébert's brigade from Forney's division, Brigadier General Francis A. Shoup's brigade from M. L. Smith's division, and Cockrell's brigade from Bowen's division. Once again, Blair's division would form the main effort in Sherman's assault. The attack was set for 1000 on 22 May.

In the predawn hours on the day of the attack, Union sharpshooters worked their way into the ravine in front of Stockade Redan. From these advanced positions, they would attempt to suppress Confederate rifle fire. At dawn, twenty-seven carefully sited artillery pieces opened fire on the redan. They succeeded in partially breaking down the parapet and silencing the only Confederate artillery piece within the work. At 1000, the Union artillery shifted fire to the Confederate rifle pits flanking Stockade Redan, just as the infantry assault began.

To avoid the obstacles presented by the ravine, this assault came straight down Graveyard Road. First, a "storming party" of 150 volunteers dashed forward with scaling ladders. Those who reached the redan prepared to assist follow-on forces in crossing the parapet. Close behind came Ewing's brigade of Blair's division in a column four men abreast. The lead regiment advanced rapidly to the road cut, 100 yards from the redan, but when it emerged from the cut, Confederate fire from the front and both flanks mowed it down. Only a handful of men reached the ditch. Soldiers in the following regiment dove for cover within and around the cut, which was soon choked with dead, wounded, and demoralized men. Blair's attack had been stopped cold.

With his carefully prepared attack in a shambles, Blair began to improvise. He shifted one brigade into the ravine south of Graveyard Road and directed it to attack Green's Lunette. By accident, these men found themselves cooperating with troops from McArthur's division of McPherson's corps, Blair's neighbor on the left. But the ravines proved to be just as impenetrable on 22 May as they had been three days earlier.

Late in the afternoon, Sherman decided to make one more assault down Graveyard Road. Tuttle's division, unengaged until now, formed into column and moved out toward the redan. Once again, the lead regiment was shot down upon exiting the road cut, and the follow-on troops again broke ranks and sought cover. Sherman is reported to have said, "This is murder. Stop those men."

Sherman's corps lost 150 killed, 666 wounded, and 42 missing on 22 May. The Union army as a whole lost 502 killed, 2,550 wounded, and 147 missing. Many of the wounded remained in no man's land for two days after the battle—Grant refused to request a cease-fire to retrieve the Union dead and wounded. Finally, on 25 May, Pemberton proposed a truce "in the name of humanity," which Grant accepted. Pemberton's losses were only about 500.

Vignette 1 (an account from the volunteer "storming party"): "At 10 a.m. precisely we started, and proceeded rapidly, occupying but three minutes from the ravine to the bastion. Just as we entered the ditch, a captain and a lieutenant from the Sixth Missouri were shot by sharpshooters on our flank, severely wounding both. I immediately assumed command... Some men of Ewing's brigade came up, but not sufficient to warrant my thrusting them over the ramparts, to be either slaughtered or taken prisoners. We remained in this position, exposed to the fire from the flanks of the enemy, and a direct fire from the skirmishers of the First Brigade, till 4.30 p. m., when about 30 of the Eleventh Missouri... succeeded in reaching us... The rebels, in trying to dislodge us, commenced to use 12-pounder shells, burning the fuse and then rolling them into the ditch. We succeeded in throwing back three with our bayonets, which burst on the inside, causing the same effect they intended for us. One shell, however, exploded, killing Sergt. Richard Haney, Company F, Fifty-fifth Illinois Infantry, and wounding 4 privates severely. At about 7.30 p. m. I received a verbal order from Major-General Blair to fall back, which we did, but not till I had all my wounded safely removed." (Report of Lieut. William C. Porter, 23 May 1863, in *O.R.*, Vol. 24, pt. 2, 272-74.)

Vignette 2 (Confederate perspective, as reported by Col. Cockrell): "This assault was preceded by a most furious fire from the enemy's numerous batteries, of shell, grape and canister. The air was literally burdened with hissing missiles of death... Nobly did the officers and soldiers of this brigade greet every assault of the enemy with defiant shouts and a deliberately aimed fire, and hurled them back in disorder. The enemy gained the ditch around the redan to the right of the stockade and occupied it for some time. Colonel Gause, of the Third Missouri Infantry, procured some fuse-shell, and, using them as hand-grenades, threw them into the ditch, where they exploded, killing and wounding some 22 of the enemy." (Report of Col. Francis M. Cockrell, 1 August 1863, in *O.R.*, vol. 24, pt. 2, 414-17.)

Teaching Points: Synchronization, deliberate assault over difficult terrain, face of battle, commander's callousness.

Situation 2: McClernand's Relief. The attacks mounted by McClernand's and McPherson's corps on 22 May also fell short of success. In McPherson's sector, Logan's division assaulted but failed to reach Great Redoubt. McClernand's attack against Railroad Redoubt fared somewhat better. Elements of two brigades reached the ditch in front of the redoubt, and about a dozen men of the 22d Iowa (Carr's division) actually fought their way into the interior of the work. Eventually, Colonel Thomas Waul's Texas Legion counterattacked and cleared both the redoubt and the ditch of Union troops.

Meanwhile, however, McClernand informed Grant that his troops had captured portions of the enemy line. He asked for reinforcements and for the other two corps to create diversions in their sectors. Grant doubted the validity of McClernand's claims, but he ordered McPherson to send reinforcements (Brigadier General Isaac F. Quinby's division) and authorized the renewal of attacks along McPherson's and Sherman's lines (most notably, Tuttle's afternoon assault against Stockade Redan). Neither the reinforcements nor the diversions had any discernible impact on the battle for Railroad Redoubt.

Afterwards, McClernand blamed Grant, Sherman, and McPherson for the failure to take and hold Railroad Redoubt. In a congratulatory order to his troops, McClernand implied that the other two corps had failed to do their part in the 22 May assault, leaving McClernand's corps to fend for itself against the bulk of the Confederate army. Sherman and McPherson were furious when they learned of McClernand's insinuations. Both wrote formal letters of protest to Grant.

Ultimately, the congratulatory order provided Grant with the pretext to remove McClernand altogether. The order was, in fact, a thinly disguised press release, which subsequently appeared in several Northern papers. Standing orders required corps commanders to clear such releases through Grant's headquarters. McClernand had neglected to do this. On 18 June, Grant relieved McClernand and ordered him back to Illinois. Major General Edward O. C. Ord assumed command of his corps.

McClernand's presence had been a source of friction from the very beginning of the campaign, when Grant incorporated McClernand's independent command into the Army of the Tennessee. The incidents of 22 May were merely the last of several episodes in which McClernand found himself at odds with Grant. Grant tolerated McClernand's presence because of the political general's high-level connections and because McClernand was in fact an enthusiastic and aggressive campaigner. But as the campaign progressed, Grant's prestige rose, meaning that McClernand's political immunity declined. By mid-June, with Vicksburg nearly in his hands, Grant could afford to eliminate the quarrelsome and bombastic McClernand. After the ax fell, McClernand spent several months unsuccessfully pleading his case with Grant's superiors in Washington. His military career ended altogether in 1864.

Vignette 1 (After 22 May, Grant saw only McClernand's negative characteristics): "General McClernand's dispatches misled me as to the real state of facts, and caused much of this loss [on 22 May]. He is entirely unfit for the position of corps commander, both on the march and on the battle-field. Looking after his corps gives me more labor and infinitely more uneasiness than all the remainder of my department." (Grant to Halleck, 24 May 1863, in *O.R.*, vol. 24, pt. 1, 37-39.)

Vignette 2 (McClernand lobbies vigorously for reinstatement): "Having opened the way from Milliken's Bend above to Perkins' plantation, 40 miles below, Vicksburg; having led the advanced corps to Port Gibson and to Champion's Hill, and borne the brunt of both of these battles, as statistics will prove; having fought the battle of Big Black unassisted by any other corps; having made the first and perhaps only lodgments in the enemy's works at Vicksburg on the 22d ultimo, and demonstrated the vigor and persistency of my assault by the greatest loss, I ask, in justice, that I may be restored to my command at least until Vicksburg shall have fallen." (McClernand to Halleck, 27 June 1863, in *O.R.*, vol. 24, pt. 1, 165.)

Teaching Points: Selfless service, relief of subordinate.

Stand 22
Logan's Approach

Directions: Drive south along the battlefield tour road to the parking area for Great Redoubt (stop 11). Backtrack on foot past Pemberton Avenue to the old Jackson Road, a gravel path bearing off to the right through a cut. Go east to the Shirley House (stop 2) (see map 16 on page 160).

Orientation: Great Redoubt was the largest Confederate fortification at Vicksburg. (A redoubt was a fortification enclosed on all sides by a defensible parapet.) It occupied the highest ground along the

The Shirley House, starting point for Logan's approach, which extended to the left.

Confederate line. In conjunction with the 3d Louisiana Redan, Great Redoubt guarded the Jackson Road approach into Vicksburg. From Great Redoubt, you can see Battery De Golyer on the Union lines (stop 1 on the battlefield tour). Battery De Golyer massed twenty-two guns against Great Redoubt. By the end of the siege, Union artillerymen had concentrated about one hundred guns in the Jackson Road sector.

The 3d Louisiana Redan was located just north of the Jackson Road, where the road passes through the cut. A large red marker and two artillery pieces, which you passed while walking through the road cut and which are visible from the vicinity of the Shirley House, show its location.

The reverse slope immediately east of the Shirley House was the Union line of departure for siege operations in this sector. Dugouts and shelters covered this slope during the siege.

Situation 1: Union Reinforcements. To conduct a traditional siege operation, the besieger requires two distinct forces—one facing in toward the besieged place and one facing out to prevent an enemy relief force from breaking the siege. Thus, when Grant decided to lay siege to Vicksburg, he needed more troops, though he already outnumbered Pemberton 50,000 to 30,000. From his own XVI Corps in Tennessee, Grant called up three divisions that had not previously participated in the Vicksburg campaign (Brigadier General Jacob

Lauman, Brigadier General Nathan Kimball, and Brigadier General William "Sooey" Smith). The Union General in Chief, Henry W. Halleck, ordered other departments to send additional troops to Grant. The Department of the Missouri sent Major General Francis J. Herron's division. The Department of the Ohio contributed a detachment from IX Corps, commanded by Major General John G. Parke. The IX Corps contingent consisted of Brigadier General Thomas Welsh's and Brigadier General Robert B. Potter's divisions. Together, these reinforcements, raised Grant's strength to over 90,000 (70,000 men present for duty) and 260 pieces of artillery.

Grant used Lauman's and Herron's divisions to extend the lines of investment from McClernand's left flank to the river below Vicksburg. The other four divisions joined the "Army of Observation," a force of approximately 36,000 men commanded by Sherman (Major General Frederick Steele assumed command of Sherman's sector of the siege lines). The "Army of Observation" had the mission of blocking any Confederate attempt to break the siege from the outside. During the siege, this force conducted "scorched earth" raids north and east of Vicksburg to impede the approach of Confederate relief forces.

Vignette 1 (Grant's orders to begin siege operations): "Corps commanders will immediately commence the work of reducing the enemy by regular approaches. It is desireable that no more loss of life shall be sustained in the reduction of Vicksburg and the capture of the garrison." (Special Orders, No. 140, 25 May 1863, in *O.R.,* vol. 24, pt. 3, 348.)

Vignette 2 (General in Chief Halleck expresses his concerns regarding the siege): "I hope you fully appreciate the importance of time in the reduction of Vicksburg. The large re-enforcements sent to you have opened Missouri and Kentucky to rebel raids. The siege should be pushed night and day with all possible dispatch." (Halleck to Grant, 12 June 1863, in *O.R.,* vol. 24, pt. 1, 42.)

Teaching Points: Reinforcing operational success.

Situation 2: Johnston's "Army of Relief." With Pemberton's army besieged in Vicksburg, Confederate hopes to regain the initiative rested upon General Joseph E. Johnston. Establishing his headquarters in Jackson, Johnston assembled an army out of reinforcements sent to him from various parts of the Confederacy. This force included four infantry divisions (Major General John C. Breckenridge, Major General Samuel G. French, Major General William W. Loring, and

Major General William H. T. Walker) and one cavalry division (Brigadier General William H. Jackson. Loring's division had been part of Pemberton's army until the retreat from Champion Hill.) Johnston's force numbered about 36,000 men, although it lacked a full complement of artillery and transport.

If Johnston and Pemberton could have found some way to combine their efforts, they might have posed a serious threat to the Union siege operation. Although they could and did communicate with each other by way of couriers slipped through the Union encirclement, the two never agreed on a course of action. Pemberton expected Johnston to break into Vicksburg, and Johnston expected Pemberton to break out. Thus, Johnston remained inactive, even after the Confederate government gave him a direct order to attack Grant. Not until 1 July did he move his force in the direction of Vicksburg. Pemberton surrendered before he arrived.

Vignette 1 (the Confederate president reassures Pemberton): "I made every effort to re-enforce you promptly, which I am grieved was not successful. Hope that General Johnston will join you with enough force to break up the [siege] and defeat the enemy." (Davis to Pemberton, 23 May 1863, in *O.R.,* vol. 24, pt. 3, 909.)

Vignette 2 (Johnston offers Pemberton less encouragement): "I am too weak to save Vicksburg. Can do no more than attempt to save you and your garrison. It will be impossible to extricate you, unless you co-operate, and we make mutually supporting movements. Communicate your plans and suggestions, if possible." (Johnston to Pemberton, 29 May 1863, in *O.R.,* vol. 24, pt. 3, 929.)

Vignette 3 (an apocryphal tale about a prewar hunting trip that may explain Johnston's inactivity):

"He was a capital shot, better than Wade or I; but with . . . Johnston . . . the bird flew too high or too low, the dogs were too far or too near. Things never did suit exactly. He was too fussy, too hard to please, too cautious, too much afraid to miss and risk his fine reputation for a crack shot. Wade and I . . . came home with a heavy bag. We shot right and left, happy-go-lucky. Joe Johnston did not shoot at all. The exactly right time and place never came." (Hamilton Boykin, quoted in Mary Boykin Chesnut, *A Diary from Dixie,* Ben A. Williams, ed. [Boston: Houghton Mifflin, 1949], 175.)

Teaching Points: Lack of intent, absence of synchronization.

Situation 3: Trans-Mississippi Relief Effort. Across the river from Vicksburg was the Confederate Department of the Trans-Mississippi under the command of General Edmund Kirby Smith. Throughout the Vicksburg campaign, the government in Richmond had prodded Smith to provide some assistance to Pemberton. It was not until the siege was under way that Smith felt able to do so. He dispatched a division-size force commanded by Major General Richard Taylor to attack Union bases on the west bank of the Mississippi. On 31 May, Taylor's men captured New Carthage, and on 5 June, they occupied the Lake Saint Joseph area. Neither of these locations, however, was of any particular importance so late in the campaign.

Between 7 and 10 June, Taylor undertook a series of attacks upon the much more important Union bases at Milliken's Bend, Young's Point, and Lake Providence. These piecemeal attacks failed, due in part to Union gunboat firepower, and in part to the stout resistance mounted by the Union garrisons. Some of the Union regiments involved in these actions were locally raised units consisting of freed slaves.

Teaching Points: Failure to coordinate across unit boundaries.

Situation 4: Logan's Approach.. In a traditional siege, the besieging force first fortifies its own positions to protect itself from counterattacks and then begins to dig approaches (saps) to advance its men and guns toward the enemy works. (An approach is a zigzag trench with angles laid out so that no section of the trench is exposed to direct enemy fire down its length.) During the siege of Vicksburg, Union soldiers dug ten separate approaches at various points along their twelve-mile line. Logan's division of McPherson's corps dug one of these approaches, which ran from the Shirley House toward the 3d Louisiana Redan. Captain Andrew Hickenlooper, McPherson's chief engineer, supervised the work. The trench was eight feet wide and seven feet deep so that artillery could pass through. A railroad car loaded with bales of cotton served as moveable cover for the digging parties. (Usually, a large bundle of brush called a "sap roller" would be used for this purpose.)

(Follow the route of Logan's approach.) Logan's men began digging on 26 May. Work parties numbered 300 men at the outset but diminished in size as the approach neared the enemy. The approach began at the battery opposite the Shirley House and ran up to the front porch of the house. There, it angled left, along the front of the house, to

a position behind the current site of the Illinois monument. Logan's men constructed an artillery battery position at this angle. From this battery, the approach ran left across the Jackson Road. At the road, the small knoll in front provided cover from the 3d Louisiana Redan, so the workers were able to dig straight ahead to the base of the knoll. They reached the knoll on 3 June.

On this knoll, the Union work parties established Battery Hickenlooper—two 30-pounder Parrott guns situated less than 150 yards from the parapet of 3d Louisiana Redan. They also dug a "parallel" extending left from the knoll. (A parallel is a trench running parallel to the enemy front within which the besiegers may mass troops and guns.)

The approach then continued from the right-hand side of the knoll to the point where Hickenlooper's statue stands today. Here, the Union troops put out another parallel to the right and left of the approach. Driving the approach forward, Logan's men reached the base of the enemy redan on 22 June.

Then, the digging parties began mining under the redan. They excavated a tunnel forty-five feet long, which branched at the end into three galleries, each fifteen feet long. Into these galleries, Logan's men placed 2,200 pounds of black powder.

At 1530 on 25 June, the mine was detonated, creating a crater forty feet wide and twelve feet deep, where the point of the redan had once stood. Brigadier General Mortimer D. Leggett's brigade of Logan's division sent a regiment charging into the crater, supported by every gun within firing range. But the defenders of the redan, Hébert's brigade of Forney's division, had detected the mining operation and evacuated the work before the mine exploded. They stopped Leggett's attack from a newly constructed position in the rear of the damaged redan. Fighting continued in and around the crater well into the night, but when Cockrell's brigade (Bowen's division) arrived to reinforce the Confederate line, any chance of a Union breakthrough vanished. The engagement cost Logan 34 killed and 209 wounded. Confederate losses were 21 killed and 73 wounded. Logan's men immediately started another mine under the remnants of the redan. Detonated on 1 July, this mine completed the destruction of the redan, but there was no Union assault.

Although labor intensive, the siege phase of the Vicksburg campaign was not particularly bloody. Excluding the assaults of 19 and 22 May, six weeks of siege warfare resulted in only 530 Union casualties—104 killed, 419 wounded, and 7 missing. Confederate casualties were higher, owing to the overwhelming Union superiority in artillery. Pemberton's men sustained approximately 2,500 total casualties in the siege. In addition, Union shelling killed three Vicksburg citizens and wounded another twelve.

Vignette 1 (a Confederate attempt to interrupt Logan's siege operations): "I have the honor to report that, for two days before, the enemy had been advancing their works on the Jackson road, under the cover of cotton bales placed on a [railroad] car, which car was moved along at will. Yesterday I directed Lieutenant-Colonel Russell, of the Third Louisiana Regiment, to make an attempt to destroy this cotton, and, if necessary, I would order some volunteers to dash forward and fire the cotton. The lieutenant-colonel, however, invented a safer and a much simpler course. He procured spirits of turpentine and tow [flax or hemp fibers], and, wrapping his musket-balls with the same, fired them, with light charges, into the cotton bales. His attempt succeeded admirably. The cotton was soon burning, and our sharpshooters, having been well instructed, prevented the fire from being extinguished or the cotton rolled away. Lieutenant-Colonel Russell reports that the car and over twenty bales of cotton on it were destroyed ... The car was at a distance of some 75 yards from our works when destroyed, at 10 p. m. yesterday." (Report of Brig. Gen. Louis Hébert, 9 June 1863, in *O.R.,* vol. 24, pt. 2, 371.)

Vignette 2 (an account of Logan's assault following the explosion of the mine): "At 4.30 o'clock the mine was sprung, and before the dirt and smoke was cleared away the Forty-fifth Illinois had filled the gap made by the explosion and were pouring deadly volleys into the enemy. As soon as possible, loop-hole timber was placed upon the works for the sharpshooters, but the enemy opened a piece of artillery at very close range on that point, and the splintering timbers killed and wounded more men than did balls, and I ordered the timbers to be removed. Hand-grenades were then freely used by the enemy, which made sad havoc amongst my men, for, being in the crater of the exploded mine, the sides of which were covered by the men, scarcely a grenade was thrown without doing damage, and in most instances horribly mangling those they happened to strike. The Forty-fifth Illinois, after holding the position and fighting desperately until their guns were too hot for further use, were relieved by the Twentieth

Illinois..." (Report of Brig. Gen. Mortimer D. Leggett, 6 July 1863, in *O.R.*, vol. 24, pt. 2, 293-95.)

Vignette 3 (Confederate account of the crater battle): "At that hour the enemy sprang his mine under the main redan, on the left of the road, and advanced to the assault. His attempt was a feeble one, and was easily defeated; but few of his men could be brought to mount the breach, and, with the exception of one officer (supposed to be a field officer, leading the forlorn hope), evinced [no] determination. He mounted the parapet, waved and called his men forward, but was instantly shot down. After his repulse, the enemy occupied the outer slope of our works, and from there commenced, accompanied by musketry fire, a terrific shower of hand-grenades upon our men. We replied with grenades and sharpshooters, and this species of combat is still going on this morning...

"After the first charge, the enemy attempted to advance by covering himself with logs and pieces of timber. He was made to fall back several times by the rapid and well-directed fire of a piece of our artillery commanded by Lieutenant Scott (Appeal Battery) . . .

"At the time of the explosion, 6 enlisted men of the Forty-third Mississippi Regiment were at work in the shaft, which our engineers were digging in the redan to meet the enemy's [tunnel]. These soldiers were necessarily lost. Not another man was injured by the explosion. This is attributable to the shaft in question, which served as a vent upward to the force of the blast . . . " (Report of Brig. Gen. Louis Hébert, 26 June 1863, in *O.R.*, vol. 24, pt. 2, 371-73.)

Teaching Points: Terrain analysis, "Plan, Prepare, Execute."

Stand 23
Surrender Interview Site

Directions: Backtrack west to the battlefield tour road, then south to Pemberton Avenue. Turn left on Pemberton Avenue to the surrender interview site (see map 16 on page 160).

Orientation: The surrender interview site is located in no-man's-land between the Union and Confederate lines. A small oak tree stood at this spot in 1863.

Situation: By the end of June, Pemberton realized that the siege of Vicksburg was about to reach its climax with a general Union assault (which, in fact, was scheduled for 6 July). He was no longer confident

This artillery piece standing on its base (center of photo) marks the location of the interview between Grant and Pemberton.

that his army could withstand such a blow. Of his 30,000 men, about 6,000 lay in hospitals recuperating from wounds and disease. The remainder was exhausted and demoralized. Six weeks of continuous duty in the trenches, subjected to incessant Union mortar boat, artillery, and rifle fire, had taken their toll. Pemberton had been compelled to reduce rations, and much of the food being issued to the troops was of poor quality. On 28 June, Pemberton received a mysterious letter signed "Many Soldiers" which warned that the army was "ripe for mutiny."

Clearly, a prolongation of the siege was not a viable option. On 1 July, Pemberton issued a circular letter to his division and brigade commanders asking whether their troops were capable of attempting a breakout. Only one of his generals believed that a breakout was feasible. At a council of war held the following day, all of his division commanders urged Pemberton to surrender.

On 3 July, Pemberton wrote a letter to Grant proposing the appointment of commissioners to negotiate terms of surrender. Bowen, who strongly favored an immediate surrender, carried the message into Union lines under a flag of truce. Grant refused to meet personally with Bowen, even though the two had been neighbors in

Missouri before the war. (Bowen had been a successful architect, while Grant sold firewood door to door.) Nor did Grant accept Pemberton's proposal to appoint commissioners. Bowen then suggested, on his own initiative, that Grant and Pemberton meet in person later that day. To this, Grant agreed. When he returned to Pemberton's headquarters, Bowen implied that Grant had been the one to request the meeting. Perceiving this to be a concession on Grant's part, Pemberton accepted.

At 1500, Grant and Pemberton, along with some of their key subordinates, met in the shade of a small oak tree near the point where the Jackson Road entered Confederate lines. When it became obvious that Bowen had manipulated the two into meeting each other, the conference nearly broke off. Grant made it clear that he would accept nothing short of an unconditional Confederate surrender, to which Pemberton replied that he was willing and ready to keep on fighting. Rather than have the talks break off, though, Grant suggested that he and Pemberton step aside so that their subordinates could do some informal negotiating. Finally, it was agreed that Grant would write out terms of surrender and send them to Pemberton that night.

Upon returning to his headquarters, Grant called together his corps and division commanders to discuss the terms he should offer—unconditional surrender or parole. Should Grant demand unconditional surrender, Pemberton would most likely refuse and the siege would continue. If Pemberton, however, accepted, Grant would have to feed and guard 30,000 prisoners until they could be transported north. Under the terms of parole, on the other hand, Pemberton's soldiers would be listed by name and then returned to Confederate control under the agreement that they would not bear arms until "exchanged" for paroled Union soldiers. Ultimately, Grant decided to offer parole. Pemberton accepted early the next morning.

At 1000 on 4 July, white flags appeared all along the Confederate line. Pemberton's soldiers then marched out of their works, stacked their arms in no-man's-land, and returned to their camps. Logan's division of McPherson's corps entered Vicksburg and raised the United States flag over the Warren County courthouse.

It took a week for the Confederates to fill out and sign their parole papers. (About 700 of Pemberton's men refused to sign, preferring to go north as prisoners rather than remain in Confederate service.) Finally, on 11 and 12 July, the disarmed Confederates marched out of

Vicksburg, bound for a camp in Demopolis, Alabama, where they would await exchange.

Meanwhile, Sherman led a strong force in pursuit of Johnston's would-be army of relief, and the Civil War went on.

Vignette 1 (excerpt from the "Many Soldiers" letter sent to Pemberton): "Men don't want to starve, and don't intend to, but they call upon you for justice, if the commissary department can give it; if it can't, you must adopt some means to relieve us very soon. The emergency of the case demands prompt and decided action on your part.

"If you can't feed us, you had better surrender us, horrible as the idea is, than suffer this noble army to disgrace themselves by desertion.

I tell you plainly, men are not going to lie here and perish, [even] if they do love their country dearly. Self-preservation is the first law of nature, and hunger will compel a man to do almost anything.

"You had better heed a warning voice, though it is the voice of a private soldier.

"This army is now ripe for mutiny, unless it can be fed.

"Just think of one small biscuit and one or two mouthfuls of bacon per day. General, please direct your inquiries in the proper channel, and see if I have not stated stubborn facts, which had better be heeded before we are disgraced." ("Many Soldiers" to Pemberton, 28 June 1863, in *O.R.*, vol. 24, pt. 3, 982-83.)

Vignette 2 (Pemberton's circular letter to his division commanders): "Unless the siege of Vicksburg is raised or supplies are thrown in, it will be necessary very shortly to evacuate the place. I see no prospect of the former, and there are very great, if not insuperable, obstacles in the way of the latter. You are, therefore, requested to inform me, with as little delay as possible, as to the condition of your troops, and their ability to make the marches and undergo the fatigues necessary to accomplish a successful evacuation. You will, of course, use the utmost discretion while informing yourself through your subordinates upon all points tending to a clear elucidation of the subjects of my inquiry." (Pemberton to Stevenson, 1 July 1863, in *O.R.*, vol. 24, pt. 2, 347.)

Vignette 3 (Bowen's reply): "I have the honor to state that my men are in as good, if not better spirits, than any others in the line, and able to stand as much fatigue, yet I do not consider them capable (physically) of enduring the hardships incident to such an undertaking . . . I am satisfied they cannot give battle and march over 10 or 12 miles in the same day. In view of the fact that General Johnston has never held out the slightest hope to us that the siege could be raised . . . I see no alternative but to endeavor to rescue the command by making terms with the enemy. Under the most favorable circumstances, were we to cut our way out, we could not, in my opinion, save two-thirds of our present effective strength." (Bowen to Pemberton, 2 July 1863, in *O.R.*, vol. 24, pt. 1, 282-83.)

Vignette 4 (the terms of capitulation proposed by Grant): "In conformity with agreement of this afternoon, I will submit the following proposition for the surrender of the city of Vicksburg, public stores, &c:

"On your accepting the terms proposed, I will march in one division as a guard, and take possession at 8 A.M. to-morrow. As soon as rolls can be made out, and paroles signed by officers and men, you will be allowed to march out of our lines, the officers taking with them their side-arms and clothing, and the field, staff, and cavalry officers one horse each. The rank and file will be allowed all their clothing, but no other property. If these conditions are accepted, any amount of rations you may deem necessary can be taken from the stores you now have, and also the necessary cooking utensils for preparing them. Thirty wagons also, counting two two-horse or mule teams as one, will be allowed to transport such articles as cannot be carried along.

"The same conditions will be allowed to all sick and wounded officers and soldiers as fast as they become able to travel.

"The paroles for these latter must be signed, however, while officers are present authorized to sign the roll of prisoners." (Grant to Pemberton, 3 July 1863, in *O.R.*, vol. 24, pt. 1, 60.)

Vignette 5 (Grant sends Washington the good news): "The enemy surrendered this morning. The only terms allowed is their parole as prisoners of war. This I regarded as of great advantage to us at this juncture. It saves probably several days in the captured town; leaves troops and transports ready for immediate service. General Sherman, with a large force, will face immediately on Johnston and drive him from the State. I will send troops to the relief of General Banks, and return the Ninth Corps to General Burnside." (Grant to Halleck, 4 July 1863, in *O.R.*, vol. 24, pt. 1, 44.)

Vignette 6 (a congratulatory letter to Grant): "I do not remember that you and I ever met personally. I write this now as a grateful acknowledgement for the almost inestimable service you have done the country. I wish to say a word further. When you first reached the vicinity of Vicksburg, I thought you should do, what you finally did—march the troops across the neck, run the batteries with the transports, and thus go below; and I never had any faith, except a general hope that you knew better than I, that the Yazoo Pass expedition, and the like, could succeed. When you got below, and took Port-Gibson, Grand Gulf, and vicinity, I thought you should go down the river and join Gen. Banks; and when you turned Northward East of the Big Black, I feared it was a mistake. I now wish to make the personal acknowledgement that you were right, and I was wrong. Yours very truly, [Abraham Lincoln]." (Lincoln to Grant, 13 July 1863, in *Abraham Lincoln, Speeches and Writings, 1859-1865* [New York: Library of America, 1989], 477-78.)

Teaching Points: Erosion of warrior ethos, surrender protocols, placing trust in subordinates.

IV. SUPPORT FOR A STAFF RIDE TO VICKSBURG

1. Information and Assistance.

a. The Staff Ride Committee of the Combat Studies Institute at Fort Leavenworth has conducted Vicksburg Staff rides for numerous military groups and can provide advice and assistance on every aspect of the campaign. Resources include files of historical data, detailed knowledge of the campaign and battles, and familiarity with the Vicksburg battlefield park and surrounding areas.

>Address: U.S. Army Command and General Staff College
>Combat Studies Institute
>ATTN: ATZL-SWI
>Fort Leavenworth, Kansas 66027-6900
>
>Telephone: DSN: 552-2078
>Commercial: (913) 684-2078
>
>Web site: cgsc.army.mil/csi/index.htm

b. The National Park Service, which maintains the Vicksburg National Military Park, can provide advice and assistance to any group desiring to visit the park. In addition, the park historian can help coordinate visits to the sites of the preliminary battles, many of which are on private land. The park also controls a portion of Grant's Canal, on the west side of the Mississippi River. The Visitor Center includes a small museum, bookstore, and restrooms. The *Cairo* museum, located in the north end of the park, features this Civil War ironclad, which was recovered from the Yazoo River, as well as a museum of naval artifacts found on the ship. No other picnic areas or restrooms are available within the park. Although there is a small fee to enter the park, military groups can be exempted. Coordinate group plans with park headquarters in advance of your visit.

>Address: Superintendent
>Vicksburg National Military Park
>3201 Clay Street
>Vicksburg, Mississippi 39180
>
>Telephone: (601) 636-0583
>
>Web site: www.nps.gov/vick/index.htm

c. The Grand Gulf Military Monument Park, not affiliated with the National Park Service, maintains the site of the Grand Gulf batteries. Facilities include a small museum, restrooms, picnic and camp areas, as well as several other buildings and displays. No food is available for purchase. Park personnel can assist with brochures and information about this portion of the campaign. Prior coordination, especially for large groups, is recommended.

Address: Grand Gulf Military Monument Park
Route 2, Box 389
Port Gibson, Mississippi 39150

Telephone: (601) 437-5911

Web site: www.grandgulfpark.state.ms.us

2. Logistics.

a. Meals. No facilities exist within the parks themselves, but several restaurants, grocery stores, and fast-food establishments are within a five-minute drive of the Vicksburg Visitor Center. Grand Gulf is in a rural area, as are most of the other campaign battle sites, with no such facilities nearby, although there are fast-food restaurants in Port Gibson. Groups visiting the national battlefield can easily drive to Vicksburg for meals. When visiting the campaign area, however, plan to bring along food and drinks or arrange catering from one of several establishments in Vicksburg.

b. Lodging. Vicksburg offers plentiful hotel and motel accommodations, to include several facilities within walking distance of the Visitor Center. Many motels offer reduced rates for large groups. Camping sites are available at Grand Gulf but not in the Vicksburg National Military Park.

3. Medical. The nearest civilian hospital is in Vicksburg, within minutes of the Visitor Center. During portions of the staff ride, Jackson offers the closest medical facilities. There are no military health care facilities in the immediate area.

4. Other considerations.

a. *Note: Except for those areas preserved within the National Military Park, and state or local parks, much of the Vicksburg campaign area and most of the battlefield sites are in private hands.*

Do not trespass on private property without prior approval from the owner. The Vicksburg National Military Park historian can help with any necessary permissions for military groups.

   b. Make provisions for liquids and food since much of the campaign area is rural.

   c. Ensure that your group has proper clothing for inclement weather. Violent thunderstorms can occur in any season.

   d. Mosquitoes, fire ants, chiggers, and ticks are prevalent from March to November; insect repellent is advised.

   e. Maintain good relations with the Vicksburg National Military Park by coordinating unusual requirements well in advance. Be sure to obey the rules.

   f. Because of the long driving distances involved when following the progress of the campaign, it is virtually impossible to follow the entire campaign in less than two full days. Plan your driving routes and timetables carefully (the Combat Studies Institute or Vicksburg National Military Park historian can help).

   g. Roads and bridges, particularly in the rural areas, are sometimes closed due to flooding or construction. Park personnel at Vicksburg and Grand Gulf can provide up-to-date information on routes.

APPENDIX A.
ORDERS OF BATTLE

Order of Battle: Chickasaw Bayou, 29 December 1863

Union Forces:

EXPEDITIONARY FORCE, ARMY OF THE TENNESSEE
Major General William T. Sherman

1ST DIVISION
Brig. Gen. Andrew J. Smith

1st Brigade, Brig. Gen. Stephen G. Burbridge
2d Brigade, Col. William J. Landram

2D DIVISION
Brig. Gen. Morgan L. Smith
Brig. Gen. David Stuart

1st Brigade, Col. Giles A. Smith
4th Brigade, Brig. Gen. David Stuart, Col. T. Kilby Smith

3D DIVISION
Brig. Gen. George W. Morgan

1st Brigade, Col. Lionel A. Sheldon
2d Brigade, Col. Daniel W. Lindsey
3d Brigade, Col. John F. DeCourcy

4TH DIVISION
Brig. Gen. Frederick Steele

1st Brigade, Brig. Gen. Frank P. Blair
2d Brigade, Brig. Gen. Charles E. Hovey
3d Brigade, Brig. Gen. John H. Thayer

Confederate Forces:
DEPARTMENT OF MISSISSIPPI AND EAST LOUISIANA
Lt. Gen. John C. Pemberton

SECOND MILITARY DISTRICT
Maj. Gen. Martin L. Smith

Barton's Brigade, Brig. Gen. Seth M. Barton
Vaughn's Brigade, Brig. Gen. John C. Vaughn
Gregg's Brigade, Brig. Gen. John Gregg

PROVISIONAL DIVISION
Brig. Gen. Stephen D. Lee

Provisional Brigade, Col. William T. Withers
Provisional Brigade, Col. Allen Thomas
Provisional Brigade, Col. Edward Higgins

Order of Battle: Port Gibson, 1 May 1863

Union Forces:

ARMY OF THE TENNESSEE
Maj. Gen. Ulysses S. Grant

XIII ARMY CORPS
Maj. Gen. John A. McClernand

9TH DIVISION
Brig. Gen. Peter J. Osterhaus

1st Brigade, Brig. Gen. Theophilus T. Garrard
2d Brigade, Col. Lionel A. Sheldon

10TH DIVISION
Brig. Gen. Andrew J. Smith

1st Brigade, Brig. Gen. Stephen G. Burbridge
2d Brigade, Col. William J. Landram

12TH DIVISION
Brig. Gen. Alvin P. Hovey

1st Brigade, Brig. Gen. George F. McGinnis
2d Brigade, Col. James R. Slack

14TH DIVISION
Brig. Gen. Eugene A. Carr

1st Brigade, Brig. Gen. William P. Benton
2d Brigade, Col. William N. Stone

XVII ARMY CORPS
Maj. Gen. James B. McPherson

3D DIVISION
Maj. Gen. John A. Logan

1st Brigade, Brig. Gen. John E. Smith
2d Brigade, Brig. Gen. Elias S. Dennis
3d Brigade, Brig. Gen. John D. Stevenson

Confederate Forces:

BOWEN'S DIVISION
Brig. Gen. John S. Bowen

1st (Missouri) Brigade, Col. Francis M. Cockrell
2d Brigade, Brig. Gen. Martin E. Green
Baldwin's Brigade,* Brig. Gen. William E. Baldwin
2d Brigade, ** Brig. Gen. Edward D. Tracy, Col. Isham W. Garrott

* Attached from Smith's Division
** Attached from Stevenson's Division

Order of Battle: Raymond, 12 May 1863

Union Forces:

XVII ARMY CORPS
Maj. Gen. James B. McPherson

3D DIVISION
Maj. Gen. John A. Logan

1st Brigade, Brig. Gen. John E. Smith
2d Brigade, Brig. Gen. Elias S. Dennis
3d Brigade, Brig. Gen. John D. Stevenson

7TH DIVISION
Brig. Gen. Marcellus M. Crocker

1st Brigade, Col. John B. Sanborn
2d Brigade, Col. Samuel A. Holmes
3d Brigade,* Col. George B. Boomer

*In reserve, not engaged.

Confederate Forces:

Gregg's Brigade, Brig. Gen. John Gregg

3d Tennessee Infantry
10th and 30th Tennessee Consolidated Infantry
41st Tennessee Infantry
50th Tennessee Infantry
1st Tennessee Infantry Battalion
7th Texas Infantry
Wirt Adams' Mississippi Cavalry Squadron*
1st Mississippi Battalion State Troops (Mounted)*

* Attached.

Order of Battle: Jackson, 14 May 1863

Union Forces:

ARMY OF THE TENNESSEE
Maj. Gen. Ulysses S. Grant

XV ARMY CORPS
Maj. Gen. William T. Sherman

1ST DIVISION*
Maj. Gen. Frederick Steele

1st Brigade, Col. Francis H. Manter
2d Brigade, Brig. Gen. Charles E. Hovey
3d Brigade, Brig. Gen. John M. Thayer

3D DIVISION
Brig. Gen. James M. Tuttle

1st Brigade, Brig. Gen. Ralph P. Buckland
2d Brigade, Brig. Gen. Joseph A. Mower
3d Brigade, Brig. Gen. Charles L. Matthies

XVII ARMY CORPS
Maj. Gen. James B. McPherson

3D DIVISION*
Maj. Gen. John A. Logan

1st Brigade, Brig. Gen. John E. Smith
2d Brigade, Brig. Gen. Elias S. Dennis
3d Brigade, Brig. Gen. John D. Stevenson

7TH DIVISION
Brig. Gen. Marcellus M. Crocker

1st Brigade, Col. John B. Sanborn
2d Brigade, Col. Samuel A. Holmes
3d Brigade, Col. George B. Boomer

*In reserve, not engaged.

Confederate Forces:
DEPARTMENT OF THE WEST
Gen. Joseph E. Johnston

GREGG'S COMMAND*
Brig. Gen. John Gregg

Gregg's Brigade, Col. Robert Farquharson
Gist's Brigade, Col. Peyton H. Colquitt
Walker's Brigade, Brig. Gen. W. H. T. Walker

* Rear-guard task force.

Order of Battle: Champion Hill, 16 May 1863

Union Forces:

ARMY OF THE TENNESSEE
Maj. Gen. Ulysses S. Grant

XIII ARMY CORPS
Maj. Gen. John A. McClernand

9TH DIVISION
Brig. Gen. Peter J. Osterhaus

1st Brigade, Brig. Gen. Theophilus T. Garrard
2d Brigade, Col. Daniel W. Lindsey

10TH DIVISION
Brig. Gen. Andrew J. Smith

1st Brigade, Brig. Gen. Stephen G. Burbridge
2d Brigade, Col. William J. Landram

12TH DIVISION*
Brig. Gen. Alvin P. Hovey

1st Brigade, Brig. Gen. George F. McGinnis
2d Brigade, Col. James R. Slack

14TH DIVISION
Brig. Gen. Eugene A. Carr

1st Brigade, Brig. Gen. William P. Benton
2d Brigade, Brig. Gen. Michael K. Lawler

XV ARMY CORPS

2D DIVISION**
Maj. Gen. Frank P. Blair

1st Brigade, Col. Giles A. Smith
2d Brigade, Col. T. Kilby Smith

* Operated in XVII Corps sector on 16 May.
** Operated in XIII Corps sector on 16 May.

XVII ARMY CORPS
Maj. Gen. James B. McPherson

3D DIVISION
Maj. Gen. John A. Logan

1st Brigade, Brig. Gen. John E. Smith
2d Brigade, Brig. Gen. Mortimer D. Leggett
3d Brigade, Brig. Gen. John D. Stevenson

7TH DIVISION
Brig. Gen. Marcellus M. Crocker

1st Brigade, Col. John B. Sanborn
2d Brigade, Col. Samuel A. Holmes
3d Brigade, Col. George B. Boomer

Confederate Forces:
DEPARTMENT OF MISSISSIPPI AND EAST LOUISIANA
Lt. Gen. John C. Pemberton

LORING'S DIVISION
Maj. Gen. William W. Loring

1st Brigade, Brig. Gen. Lloyd Tilghman, Col. Arthur E. Reynolds
2d Brigade, Brig. Gen. Winfield S. Featherston
3d Brigade, Brig. Gen. Abraham Buford

STEVENSON'S DIVISION
Maj. Gen. Carter L. Stevenson

1st Brigade, Brig. Gen. Seth M. Barton
2d Brigade, Brig. Gen. Alfred Cumming
3d Brigade, Brig. Gen. Stephen D. Lee
4th Brigade, Col. Alexander W. Reynolds

BOWEN'S DIVISION
Brig. Gen. John S. Bowen

1st (Missouri) Brigade, Col. Francis M. Cockrell
2d Brigade, Brig. Gen. Martin E. Green

Order of Battle: Big Black River, 17 May 1863

Union Forces:

ARMY OF THE TENNESSEE
Maj. Gen. Ulysses S. Grant

XIII ARMY CORPS
Maj. Gen. John A. McClernand

9TH DIVISION
Brig. Gen. Peter J. Osterhaus
Brig. Gen. Albert L. Lee

1st Brigade, Brig. Gen. Theophilus T. Garrard
2d Brigade, Col. Daniel W. Lindsey

10TH DIVISION
Brig. Gen. Andrew J. Smith

1st Brigade, Brig. Gen. Stephen G. Burbridge
2d Brigade, Col. William J. Landram

14TH DIVISION
Brig. Gen. Eugene A. Carr

1st Brigade, Brig. Gen. William P. Benton
2d Brigade, Brig. Gen. Michael K. Lawler

Confederate Forces:

DEPARTMENT OF MISSISSIPPI AND EAST LOUISIANA
Lt. Gen. John C. Pemberton

BOWEN'S DIVISION
Brig. Gen. John S. Bowen

1st (Missouri) Brigade, Col. Francis M. Cockrell
2d Brigade, Brig. Gen. Martin E. Green

Vaughn's Brigade,* Brig. Gen. John C. Vaughn

* (Attached from Smith's Division)

Order of Battle: Siege of Vicksburg, 18 May-4 July 1863

Union Forces:

ARMY OF THE TENNESSEE
Maj. Gen. Ulysses S. Grant

HERRON'S DIVISION*
Maj. Gen. Francis J. Herron

1st Brigade, Brig. Gen. William Vandever
2d Brigade, Brig. Gen. William W. Orme

*Attached from the Department of the Missouri, not assigned to a corps.

IX ARMY CORPS DETACHMENT
Maj. Gen. John G. Parke

1ST DIVISION
Brig. Gen. Thomas Welsh

1st Brigade, Col. Henry Bowman
3d Brigade, Col. Daniel Leasure

2D DIVISION
Brig. Gen. Robert B. Potter

1st Brigade, Col. Simon G. Griffin
2d Brigade, Brig. Gen. Edward Ferrero
3d Brigade, Col. Benjamin C. Christ

XIII ARMY CORPS
Maj. Gen. John C. McClenand
Maj. Gen. Edward O. C. Ord

9TH DIVISION
Brig. Gen. Peter J. Osterhaus

1st Brigade, Brig. Gen. Albert L. Lee; Col. James Keigwin

2d Brigade, Col. Daniel W. Lindsey

10TH DIVISION
Brig. Gen. Andrew J. Smith

1st Brigade, Brig. Gen. Stephen G. Burbridge
2d Brigade, Col. William J. Landram

12TH DIVISION
Brig. Gen. Alvin P. Hovey

1st Brigade, Brig. Gen. George F. McGinnis
2d Brigade, Brig. Gen. James R. Slack

14TH DIVISION
Brig. Gen. Eugene A. Carr

1st Brigade, Brig. Gen. William P. Benton; Col. Henry D. Washburn; Col. David Shunk
2d Brigade, Brig. Gen. Michael K. Lawler

XV ARMY CORPS
Maj. Gen. William T. Sherman

1ST DIVISION
Maj. Gen. Frederick Steele

1st Brigade, Col. Francis H. Manter; Col. Bernard G. Farrar
2d Brigade, Col. Charles R. Woods
3d Brigade, Brig. Gen. John M. Thayer

2D DIVISION
Maj. Gen. Frank P. Blair

1st Brigade, Col. Giles A. Smith
2d Brigade, Col. Thomas Kilby Smith; Brig. Gen. Joseph A. Lightburn
3d Brigade, Brig. Gen. Hugh Ewing

3D DIVISION
Brig. Gen. James M. Tuttle

1st Brigade, Brig. Gen. Ralph P. Buckland; Col. William L. McMillen
2d Brigade, Brig. Gen. Joseph A. Mower
3d Brigade, Brig. Gen. Charles L. Matthies

XVI ARMY CORPS DETACHMENT
Maj. Gen. Cadwallader C. Washburn

1ST DIVISION
Brig. Gen. William Sooy Smith

1st Brigade, Col. John M. Loomis
2d Brigade, Col. Stephen G. Hicks
3d Brigade, Col. Joseph R. Cockerill
4th Brigade, Col. William W. Sanford

4TH DIVISION
Brig. Gen. Jacob G. Lauman

1st Brigade, Col. Issac C. Pugh
2d Brigade, Col. Cyrus Hall
3d Brigade, Col. George E. Bryant; Col. Amory K. Johnson

PROVISIONAL DIVISION
Brig. Gen. Nathan Kimball

Engelmann's Brigade, Col. Adolph Engelmann
Richmond's Brigade, Col. Jonathan Richmond
Montgomery's Brigade, Col. Milton Montgomery

XVII ARMY CORPS
Maj. Gen. James B. McPherson

3D DIVISION
Maj. Gen. John A. Logan

1st Brigade, Brig. Gen. John E. Smith; Brig. Gen. Mortimer D. Leggett
2d Brigade, Brig. Gen. Mortimer D. Leggett; Col. Manning F. Force

3d Brigade, Brig. Gen. John D. Stevenson

6TH DIVISION
Brig. Gen. John McArthur

1st Brigade, Brig. Gen. Hugh T. Reid
2d Brigade, Brig. Gen. Thomas E. G. Ransom
3d Brigade, Col. William Hall; Col. Alexander Chalmers

7TH DIVISION
Brig. Gen. Issac F. Quinby
Brig. Gen. John E. Smith

1st Brigade, Col. John Sanborn
2d Brigade, Col. Samuel A. Holmes; Col. Green B. Raum
3d Brigade, Col. George B. Boomer; Col. Holden Putnam

Confederate Forces:
DEPARTMENT OF MISSISSIPPI AND EAST LOUISIANA
Lt. Gen. John C. Pemberton

STEVENSON'S DIVISION
Maj. Gen. Carter L. Stevenson

1st Brigade, Brig. Gen. Seth M. Barton
2d Brigade, Brig. Gen. Alfred Cumming
3d Brigade, Brig. Gen. Stephen D. Lee
4th Brigade, Col. Alexander W. Reynolds
Waul's Texas Legion, Col. Thomas N. Waul

FORNEY'S DIVISION
Maj. Gen. John H. Forney

Hébert's Brigade, Brig. Gen. Louis Hébert
Moore's Brigade, Brig. Gen. John C. Moore

SMITH'S DIVISION
Maj. Gen. Martin L. Smith

Baldwin's Brigade, Brig. Gen. William E. Baldwin
Vaughn's Brigade, Brig. Gen. John C. Vaughn
Shoup's Brigade, Brig. Gen. Francis A. Shoup
Mississippi State Troops, Brig. Gen. Jeptha V. Harris

BOWEN'S DIVISION
Maj. Gen. John S. Bowen

1st (Missouri) Brigade, Col. Francis M. Cockrell
2d Brigade, Brig. Gen. Martin E. Green; Col. Thomas P. Dockery

RIVER BATTERIES
Col. Edward Higgins

APPENDIX B.
BIOGRAPHICAL SKETCHES

Principal Union Commanders

Grant, Ulysses S. Born Hiram Ulysses Grant in Point Pleasant, Ohio, on 27 April 1822, Grant graduated from the U.S. Military Academy in 1843, twenty-first in a class of thirty-nine. He served under both Zachary Taylor and Winfield Scott in the Mexican War. Of the two generals, Grant would later pattern himself after the unpretentious, straightforward Taylor. Grant distinguished himself in action under both generals and received two brevet promotions for his role in the conflict.

Grant resigned from the army in 1854, unable to cope with the boredom of garrison life. He sought refuge from boredom in drink, a problem that would resurface on occasion throughout his later military career. Rumor notwithstanding, Grant was apparently not a full-blown alcoholic but rather a binge drinker who could not put down the bottle once he raised it. After his resignation from the Army, Grant failed at a number of civilian vocations. When the Civil War began, he was a clerk in his family's hardware store in Galena, Illinois.

In June 1861, Grant was appointed colonel of an Illinois volunteer infantry regiment. An appointment to the rank of brigadier general came in August. His first action occurred in November 1861, when he led a raid against a Confederate camp at Belmont, Missouri. Grant catapulted to national prominence in February 1862 when he commanded the Army component in a joint offensive that resulted in the capture of Forts Henry and Donelson in Tennessee, opening the door for the occupation of Nashville. This victory earned Grant a promotion to the rank of major general.

His reputation quickly suffered a setback when a Confederate army under Albert Sidney Johnston surprised and nearly defeated Grant's force in its camps at Shiloh, Tennessee. Grant's superior, Henry W. Halleck, essentially relieved him of command after this near disaster. Halleck moved to Washington (D.C.) in the summer of 1862 to take over the role of general in chief, and Grant resumed direct control of his troops, by now designated the Army of the Tennessee.

Operations against Vicksburg occupied Grant and his army from November 1862 to July 1863. In November, Grant transferred to Tennessee and became, in effect, an army group commander. He succeeded in breaking the Confederate siege of Chattanooga and routing the enemy forces under Braxton Bragg. This success cemented Grant's position as the Union's foremost general. He was promoted to the rank of lieutenant general (the only Union three-star general of the Civil War)) and assumed command of all the Union armies.

Moving his headquarters to Virginia, Grant accompanied the Army of the Potomac for the rest of the war. The heavy casualties sustained by this army in 1864 once again tarnished Grant's image, but the surrender of Robert E. Lee's army at Appomattox in April 1865 made Grant a national hero.

Following the war, Grant was promoted to full general and, in 1868, was elected president of the United States. Unfortunately, his two terms as president are commonly regarded as a low point in American politics. After the presidency, Grant failed in business yet again. He died of throat cancer in July 1885, shortly after completing his memoirs.

Today, military historians regard Grant as an indifferent tactician, but one of the masters of operational art. Unlike most of his contemporaries, Grant thought in terms of campaigns rather than battles. To put it succinctly, even if a battle went against him, Grant always had a "Plan B" with which to continue toward his ultimate objective.

Porter, David Dixon. Born in Chester, Pennsylvania, on 8 June 1813, Porter was a member of a prominent Navy family. His father and brother were both career officers. David G. Farragut, famous commander of the Western Gulf Blockading Squadron in the Civil War, was Porter's adopted brother.

Porter received his formal education at Columbia University in Washington (D.C.). In 1829, he was appointed a midshipman, in which capacity he acquired his professional education. (The naval academy at Annapolis did not open until 1845.) As a lieutenant, he saw action at Vera Cruz in the war with Mexico. Over the next fourteen years, Porter acquired the reputation of being an ambitious, and at times, quarrelsome officer. He was plagued by ill health and frustrated by slow advancement in the peacetime Navy.

The outbreak of the Civil War found Porter on the verge of resigning his commission, but the prospect of rapid advancement kept him in the service. His first wartime command was with the USS *Powhatan* in the Gulf of Mexico. In April 1862, Commander Porter led a flotilla of mortar schooners in the bombardment and reduction of the forts guarding New Orleans. (His commanding officer was his adopted brother, David Farragut.) In October 1862, Porter took command of the Western Flotilla, which was soon renamed the Mississippi River Squadron. This assignment carried with it the lofty rank of acting rear admiral. In this capacity, Porter became U.S. Grant's partner in the campaign against Vicksburg.

Following Vicksburg, Porter participated in an ill-fated campaign up the Red River in 1864 that nearly resulted in the loss of his gunboats because of falling water levels. He then returned to blue water and command of the North Atlantic Blockading Squadron. Porter commanded the naval component of a joint attack against Fort Fisher, North Carolina, in January 1865. This action was perhaps the best-run amphibious operation of the war.

After the Civil War, Porter served as superintendent of the Naval Academy and in other positions within the Navy Department. He died in 1891.

McClernand, John Alexander. Born in Hardinsburg, Kentucky, on 30 May 1812, McClernand grew up in Illinois. He became a lawyer and a politician, serving in both the Illinois assembly and the United States Congress. In 1860, he lost a bid to become speaker of the house. Although opposed to the abolition of slavery and a staunch Democrat, McClernand supported the Lincoln administration's war aims and helped secure the loyalty of southern Illinois, a region known for its strong pro-Southern sympathies. As a reward, he was appointed brigadier general of volunteers in May 1861. His only prior military service had been as a militia private in the Black Hawk War of 1832.

McClernand commanded a division in the Henry-Donelson campaign of February 1862 and won a promotion to the rank of major general. He also performed capably in the near disaster at Shiloh in April.

In August 1862, McClernand returned to Illinois to aid in recruitment efforts. He also obtained authorization from Lincoln to conduct an independent campaign aimed at opening the Mississippi River to Northern shipping, an objective much favored by

McClernand's Illinois constituency. Sherman used some of McClernand's newly recruited troops in the Chickasaw Bayou campaign—without the latter's knowledge. McClernand had no sooner regained control of his supposedly independent command than he was again subordinated to Grant, this time as the commander of XIII Corps within the Army of the Tennessee. McClernand eventually got to Vicksburg, but not as an independent commander.

Grant relieved McClernand of his command during the siege of Vicksburg. The two had clashed on many occasions during their association, and with Vicksburg within his grasp, Grant felt secure enough to dispose of him. McClernand later commanded XIII Corps again in Louisiana and Texas but found himself on the outer fringes of the war. He resigned from the army in November 1864 and returned to politics. He died in September 1890.

The historical record has not been kind to McClernand. He was by no means an incompetent general, but he was a quarrelsome glory seeker. He also complained loudly about a West Point conspiracy against political generals such as himself. This proved to be a self-fulfilling prophecy. When Regulars such as Grant wrote their memoirs, they were not inclined to give McClernand much credit. Most subsequent historians have followed their example.

Sherman, William Tecumseh. Sherman was born in Lancaster, Ohio, on 8 February 1820, into a prominent family. After the death of his father, Sherman grew up in the family of a U.S. senator, whose daughter he eventually married. He graduated sixth in the West Point class of 1840 but did not see combat in the Mexican War. He resigned from the Army in 1853 and tried his hand at banking and the legal profession, without much success. The outbreak of the Civil War found him serving as superintendent of a college in Louisiana.

In May 1861, Sherman became colonel of the 13th U.S. Infantry (which later fought in the Vicksburg campaign under his corps). He commanded a brigade at the First Battle of Bull Run and was subsequently promoted to brigadier general. In 1862, Sherman commanded a division at Shiloh, and soon after gained promotion to major general. During the 1863 Vicksburg campaign, he commanded XV Corps under Grant's Army of the Tennessee.

Immediately after the surrender of Vicksburg, Sherman conducted a raid into the heart of Mississippi and then accompanied Grant on the campaign to relieve Chattanooga. When Grant assumed command of all Union armies, Sherman took over Grant's role as western theater commander. The forces under his command proceeded to capture Atlanta in 1864 and conducted the famous "March to the Sea." Then, he drove his armies north through the Carolinas in the winter of 1865. Sherman closed out the war in the east by accepting the surrender of the Confederate Army of Tennessee two weeks after Appomattox.

Sherman remained in the Army after the war, advancing to the grade of full general and the post of commander in chief of the Army in 1869. He retired in 1884 and died in February 1891.

Although accused by his opponents of exhibiting barbaric behavior during the war, Sherman was actually one of the most intelligent and articulate generals who ever served in the U.S. Army. Some historians credit him with inventing "total war," while others point out that Sherman was merely applying the "scorched earth" techniques against the Confederacy that the Army had already used with great effect against some of its Indian adversaries. Never a gifted tactician, Sherman understood better than most the nature of the war in which he was engaged and the measures that must be undertaken to win it.

McPherson, James Birdseye. Born 14 November 1828 near Clyde, Ohio, McPherson's family was poor, compelling him to work at an early age. He was educated at an academy in Ohio and graduated first in the West Point class of 1853. Commissioned into the Engineers (which was the branch of choice for top Academy graduates), McPherson began the Civil War as a first lieutenant. He served as an aide to the commander of the western theater, Henry W. Halleck, then became Grant's chief engineer during the 1862 campaigns in Tennessee. In August 1862, McPherson became a brigadier general, then was promoted to major general in October, all without commanding in battle. He commanded XVII Corps in the Vicksburg campaign. McPherson was thirty-five years old at the time.

Although his performance as a corps commander was less than spectacular, McPherson continued to rise. He became an army commander when Grant went east in 1864 and Sherman became a theater commander. He was killed in action near Atlanta in July 1864.

McPherson's phenomenal ascent to the top ranks of the Army seems strange today. He was a bright, energetic protégé to both Grant and Sherman, but he never demonstrated any particular genius for command.

Principal Confederate Commanders

Pemberton, John Clifford. Born in Philadelphia on 10 August 1814, Pemberton traced his lineage to one of the original Quaker founders of Pennsylvania. He completed two years of study at the University of Pennsylvania before entering the U.S. Military Academy. He graduated from West Point in 1837, twenty-seventh in a class of fifty. Pemberton saw action in the Seminole War and performed with distinction in the war with Mexico. Although he led troops in combat, his strongest skills were in staff work. In 1848, Pemberton married a well-to-do woman from Norfolk, Virginia, and thereafter felt strong ties to Virginia and to the Southern aristocracy. With the outbreak of the Civil War, Pemberton resigned from the U.S. Army, over the protests of his family in Philadelphia, and accepted a commission in the Confederate service. It does not appear that Pemberton's political beliefs played much of a role in his decision one way or the other. Torn between his wife and his family, he ultimately sided with his wife.

Pemberton's rise to high rank in the Confederate Army was not a result of demonstrated proficiency on the battlefield. He began service as a lieutenant colonel in May 1861, but by mid-June, he was a brigadier general. Pemberton was assigned to South Carolina under Robert E. Lee and won another promotion in January 1862. He replaced Lee in command of the Department of South Carolina and Georgia in March. His tenure as department commander was not a success. He managed to alienate the leaders of South Carolina with his heavy-handed bureaucratic methods. Worst of all, Pemberton made it clear that he would not sacrifice his army to defend Charleston, the "Cradle of Secession." The governor of the state consequently mounted a successful campaign to have Pemberton relieved. The popular P. G. T. Beauregard replaced him in August 1862.

This setback in Pemberton's career was temporary. For reasons that are not completely understood, Pemberton was, by this time, a favorite of President Jefferson Davis. In October, Pemberton received command of the Department of Mississippi and East Louisiana. Since there were already two major generals within the department who had seniority over Pemberton, the new assignment brought with it a promotion to three-star rank. Pemberton's instructions from the War Department contained two clauses that were to have profound implications for the future. First, Pemberton's top priority was to defend the *territory* of his department. Second, he was to report directly to Richmond. Neither provision was ever rescinded.

Pemberton's considerable skills as an organizer helped bring order out of the chaos of this new department. He was, first and foremost, an administrator operating out of his headquarters in Jackson, Mississippi. The troops rarely saw him. Even after Grant commenced operations against Vicksburg, Pemberton stayed in the role of a behind-the-scenes department commander. He did not take to the field until shortly before the Battle of Champion Hill.

The loss of Vicksburg ended Pemberton's career as a Confederate general. Davis attempted to find another command for him, apparently considering him as a replacement for Braxton Bragg as head of the Army of Tennessee. In April 1864, Pemberton voluntarily gave up the rank of lieutenant general and accepted an appointment as lieutenant colonel and command of an artillery battalion. He ended the war as General Inspector of Artillery and Ordnance for the Confederate Army. Vilified by Northerners and Southerners alike after the war, Pemberton took up farming in Virginia, but later moved back to Pennsylvania, where he died in 1881.

History has dealt harshly with John C. Pemberton. The literature on the Vicksburg campaign has generally reflected the views of two men—Ulysses S. Grant and Joseph E. Johnston. Johnston's self-serving account of the campaign pinned all of the blame on Pemberton, and most subsequent historians have followed Johnston's lead. Pemberton never succeeded in publishing a defense. In reality, Pemberton did no worse than many Civil War generals in their first battles. Pemberton's misfortune was that his first battle came in 1863 and that his opponent was U. S. Grant.

Johnston, Joseph Eggleston. Born in Farmville, Virginia, on 3 February 1807, Johnston graduated from West Point in 1829, thirteenth in a class of 46. (Robert E. Lee graduated second in this class.) Johnston served in the Seminole War, resigned from the Army, and then returned to service after a brief interlude as a civilian. Johnston served with distinction in the Mexican War, receiving five wounds in the process. In 1860, he was appointed quartermaster general, a post that carried with it the rank of brigadier general.

Johnston resigned his commission and joined the Confederacy when Virginia seceded in 1861. He received the rank of brigadier general but was junior to several officers who he had outranked in the

U.S. Army. By a curious convolution of logic, Johnston insisted that seniority in U.S. service should carry over in the Confederate Army. This was but the first dispute that alienated Johnston from the Davis administration.

Johnston became one of the Confederacy's first heroes at the First Battle of Bull Run in 1861. Commanding a corps-size force in the Shenandoah Valley, Johnston moved forces to Mannassas in time to reinforce Beauregard's army there, thus providing the Confederacy with its first major victory. Part of the troop movement took place by rail, marking a turning point in military logistics.

Promoted to full general, Johnston commanded the Army of Northern Virginia in the Peninsula campaign of 1862. Outnumbered heavily by the Union army under George McClellan, Johnston gave ground steadily until the Federals were within sight of Richmond. Only then did Johnston attempt to seize the initiative with an attack (the Battle of Fair Oaks or Seven Pines) in which he was severely wounded. Robert E. Lee replaced him as commander of the Army of Northern Virginia and went on to great fame in that capacity.

In November 1862, Johnston was assigned to a new departmental command that encompassed all of the military departments between the Appalachian Mountains and the Mississippi River. Johnston apparently resented this assignment, believing that he had been "kicked upstairs" to make way for Davis' favorites. The subordinate departments within Johnston's command (including Pemberton's Department of Mississippi and East Louisiana) continued to report directly to Richmond. When Grant moved against Vicksburg in force, Johnston did not come to Pemberton's assistance until ordered by Richmond to do so.

After the fall of Vicksburg, Johnston embarked upon a bizarre "war of letters" with Jefferson Davis in which he denied responsibility for the events in Pemberton's department prior to mid-May and was, by implication, blameless in the calamity. Clearly, Davis would have liked to fire Johnston for good, but the Confederacy was running short of general officers. Moreover, Johnston had powerful friends in the Confederate Congress.

In December 1863, Davis reluctantly assigned Johnston to command of the Army of Tennessee. When Sherman commenced his 1864 campaign into Georgia, Johnston refused to take offensive action and instead gave ground until the Federals had nearly reached Atlanta.

Davis relieved Johnston in favor of John Bell Hood, who proceeded to wreck the Army of Tennessee in a series of impetuous attacks. Johnston returned to command of the army in February 1865, fought the last major battle of the war at Bentonville, North Carolina, and surrendered to Sherman on 18 April.

Joseph Johnston is a historical paradox. Some historians call him one of the most brilliant generals of the war, citing his skill in delaying actions against greatly superior forces. This favorable interpretation might be a result of the fact that Johnston published his own views of the war early and often. Other historians assert that his greatest military talents involved conducting retreats and quarreling with his superiors.

Bowen, John Stevens. Born 30 October 1829, near Savannah, Georgia, Bowen graduated thirteenth out of fifty-two in the West Point class of 1853. (The top graduate was James McPherson. The academy's new superintendent that year was Robert E. Lee.) Bowen married a woman from Missouri in 1854 and resigned his commission two years later. The Bowens took up residence near St. Louis, where John became a successful architect. He trained a regiment of prosecession militia troops in 1859-60, reportedly imposing Regular Army standards upon his command. Shortly after the outbreak of war, Bowen and his troops were captured in their camps. Paroled and exchanged, Bowen received a Confederate colonelcy and command of a regiment. Promotion to brigadier general and command of a brigade soon followed, based in large part on Bowen's demonstrated talents as a trainer. In 1862, he fought with distinction at Shiloh, where he was wounded, and he participated in the Battle of Corinth.

Later that year, Bowen and his brigade came under the command of John C. Pemberton. In March 1863, Pemberton sent Bowen to Grand Gulf with orders to fortify the place against the passage of Union vessels on the Mississippi. This was an independent command, in which Bowen answered directly to Pemberton. Bowen's force and command responsibilities expanded in the course of Vicksburg operations, elevating him to the status of division commander.

Bowen contracted dysentery during the siege of Vicksburg and was too ill to ride a horse by the time paroles had been signed. He left Vicksburg in an ambulance and died at a farmhouse on the Raymond Road on 13 July.

Historians generally consider Bowen to be the best Confederate battle commander in the Vicksburg campaign. He was a superb trainer of troops and an imaginative tactician. If nothing else, Bowen began the Vicksburg campaign with more Civil War battle experience than either of Pemberton's other division commanders, not to mention Pemberton himself.

Stevenson, Carter Littlepage. Born 21 September 1817 near Fredericksburg, Virginia, Stevenson graduated from West Point in 1838. He served in the Mexican War and became the colonel of a Virginia regiment at the onset of the Civil War. In February 1862, Stevenson was promoted to brigadier general and was transferred to the western theater, where he participated in the Kentucky campaign of that year, receiving a promotion to major general in October. Stevenson commanded the largest of Pemberton's divisions during the Vicksburg campaign. He may well have been Pemberton's most trusted subordinate.

After the surrender of Vicksburg, Stevenson commanded a division in the Army of Tennessee. Although he had little battle experience at the time of the Vicksburg operations, he made up for it with an extensive campaign record thereafter. After the war, Stevenson worked as a civil engineer. He died in August 1888.

Loring, William Wing. Born 4 December 1818 in Wilmington, North Carolina, Loring grew up in Florida. He became a lawyer and Florida state legislator. Loring acquired a direct commission into the regular Army in 1846 as a captain and served with distinction in the Mexican War, receiving two brevets and losing an arm. He was a colonel in the U.S. Army when he resigned in 1861 to join the Confederacy.

Loring entered Confederate service as a brigadier general. He served under "Stonewall" Jackson in the Romney campaign and had the poor judgment to quarrel with one of the Confederacy's most popular generals. Loring was transferred away from Virginia, eventually being assigned to Pemberton's department (December 1862). He also received a promotion to the rank of major general.

To a man who could argue with "Stonewall" Jackson, bickering with John Pemberton must have come naturally, and Loring contributed materially to the deterioration of the command climate under Pemberton. After Vicksburg, he commanded a division in the Army of Tennessee. With the collapse of the Confederacy in 1865, Loring left the United States and eventually became a division commander in the Egyptian Army. He returned to the U.S. in 1879 and died in December 1886.

APPENDIX C.
MEDAL OF HONOR CONFERRALS IN THE VICKSBURG CAMPAIGN

The Vicksburg campaign resulted in 121 known conferrals of the Medal of Honor. The Chickasaw Bayou campaign produced one recipient—the colonel of the 4th Iowa. Twelve Medals of Honor went to Army volunteers who manned unarmed riverboats on various attempts to run the Vicksburg batteries. Three other medals went to soldiers who performed a similar mission during the passage of the Grand Gulf batteries. The battle of Champion Hill produced two recipients, both from McClernand's corps (one each from Hovey's and Carr's divisions). Another of McClernand's soldiers earned the medal at the Big Black River battle.

Most of the Medals of Honor stemming from the Vicksburg campaign involved action against the fortifications of Vicksburg. The assault of Sherman's corps against Stockade Redan on 19 May led to three conferrals, all to soldiers in Blair's division. One of these was Orion P. Howe, a fourteen-year-old drummer. The general assault of 22 May produced no fewer than ninety-eight conferrals of the Medal of Honor. (By contrast, the entire battle of Gettysburg produced sixty-one.) Eighty-two medals went to members of the "volunteer storming party" that led Sherman's assault upon Stockade Redan. Five other soldiers in Sherman's corps also won the medal that day. In McClernand's corps, seven soldiers received the medal for pushing a six-pounder cannon up to the parapet of the 2d Texas Lunette and firing into the interior of the work through an embrasure. Three additional soldiers from McClernand's corps and one from McPherson's corps also received the medal for their actions on 22 May. Another of McPherson's soldiers, a sergeant from Logan's division, won the award on 25 June for planting the national colors on the 3d Louisiana Redan following the explosion of the mine. Finally, a musician in Sherman's "Army of Observation" received the medal for bravery under fire near Mechanicsburg, Mississippi, on 4 June.

As the numbers cited above suggest, the criteria for conferring the Medal of Honor were less well defined in 1863 than they are today. (Some Civil War soldiers received the medal merely for reenlisting when their terms of service expired. These awards were later withdrawn.) Moreover, the great majority of medals conferred for service in the Vicksburg campaign were actually issued in the 1890s.

BIBLIOGRAPHY

This bibliography is not intended to be comprehensive. Inclusion is based upon probable availability and utility for staff ride preparation.

I. Conducting a Staff Ride.

Robertson, William G. *The Staff Ride*. Washington, D.C.: U.S. Army Center of Military History, 1987.

This pamphlet outlines the philosophy of the staff ride and offers suggestions on creating and conducting rides.

II. Campaign.

Ambrose, Stephen E. *Struggle for Vicksburg*. N.p.: Eastern Acorn Press, 1982 (1967).

This booklet, available at National Military Park bookstores, provides an excellent general overview of the campaign.

Arnold, James R. *Grant Wins the War: Decision at Vicksburg*. New York: John Wiley, 1997.

Although containing some tactical-level errors, this work is an excellent one-volume military analysis of the campaign.

Ballard, Michael B. *The Campaign for Vicksburg*. N.p.: Eastern National Park & Monument Association, 1996.

Comparable to the Ambrose work cited above, this booklet is also sold at many National Military Park bookstores.

Bearss, Edwin C. *The Vicksburg Campaign*. 3 vols. Dayton, OH: Morningside House, 1985-86.

This is the most comprehensive treatment of the campaign available. The level of detail exceeds the requirements of most staff riders.

Catton, Bruce. *Grant Moves South*. Boston: Little, Brown and Co., 1960.

Intended for a general audience, Catton's gifted prose makes an excellent introduction to the Civil War in the west, placing the Vicksburg campaign within a broader strategic context.

Carter, Samuel III. *The Final Fortress: The Campaign for Vicksburg 1862-1863*. New York: St. Martin's Press, 1980 (1963).

A narrative history for a general readership, this work is rich in anecdotes and first-person observations from participants and eyewitnesses.

Foote, Shelby. *The Beleaguered City: The Vicksburg Campaign*. New York: The Modern Library, 1995.

Excerpted from Foote's monumental three-volume popular history of the Civil War, this masterfully written account errs in attributing to Pemberton a degree of foresight that actually was hindsight. Foote utilized unquestioningly Pemberton's *postwar* recollections.

Grabau, Warren E. *Ninety-Eight Days: A Geographer's View of the Vicksburg Campaign*. Knoxville, TN: University of Tennessee Press, 2000.

Grabau's book provides a highly detailed, comprehensive study, particularly useful for tactical analysis. The chapter on geographic setting is essential reading for a full understanding of the theater of operations. The book contains sixty-eight maps showing details down to the regimental level.

Johnson, Robert U., and Clarence C. Buel, eds. *Battles and Leaders of Civil War*. Vol. 3. New York: The Century Company, 1885-87.

This collection of essays from high-ranking participants has long been a standard work and is available in various reprints. The section on Vicksburg includes a campaign account by Grant, plus other essays by Johnston, Samuel H. Lockett, Andrew Hickenlooper, and others.

Miers, Earl Schenk. *The Web of Victory: Grant at Vicksburg*. Baton Rouge, LA: Louisiana State University Press, 1984 (1955).

While a very readable narrative account of the campaign, this work is not particularly strong on military analysis.

The War of the Rebellion: A Compilation of the Official Records of the Union and Confederate Armies. Vol. 17, pts. 1-2, and Vol. 24, pts. 1-3. Washington, D.C.: U.S. Government Printing Office, 1886-87, 1899.

Originally compiled and published by the United States government, the *Official Records* have subsequently appeared in several reprints and in CD ROM format. Indispensable for any serious study, these records include a wide variety of reports and correspondence from both sides. Volume 17 encompasses the Chickasaw Bayou campaign; Volume 24 treats all subsequent actions in the struggle for Vicksburg.

West Point Atlas of American Wars. Vol 1. New York: Praeger, 1959. Also available as Griess, Thomas E., ed. *Atlas for the American Civil War*, West Point Military History Series. Wayne, NJ: Avery Publishing Group, 1986.

While possessing a useful set of campaign maps, this work contains some minor errors regarding troop strengths and dispositions.

Winschel, Terrence J.

Champion Hill: A Battlefield Guide

Chickasaw Bayou: A Battlefield Guide

Port Gibson: A Battlefield Guide

Raymond: A Battlefield Guide

This series of excellent brochures was prepared by the Vicksburg National Military Park historian and is available for purchase at the visitor center.

Winschel, Terrence J. *Triumph and Defeat: The Vicksburg Campaign.* Mason City, IA: Savas Publishing, 1999.

This collection of well-crafted, insightful essays covers key aspects of the campaign.

Winschel, Terrence J. *Vicksburg: Fall of the Confederate Gibraltar.* Abilene, TX: McWhiney Foundation Press, 1999.

This excellent introduction to the campaign is complete with biographical sketches of the key participants and is highly recommended.

III. The Navy.

Bearss, Edwin H. *Hardluck Ironclad: The Sinking and Salvage of the Cairo.* Baton Rouge: Louisiana State University Press, 1966.

Bearss provides a good understanding of naval operations on the western waters, plus fascinating background information on the *Cairo* exhibit located at the Vicksburg National Military Park.

Milligan, John D. *Gunboats Down the Mississippi.* Annapolis, MD: U.S. Naval Institute, 1965.

Milligan has authored an excellent overview of the Navy's campaigns in the western theater.

Official Records of the Union and Confederate Navies in the War of the Rebellion. Vols. 24, 25. Washington, D.C.: Government Printing Office, 1911-12.

These volumes are the Navy's counterpart to the Army's *Official Records* cited above.

Silverstone, Paul H. *Warships of the Civil War Navies.* Annapolis, MD: Naval Institute Press, 1989.

Silverstone's book is an invaluable source of technical data.

IV. Weapons and Tactics

Coggins, Jack. *Arms and Equipment of the Civil War*. Wilmington, NC: Broadfoot Publishing Company, 1987 (1962).

This very useful primer features instructive illustrations and an authoritative text. It provides a solid grounding in weapons capabilities that is essential to understanding Civil War battles.

Griffith, Paddy. *Battle in the Civil War*. Nottinghamshire, England: Fieldbooks, 1986.

This excellent booklet describes and illustrates the fundamentals of Civil War tactics in a concise, easily comprehended format. Highly recommended.

McWhiney, Grady, and Perry D. Jamieson. *Attack and Die: Civil War Tactics and the Southern Heritage*. Tuscaloosa, AL: University of Alabama Press, 1990 (1982).

McWhiney and Jamieson offer a controversial analysis of the Confederacy's predeliction for offensive operations.

Ripley, Warren. *Artillery and Ammunition of the Civil War*. 4th Edition. Charleston, SC: The Battery Press, 1984.

This comprehensive work provides technical information on artillery and ammunition, including data and photos of specific pieces on display at Vicksburg National Military Park.

Thomas, Dean S. *Cannons: An Introduction to Civil War Artillery*. Gettysburg, PA: Thomas Publications, 1985.

This book is a helpful primer on the technical characteristics of standard Civil War field artillery weapons.

V. Combat Support and Combat Service Support

Brown, Joseph Willard. *The Signal Corps, U.S.A. in the War of the Rebellion*. Boston: U.S. Veteran Signal Corps Association, 1896.

Provided in this book is general background information on organization, equipment, personnel, and techniques. It includes a section on Grant's Department of the Tennessee.

Gillett, Mary C. *The Army Medical Department 1818-1865*. Army Historical Series. Washington, D.C.: Center of Military History, Government Printing Office, 1987.

This broad survey provides general background information plus several pages dealing specifically with the Vicksburg campaign.

Huston, James A. *The Sinews of War: Army Logistics 1775-1953*. Army Historical Series, Washington, D.C.: Office of the Chief of Military History, Government Printing Office, 1970.

A standard work in the field, this survey provides helpful background data on Civil War logistics.

Lord, Francis A. *They Fought for the Union*. Harrisburg, PA: Stackpole, 1960.

A wide-ranging examination of the Civil War experience, this work details organization, training, weapons, equipment, uniforms, and soldier life.

VI. Biographies (Federal)

Warner, Ezra J. *Generals in Blue*. Baton Rouge: Louisiana State University Press, 1964.

This standard reference work provides biographical sketches (and some photographs) of Union general officers.

Grant

Grant, Ulysses S. *Personal Memoirs*. 2 vols. New York: Charles L. Webster, 1885-86.

Several reprints of this work are available, and it is considered to be the standard for military memoirs, but it should still be read with a critical eye.

Logan

Jones, James P. *"Black Jack:" John A. Logan and Southern Illinois in the Civil War Era*. Carbondale, IL: Southern Illinois University Press, 1995 (1967).

This scholarly biography explores military operations as well as the political undercurrents that influenced campaigns in the west.

McClernand

Kiper, Richard L. *Major General John Alexander McClernand: Politician in Uniform*. Kent, OH: Kent State University Press, 1999.

Kiper analyzes McClernand's conduct of tactical operations and his relationship with other Union generals during the campaign.

Porter

Hearn, Chester G. *Admiral David Dixon Porter: The Civil War Years*. Annapolis, MD: Naval Institute Press, 1996.

This book explores Porter's character and capabilities and offers a solid analysis of military operations.

Sherman

Sherman, William T. *Memoirs of William T. Sherman*. New York: Library of America, 1990 (1885).

Several reprints of Sherman's memoirs are available. This one represents Sherman's revised edition, published ten years after the initial printing. Sherman's outspoken, argumentative, but articulate nature is clearly demonstrated.

VII. Biographies (Confederate)

Warner, Ezra T. *Generals in Gray.* Baton Rouge: Louisiana State University Press, 1959.

This book contains short biographical sketches and photographs of Confederate general officers.

Woodworth, Steven E. *Jefferson Davis and His Generals: The Failure of Confederate Command in the West.* Lawrence: University Press of Kansas, 1990.

Although primarily an analysis of Confederate strategy, this work also offers key insights into the often tempestuous relationships within the high command.

Bowen

Tucker, Phillip Thomas. *The Forgotten "Stonewall of the West:" Major General John Stevens Bowen.* Macon, GA: Mercer University Press, 1997.

Although stylistically flawed, this work helps explain how Bowen came to be Pemberton's best division commander.

Johnston

Symonds, Craig L. *Joseph E. Johnston: A Civil War Biography.* New York: W. W. Norton, 1992.

Symonds' work includes a useful chapter on Vicksburg in which the author supports Johnston's actions.

Loring

Raab, James W. *W. W. Loring: Florida's Forgotten General.* Manhattan, KS: Sunflower University Press, 1996.

Intended for a popular audience, this book provides a highly partisan defense of a controversial character.

Pemberton

Ballard, Michael B. *Pemberton: A Biography*. Jackson: University Press of Mississippi, 1991.

Although not particularly strong on operational issues, this biography offers a clear portrait of Pemberton the man. The only other biography, written by Pemberton's grandson, should be avoided.

Smith, David M., ed. *Compelled to Appear in Print: The Vicksburg Manuscript of General John C. Pemberton*. Cincinnati, OH: Ironclad Publishing, 1999.

This recently discovered manuscript showcases Pemberton's rebuttal of J. E. Johnston's version of the campaign.

VIII. Vignettes and First-Person Accounts

Hoehling, A. A. *Vicksburg: 47 Days of Siege, May 18-July 4, 1863*. Englewood Cliffs, NJ: Prentice-Hall, 1969.

Wheeler, Richard. *The Siege of Vicksburg*. New York: HarperPerennial, 1991 (1978).

Wheeler treats the entire campaign, whereas Hoehling (above) focuses upon the siege of Vicksburg. Both are good sources of vignettes that add color and human interest to a staff ride.

IX. Films

Department of the Army. *The Staff Ride*. TVT 20-762 (706159DA). Thirty-six minutes.

This film presents an excellent overview of what a staff ride entails and provides advice on how to conduct one.

Department of the Army. *.58 Rifled Musket*. TVT 21-84 (705967DA). Sixteen minutes. *12 Pounder Napoleon*. TVT 21-85 (705968DA). Sixteen minutes.

Created by the Department of History at West Point, both films feature firing demonstrations of actual weapons, as well as background information.

X. Maps:

U.S. Department of the Interior Geological Survey.

1:100,000 Series:

   Brookhaven, MS 31090-E1-TF-100-00

   Tallulah, LA 32091-A1-TF-100-00

   Jackson, MS 32090-A1-TF-100-00

   Natchez, [MS] LA 31091-E1-TF-100-00

1:24,000 (7.5 Minute Series Topographic):

   Redwood, MS

   Floweree, MS

   Long Lake, MS

   Vicksburg, MS West

   Vicksburg, MS East

   Grand Gulf, MS

   Saint Joseph, LA

   Widows Creek, MS-LA

   Port Gibson, MS

   Willows, MS

   Terry, MS NW

   Raymond, MS

   Edwards, MS

   Bovina, MS

Maps can be ordered through:

Distribution Branch
U.S. Geological Survey
Box 25286
Federal Center Building 41
   Denver, Colorado 80225

www.ingramcontent.com/pod-product-compliance
Lightning Source LLC
Chambersburg PA
CBHW080459110426
42742CB00017B/2938